Desk Top Publishing with QuarkXPress 2018

Martin Turner

inGenios

Introduction	1	**The Basics**	
What is DTP?	2	Freeform to automated	12
What is QuarkXPress?	3	The User Interface	13
What's new in…	5	Doing it with style	14
History of Publishing	6	With conditions	15

By Design

Composition	19
Typography	21
Typefaces	23
Archetypefaces	25
Faking it with fonts	27
Photography	29
Colour and emotion	31
Colour and science	33
Brand	35

By Process

Text control	38
Importing text	39
Line and shape	41
Texture	43
Importing graphics	45
Importing images	47
Layering & Compositing	49
Automation	51
Exporting	53
The printed document	55
Print Processes	56

By Practice

Designing a flyer	61
Magazine publishing	63
Publishing a book	65
eBooks and Tagged PDF	67
Digital layouts	69

By Function

Tools	72
Measurements	
1 Home	76
2 Character	77
3 Paragraph	78
4 Rules	79
5 Column Flow	80
6 Tabs	81
7 Text Box	82
8 Picture Box	83
9 Border (frame)	84
10 Runaround and Clipping	85
11 Space/Align	87
12 Text Shading	88
13 Drop Shadow	89
14 Table	89

16 Hyperlinks	110
17 Image Editing	110
18 Index	121
19 Item Styles	123
20 JavaScript	124
21 JavaScript Debugger	124
22 Layers	125
23 Lists	125
24 Page Layout	126
25 Profile Information	128
26 Redline	129
27 Reflow Tagging: See Articles	
28 Scale	129
29 Style Sheets	130
30 Table Styles	133
31 Text Shading Styles	134
32 Welcome Screen	134

Palettes
1 Advanced Image Control 91
2 App Studio Publishing 91
3 Articles 92
4 Books 93
5 Callout Styles 93
6 Colours 94
7 Conditional Styles 97
8 Content 99
9 Content Variables 100
10 Footnote Styles 102
11 Glyphs 103
12 Gradients 104
13 Grid Styles 104
14 Guides 105
15 HTML5 108

Menus
1 QuarkXPress (Mac) 135
2 File 138
3 Edit 151
4 Style 160
5 Item 162
6 Page 166
7 Layout 167
8 Table 168
9 View 169
10 Utilities 171
11 Window 178
12 Script (Mac) 179
13 Help 17

Index 180

With thanks to my wife for her ever diligent proof-reading:

Scip sceal genægled, scyld gebunden,
leoht linden bord, leof wilcuma
Frysan wife, þonne flota stondeð;
biþ his ceol cumen ond hyre ceorl to ham,
agen ætgeofa, ond heo hine in ladaþ,
wæsceð his warig hrægl ond him syleþ wæde niwe,
liþ him on londe þæs his lufu bædeð.

Published by Ingenios Books
Fabrieksstraat 63, 1930 Zaventem, Belgium

Desk Top Publishing with QuarkXPress 2018
© Martin Turner 2018
All rights reserved
21 20 19 18   4 3 2 1
First Edition

No part of this book may be used or reproduced in any manner without written permission from the publisher, except in the context of reviews.

Every reasonable attempt has been made to identify owners of copyright. Errors or omissions will be corrected in subsequent editions.

ISBN-13: 9781980436423

Introduction

Desk top publishing is a craft which has been around since the 6th century. The software category, desktop publishing (DTP), has been around since the 1980s. This book is about QuarkXPress 2018, which is the most powerful DTP tool available today. But it is also about the art, craft and science of desk top publishing, and allied disciplines such as illustration, photography, marketing and branding. No man, as John Donne put it, is an island, and no discipline can afford to be insular.

Illuminated manuscript in the Plantin Museum, Antwerp, Belgium.

The image was imported straight from a Nikon Df as JPEG and colour balanced in QuarkXPress using Window>Image Editing with Selective Colour to remove a green cast, and Levels to correct contrast.

For the last ten years, QuarkXPress has been my competitive advantage. Jobs begun in other software which, through application or user shortcomings, could not be completed have come my way, and, as often as not, this has led to a long-standing commercial relationship. This book is written to help you extend your QuarkXPress advantage, or, if you're coming from other software, to give you a kick-start in making the most of it.

The book has been rewritten and redesigned since Desk Top Publishing with QuarkXPress 2017. The move to the larger format, and the introduction of colour, echo the needs of a DTP book. It simply no longer makes sense, if it ever did, to prevent a monochromatic view of a skill which is increasingly colour-led.

The book also makes use of the video series, DTP with QuarkXPress, which QuarkTV webcast in 2017. These videos offer an ideal introduction to many of the most powerful features of the software.

Many of the tips and tricks described here have come out of questions in the QuarkXPress Facebook group, www.facebook.com/groups/quarkxpress. I would strongly recommend joining that group. On it, you can discuss with Quark users worldwide, and also with the development and quality assurance team who are actively working on the application itself. On one occasion, someone reported a software bug, and the team had tested it, resolved it and issued the fix all within a single day. It's also the place where you can take part in the biannual poll of new features.

▲ *This book refers frequently to the series DTP with QuarkXPress, available free of charge on YouTube.*

▼ *Use the QR code to access it, or go to youtu.be/ZNms8Va05vQ*

The QR code was created with Utilities—Create QR Code.

What is DTP?

Desk top publishing is the discipline which gives the final shape to documents and prepares them to be widely distributed. These documents can be purely typographic or purely graphical, but usually they will be a mixture of 'art', meaning photography and illustrations, and text. When people look at DTP software, they tend to think of it as being purely about page layout, but DTP also involves other publishing tasks. Even if you are purely a layout artist, it is still worth understanding them.

Great DTP versus Terrible DTP

Great DTP manages the mind's journey around a document. It uses visual cues to support the message, to let the elements speak for themselves, and to combine them into a harmonious, coherent, aesthetic whole which is greater than the sum of the parts.

Terrible DTP distracts the mind with irrelevant complication. It draws attention to itself with spurious effects, ornamentation and clutter, as it attempts to compensate for perceived weaknesses in the source material, but the result is less than the effort required to create it.

Commissioning

Commissioning is giving the instruction to produce a document. If you are a one-man show, originating, designing and publishing your own stuff, then you may be unaware of it. Working in-house, or for external clients, the commissioning process is crucial. A properly commissioned document has clear outcomes, audiences, messages and delivery. Knowing these informs every stage of the process that follows, and tells you when the document is ready. When things go wrong, they usually go wrong with lack of clarity at the commissioning stage.

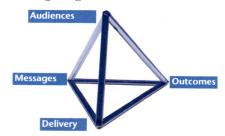

Origination

Origination is the production of the elements you will combine in DTP. Typically, these will be a combination of new text, new images and new illustrations, underpinned by an established brand guide which will specify colours, logos, brand-graphics, and may also include characteristic illustrations and images. Part of the publishing task is to marshall all of these, ensuring that you get the right materials from the right people at the right time, and that these have been signed off by the commissioners before they get to you. If this is not possible, you need to build in a clear process for sign-off, otherwise you will find yourself juggling dozens or in some case hundreds of conflicting versions which are impossible to manage. Who gets the blame when this then goes wrong? Naturally, it's you.

Layout

Layout is what DTP applications help you to do. Your aim in layout is to combine the original elements in a way which is consistent, pleasing, attractive and readable—and which satisfies the intention of the commissioners. Most of this book is about this. If you structure the document well, using style sheets, content variables, master pages and tags, then everything else will be easier.

Editing

Even when you get everything signed off before you start on the layout, there will always be editing. Editing is where the document is fully scrutinised, both by commissioners and by proofreaders. If you constructed the document well, editing is fairly painless. If you didn't, then the process is fraught, stressful, and frustrating.

Prepress Deployment

When the document is ready, you export it as final PDF artwork, or as an HTML5 publication, an ePub or Kindle, or a smartphone app.

Production and Distribution

When everything is ready, print or web-distribution is when final copies start making their way to the end customers. Remember: the job is not done until people are reading your material.

What is QuarkXPress?

QuarkXPress (QX) is powerful layout software that does most of the heavy lifting for design, editing and deployment. It can also assist with origination and production. QX has been around a long time. It quickly established itself as the leading DTP application during the 1990s, and was used for almost every magazine, newspaper, advertisement or book you could find. However, competition was on the horizon, and in the 2000s, aggressive promotion of Adobe's InDesign saw many designers switching to the new software.

Two things have happened to reverse the trend, with increasing numbers switching back to Quark.

First, the rise of subscription software has led many to seek 'buy once, own forever' applications, such as QuarkXPress. This is not just about price: discovering that software you rely on is to be discontinued has proved a bitter pill for many.

Second, and more importantly, QuarkXPress itself has gone through an astonishing renaissance, with version after version turning out highly prized features. The chart here shows it all. From 1987 to 2015, QX was upgraded significantly on average once every two years. From 2015 to 2018 the upgrades have been annual, with more and more significant new features per upgrade.

There is one thing further. Quark Inc itself has become arguably the most responsive software company in the world.

◀ The timeline was created in Bee-Docs Timeline 3D and exported as PDF. Timeline 3D offers basic styling, so we used Style>Convert to Native Objects and edited directly in QuarkXPress.

◀ The lines are made in QX with Edit>Dashes&Stripes to create a line which is just a dot at each end, and then setting the gap to the same colour, 30% transparency.

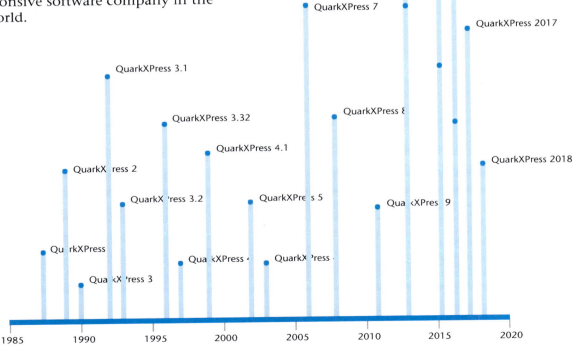

	QX2015	QX2016	QX2017	QX2018
Typography	**Inline tables** **Table styles (inline tables)** Footnotes Endnotes **Content variables** **Running headers** Import footnotes/endnotes from DOCX	Find/Change non-breaking attribute Cross-referencing Wrapping content variables Flip box to text **OpenType stylistic sets**	Merge text boxes Proportional leading **Text shading** **Text framing** **Stroke live text** Text spanning Column splitting Column rules Smart single quotes	Footnotes span GREP (via Javascript) **Preview access to OpenType functions** Apply multiple stylistic sets **Colour fonts** **Hyphenation quality** Font style list HTML5 Open Type features
Graphics and colour	Relink images in usage dialogue Crisp EPS previews **New Graphics Engine** Scale images to 5000%	Full ICC v4 colour support Colour picker **Multi-colour blends** **Convert vector import to native**	**Transparency modes** Multi-gradients all shapes Frame gradients *'Blends' now 'Gradients'* **Image editing**	*'Frames' now 'borders'* **Multi-borders** Flip groups
Tools & Management	Search in palettes **Customise keyboard commands (Mac)** Custom paper sizes Paper sizes >1.2m Format painter (text)	Trackpad Gestures Resizeable measurements panel **Change values by cursor keys**	Format painter (item) Linking tool enhanced Show recent fonts **Adaptive scaling** **Shapemaker tools** IDML import (beta)	Vertical Measurements panel (Mac) **Javascript** **IDML import**
Output	HTML5 animations **PDF/X-4 output** **Fixed-layout eBook** Style Sheets export CSS (digital)	**HTML5 publications** Locally preview HTML5 Justification, runaround, drop caps etc. in ePub and HTML5	**Create iOS app** Auto-create a table-of-content (digital) **Responsive HTML5 Publications**	**New PDF Engine** **Create Android app** **Tagged PDF export** PDF/A export Print 10% to 10000% Preview HTML5 page HTML5 interactive groups Offline HTML5 reading

29: New Tools in QuarkXPress 2017

What's new in...

QuarkXPress is on an aggressive upgrade cycle. This book has been written primarily for QuarkXPress 2018, but also with users of QuarkXPress 2015, 2016 and 2017 in mind. This page will tell you what you need to know when working from one version to another. Watch out for changes in terminology: 'blends' are now 'gradients', 'frames' are now 'borders', and ePub reflowing is now under 'articles'. Throughout the book, we have tried to indicate when a new feature became available.

2018
OpenType previews, Hyphenation quality, Multi-toppers, Colour fonts, JavaScript, Android apps, Tagged PDF

QX2018 introduces JavaScript on Windows and Mac, using the latest version of the code, so that current script-libraries can be adapted quickly and accurately. It became the first commercially available package to offer hyphenation strictness, possibly the most significant upgrade to computer typography in 20 years. Boxes can now have four different kinds of borders, Android apps can be created, as can Tagged PDF. QX previews OpenType features. On a more fun level, all types of colour fonts are supported.

Colour Fonts

▲ QX2018, at the time of writing, is the only DTP package supporting all four types of colour fonts: SVG vector, SVG bitmap, Apple SBIX and Microsoft COLR.

2017
Image Editing, Transparency Blend modes, iOS apps, Responsive HTML5, Text Shading, Text Stroking, Adaptive scaling

QX2017 introduced non-destructive image editing, and is still the only pro-level DTP application that offers this. It added transparency blend modes, as well as text shading, text framing and text stroking. HTML5 publications became responsive, behaving much more like native apps. QX2017 introduced the ability to create iOS apps freely, with no additional costs beyond those required by Apple. The ability to make apps was the first for a DTP application, and QX is still the only package providing it.

Text Stroking, Shading and Framing

▲ QX2017's new stroking, shading and framing allow self-formatting boxes.

2016
Convert vector imports to native, HTML5 publications, Multi-colour blends, OpenType Stylistic sets

QX2016 introduced two dramatic new features. The first was the conversion of imported vectors into native, editable QuarkXPress objects. This had not been seen before in a professional DTP package, and QX is still the only pro-application offering it. Whole documents could be converted, conformed to brand requirements, or edited as required. The second was HTML5 publications, allowing a QX layout to get to the web unaltered without additional software or costs.

MULTI BLENDS

▲ QX2016's multi-coloured blends (since then renamed 'gradients') are not just for creating pseudo-photographic effects like chroming.

2015
Inline tables, Table Styles, Content Variables, new graphics engine

QuarkXPress 2015 was the first of a new generation. Until then, updates were every 2-3 years named 3.3, 4.0, 5.0 etc, up to 10. Since then, updates have been yearly, named after their years. QX2015 introduced the Xenon graphics engine. For the first time, QX users were seeing the actual EPS and PDF files, not previews of them. This engine also laid the foundations for what was to follow in QX2016 with its conversion of vector imports to native.

Crisp Previews

▲ QX2015's new graphics engine closed one chapter and opened another. The crisp previews made it faster and more enjoyable to work with, but they also opened the door for direct conversion of vectors in QX2016 and later.

History of Publishers

This book is about 'Desk Top Publishing', a craft that goes back to the 6th century, not merely 'Desktop Publishing', a software category which goes back to 1983. Publishing covers a multitude of skills, from understanding of copyright to recognitiion of the impact of paper weave on cracking during the folding process. Since Peter Behrens created the first corporate visual identity for AEG in 1907, brand has become a key aspect of the publisher's craft. The Xerox Docutech, 1990, restored complete control of the printing process—if desired—to the desk top publisher, as it was in the days of Gutenberg.

▲ *36 line Bible, 1461, printed with Gutenberg letters. Plantin Museum, Antwerp*

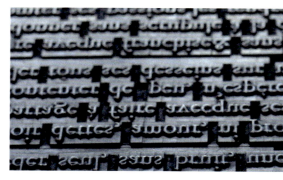

▲ *Moveable type, Plantin Museum, Antwerp.*
The invention of the printing press brought the middle ages to an end. By the 1500s, an estimated four million books had been printed and sold.

▶ *Claude Garamond*

- Lindisfarne Gospels, pencil invented
- Papermill in Baghdad
- Chinese wood-block mass printing
- Movable type invented, China
- Johannes Gutenberg: adjustable type mould
- Claude Garamond's Roan face, Paris
- Complete printed book, China
- Plantin's 5 language Bible, Antwerp
- Papermaking in Samarkand
- Gutenberg's Bible
- German newspaper
- First type specimen, Erhard Ratdolt Venice

1425 1450 1475 1500 1525 1550 1575 1600 1625

Behrens creates visual identity for AEG

DIN paper sizes introduced, Germany

Eric Gill's original artwork for Gill Sans, London Print Museum

Xerography (photocopying)

Early typefaces such as Gutenberg's and Garamond's had to be carved in wood or metal, reversed into moulds and then cast as lead letters. By the time of Paul Renner's Futura and Eric Gill's Gill (right), they were being drafted with pen, brush and ink. In 1996 Microsoft's Verdana was commissioned to exist primarily in digital space.

Phototypesetting

Inkjet printing

Image Scanner

Coloritto, by Jacob Christoph Le Blon, describes RYB three-colour process

Chromolithography (multicolour printing)

Thermal printing

Plantin-Moretus Museum, Antwerp

Graphical User Interface

Statute of Anne regulates copyright in Great Britain

Johnson's Dictionary of the English Language

Gestetner duplicator

ISO paper standard

Cylindrical printing press

Linotype automatic typesetter

Desktop publishing

Steam-powered cylindrical printing press

Wirephoto transmitted

Apple Macintosh

Sans-serif type specimen

Futura developed

Postscript

Photoengraving

Times New Roman

QuarkXPress

Paperback books

Halftone process patented

Helvetica

Xerox Docutech

Encyclopaedia Britannica

Photography

Flexography

Letraset

World Wide Web launched

Didot's point system

Rotary letterpress

CMYK process

Pantone

Kindle

Lithography

Paperfolding machine

Gill Sans

Laser Printer

iPad

1700   1725   1750   1775   1800   1825   1850   1875   1900   1925   1950   1975   2000   2025

Scip sceal genægled, scyld gebunden,
leoht linden bord, leof wilcuma
Frysan wife, þonne flota stondeð;
biþ his ceol cumen ond hyre ceorl to ham,
agen ætgeofa, ond heo hine in laðaþ,
wæsceð his warig hrægl ond him syleþ wæde niwe,
liþ him on londe þæs his lufu bædeð.

The Basics

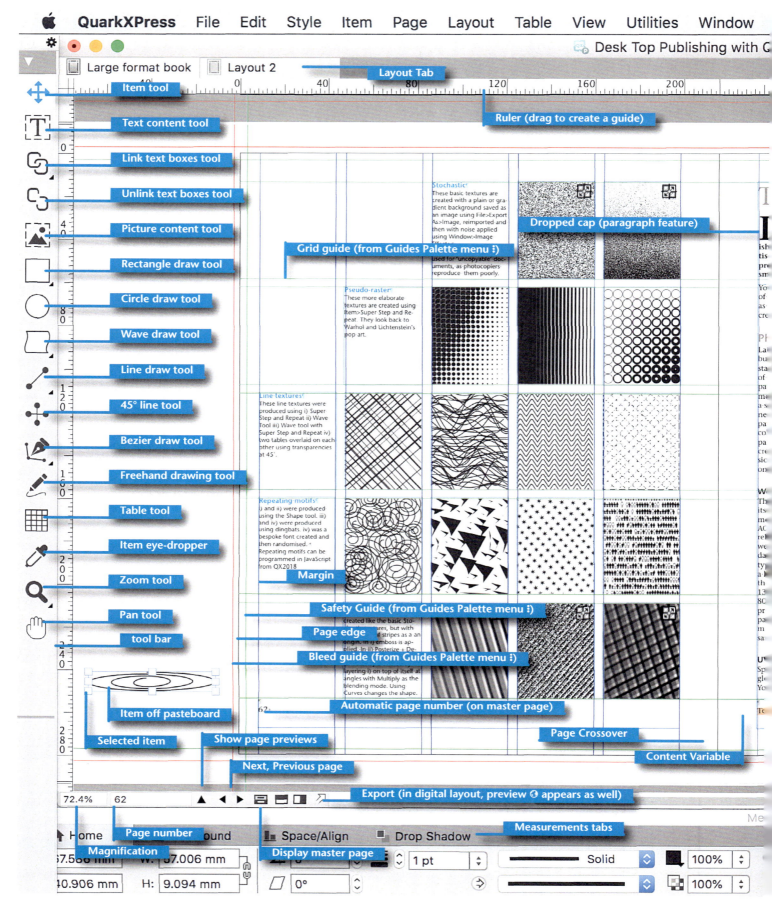

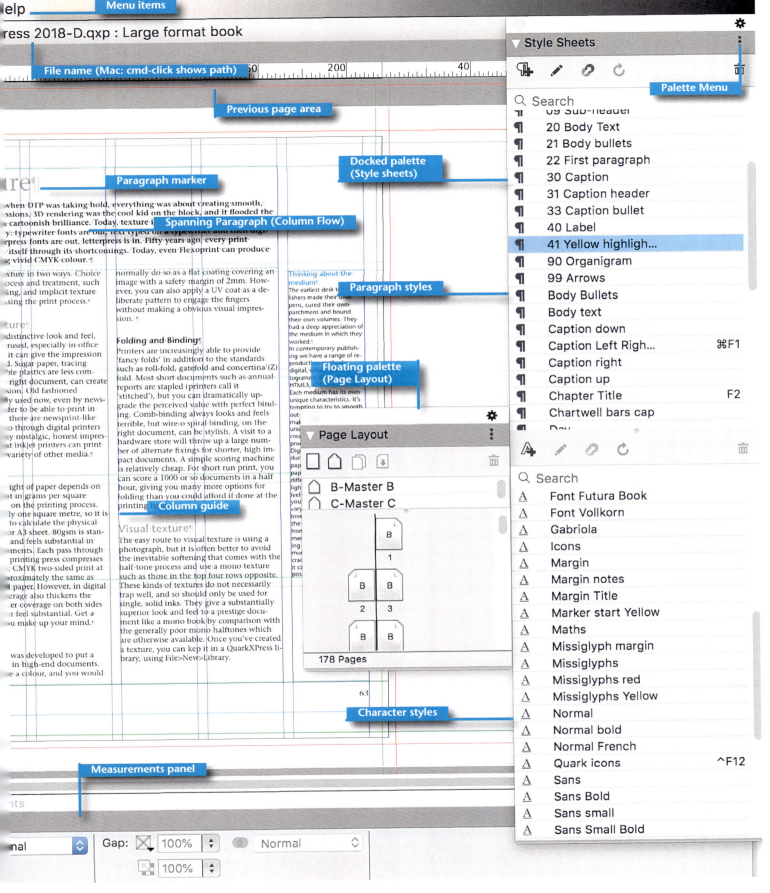

Freeform to automated

QuarkXPress allows you to work completely freeform, or with so much automation that you can lay out entire documents with minimum user involvement. Here, we look at twelve aspects which take us from totally you to totally machine.

Completely Freeform — Entirely automated

Tools—See p72
The tool bar allows you to create text boxes, graphics, shapes, lines and tables and put them wherever you want.

Use the pointer ✛ to move items around.

Measurements—See p76
The Measurements panel gives you direct access to every value that affects what appears on the page. Use this for every ad hoc change, and to see what settings have been applied in style sheets.

Find/Change—See p152
Find/Change lets you locate and exchange text throughout a story or document, and it allows you to do the same for all character attributes and style sheets. This can be dangerous, but if you get it wrong Cmd/Ctrl-Z will undo all changes. More complex searches can be done with GREP (JavaScript).

Style Sheets—See p130
Style Sheets format text. Character styles set font, size, colour, language and stroke. Paragraph styles specify a Character style and set spacing, indents, tabs, rules, column flow and what the next style is. You can quickly format an entire document clicking through styles, or with a self-defined shortcut key.

Masters and Guides—See p126
Master Pages allow you to create a consistent layout across an entire document. Using Guides (p105) you can set up a grid which then gives you freedom to design each page differently and yet retain consistency.

Item Styles—See p123
Item Styles set characteristics for objects such as picture boxes, text boxes and lines. Like Style Sheets, you can quickly format a whole document in this way. If you also use Callout Styles (p93) you can have boxes automatically move to the right place on the page as the text they refer to moves around.

Conditional Styles—See p97
Conditional Styles apply Paragraph and Character Style Sheets to conditionally based on the content of text. You can format an entire document using a Conditional Style.

Content Variables—See p100
Content Variables take text from one part of the document and insert it anywhere you want. Content Variables update automatically, and can look at changing style sheets from page to page. Using input from an Excel sheet, you can populate data intensive publications automatically.

JavaScript—See p124
JavaScript runs a potentially branching computer script which can operate on almost any aspect of QuarkXPress, effectively taking over from you, the operator, and executing a series of repetitive or complex tasks reliably. You can programme your own JavaScripts or use supplied or downloaded scripts.

Job Jackets—See p173
Job Jackets manage all of the styles and settings for an entire suite of documents, enabling you to update their formatting together, or run Job Evaluations to check that a particular document complies with the brand specifications or other requirements. A job jacket can create an entire project.

Inline Tables—See p133
Inline Tables can be automatically styled so that data-intensive Excel sheets can be fully formatted, and remain updatable from the original files. Using Inline Tables, it is possible to specify the content in an Excel file and have it fully format itself as a page layout, without any indication that it is from a table.

XPress Tags
XPress Tags are human-readable tagging files that can be prepared by an external database to completely format a full document of flowing text, specifying every paragraph and character style so that no further involment is required. Complete books can be prepared for publication from a database.

The User Interface

On the previous spread is an annotated image of the user interface, Mac version, with View>View Sets>Authoring View turned on. The Windows and Mac versions are now essentially unified, although, from QX2018, QX Mac offers a vertical measurements panel (not shown here) as an alternative to the horizontal panel. Mac and Windows now differ primarily in the shortcut keys. Usually Command on a Mac is Ctrl on Windows, and Right-Click on Windows is Ctrl-Click on a Mac. Ctrl-click/Right-click invokes the contextual menu.

▼ *Ctrl-click (Mac)/Right-click (Win_ brings up the Contextual menu, with the most useful and relevant menu items.*

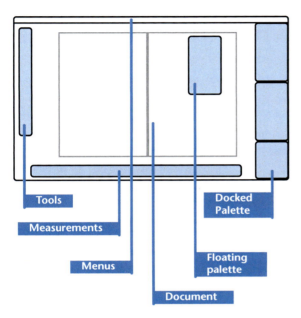

The interface has got five basic things:

Tools are how you control things with the mouse, like creating objects and selecting text.

Measurements set the characteristics of what you have selected, such as colour, font size.

Menus organise the features by header: File, Edit, Style, Item, Page, Layout, Table, View, Utitilities, Window and Help.

Docked **palettes** are tied to the side of the screen. Floating palettes can be anywhere. You open them from the Window menu.

The **document** space is where you work. To the sides is a pasteboard where you can temporarily keep unused items. You bleed into the pasteboard for bleed.

About the tools
Many of the tools also work with modifier keys. Shift usually constrains, Option/alt varies the function. You can also use the arrow keys to move objects. Opt/alt-arrow makes the movements smaller, shift-arrow makes them larger. There are shortcut keys for tools.

About measurements
The Home tab of the Measurements panel changes to match what you are doing. Other tabs will appear or disappear when relevant (or not). For any measurement, you can use the mouse keys to increment or decrement. Shift increases the amount, opt/alt reduces it. See p76.

About the palettes
Most palettes have a palette menu in the top right, ⁝. Click this for more options. This is especially important for the Style Sheets palette. You can also ctrl-click/right-click to invoke it. Cmd/Ctrl-click typically takes you to the Edit menu for that item. What this is varies by palette. See p91.

About the keyboard
You can assign shortcut keys to individual styles. This makes formatting a document very quick. There are also built-in shortcuts for many features, and they are worth memorising. On a Mac, you can change the shortcuts or create new ones.

Document space
The View Menu gives you many options for the document space, but you can select between the most common sets with View>View Sets. The Authoring View shows you almost everything, whereas the Output Preview shows you pretty much exactly what will be printed.

First Aid when things go wrong

Before you do anything else, do this:
Go to QuarkXPress>Preferences (Mac) or Edit>Preferences (Win), and from there Application>Open and Save. Turn on Auto-Save and Auto-Backup. Set the number for Auto-Backup to something unreasonably high, like 25. This means that QX will automatically save your file every few minutes, and that you will keep a large number of previous versions.

You have to set this again whenever you delete Preferences!

Sometimes, QuarkXPress will unexpectedly quit. All software does this: changes in the Operating System, bad fonts, bad graphics, power failure, bad hard-disk or memory. Whatever. If it does, you will find a folder on your Desktop called 'Quark Rescue'. It will contain the document the moment before the crash. If it's your document that caused the crash (bad font, bad graphic), then this won't help you. But usually it will rescue you. If problems persist, go to QuarkXPress/Help>Quark Cache Cleaner. Use it to clear the Image Cache and delete the Preferences. Then restart your machine.

Doing it with style

Consistency in design is the difference between professional layout and amateurishness. These days a lot of applications, including Microsoft Word and Apple Pages, can produce a result which would have required a DTP package back in the 1990s. But managing non-DTP software to do so consistently becomes a nightmare. The power of ad hoc design via the Measurements panel may delight designers, but for true publishing, it's the power of styles which set pro-DTP apart from the rest. QuarkXPress has 16 types of style that interact with each other. See page 123.

- Add other palettes
- Submenu
- Add a colour
- Edit selected colour
- Frame colour
- Picture (or text) colour
- Background colour
- Tint
- Opacity
- Search by name
- Delete a colour
- Transparency mode
- Knock-out mode
- Spot colour
- Process colour

◀ Invoke the colour palette with Window>Colours. To create a new colour, press ✥, and to edit an existing one press ✐. This applies to all of the palettes. 🗑 deletes and ⋮ invokes a submenu.

◀ Any colour you add becomes available by name in every place you can assign colours.

◀ The eye-dropper sub-palette creates colours from images.

Define a colour once, and it becomes available everywhere. This is obvious, of course, and lots of applications let you do this. But in QuarkXPress the same applies to bullets, hyphenation, paragraph styles, text styles, box styles, text shading styles, stripes and dashes, grids, hanging characters, callouts and footnotes. Not only does this give you highly consistent layout, it means you can tweak the entire document in an instant.

You name it

Whenever you create a style, such as a colour or a paragraph style, you will be able to give it a name. You can structure these any way you like, and they will appear in alphanumeric order in most contexts. For this book, we used numbered styles to show hierarchy.

You can also include tags in the names. In the colours palette above, we've added in "Brand Red" for Pantone 485. If we type the word 'Brand' into the 🔍 Search box, then only colours with 'Brand' in the name will appear.

▼ The Style Sheets palette, Window>Style Sheets, showing some of the Paragraph styles used to create this book. The numbering helps keep them in hierarchical order.

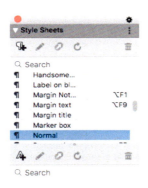

Character Style Sheets specify the look of the words: letter types, colour, size, styles, tracking, kerning, moving the baseline up and down, and stroking (outlining the letters). They also control which language applies to the words, so you can have individual words in a different language which will then hyphenate and spell check correctly according to the base language.

▶ Editing a paragraph style sheet

▼ Editing a character style sheet..

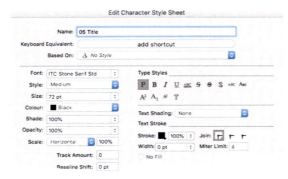

Cascading Styles:
Paragraph, Character and Item styles only

Paragraph, Character and Item style sheets have a couple of extra tricks. First, Paragraph Styles 'contain' character styles: you can either define the character style sheet from within the paragraph style, or you can assign one you already created, or you can create a new one which you can use elsewhere. Secondly, You can set a paragraph, character or item style to be 'based on' another style. If you change that other style, everything you specifically set for your new style stays the same, but everything else changes with the style it's based on.

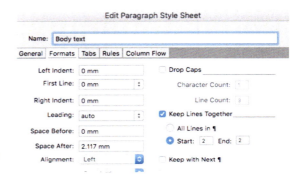

Paragraph style sheets apply to the entire paragraph. If you're wondering where to look for something, think 'if it can apply to just one word within a paragraph, then it's a character style, otherwise it's a paragraph style'. A paragraph style usually contains a character style, which specifies how the text will look.

If you're coming to QX2018 from an older version, note the new Heading Style. This is important for Tagged PDF. See page 130.

With conditions

Style sheets can do all kinds of things, but what if you want something fiendishly complicated or tediously technical, hundreds of times in the same document? For example, you want to highlight a particular actor's part in a film script, but he's got hundreds of lines of dialogue and you don't have time to wade through them. Or supposing you want to bold an abbreviation the first time it's used, but not again? Conditional styles let you move backwards and forwards through text, applying character or paragraph styles based on content, and repeating as required. See p97.

The Post-Modern dropped cap is as distant from its medieval cousin as the Internet is from the Carrier Pigeon, and the self-driving car from the horseless carriage. Truly, these are marvellous days we live in, even if our sense of irony at times overtakes our joie-de-vivre. In the words of the great Gary Larson, never forget to eat the flowers by the wayside.

◀ *The madcap colour font Color-Tube sets substantially larger than other text. You can automate it with a conditional style, which is also the best way to create a dropped-cap with an alternate letter-type. Body text Futura Medium.*

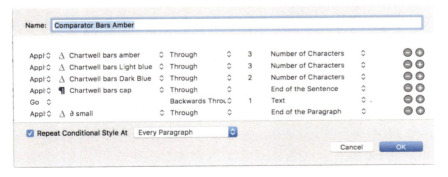

Participants under 23 with own vehicle, total vehicles already at site and total parking capacity at site.

◀ *This example uses the Chartwell fonts to create a simple bar chart. The problem is, to create the charts, you have to enter a string of numbers (easy), and then individually colour those numbers. On a good day this is tedious, on a bad day it's a nightmare, especially as you can't see the result until you turn on 'discretionary ligatures' in the Open Type settings, at which point you can no longer see the numbers.*

It will take about ten minutes to write this particular conditional style, and you need to have got one example working before you start, but, afterwards it all becomes automatic.

Just clicking on the Conditional Style you've created in the Conditional Styles palette formats the bars and the accompanying text, and it will do it consistently. You can do fifty charts like that in five minutes, and restyle all of them in 30 seconds. To edit the data afterwards, press Cmd/Ctrl-8 to enter the Story Editor.

▲ *This example is about as complicated as you will generally want to go. The available commands are 'Apply' and 'Go'. Apply sets a paragraph or character style sheet, 'Go' moves the start point for the next action. The range for each is 'Through', 'Backwards through', 'Up to' and 'Backwards to'. This is based on a numbered occurrence of something in the text.*

▼ *To change all of the 'q' followed by a space into Zapf Dingbats takes just one line in a conditional style sheet.*

Tick all that apply:
- ❏ Onions
- ❏ Lettuce
- ❏ Mauve
- ❏ Sartre
- ❏ Radishes
- ❏ Artichokes
- ❏ Potatoes
- ❏ Tuesday
- ❏ Logic errors

You can only apply one conditional style sheet at a time, but you can apply on top of each other. How does this work? Essentially, if you apply a conditional style, it leaves everything as is, except for things it is designed to change. When you click onto a new conditional style, it does not undo the work of the first—for that, use the Undo command (Cmd/Ctrl Z). Everything initially altered by the first conditional style stays, except where the second changes it. Doing it this way the first style is no longer 'live': if you change the conditional style sheet, it will not update. In other words, it runs like a simple Macro. If you want something more advanced, look at Java Scripting, new in QX2018. See p124.

33: Conditional Styles

By Design

1 The eye moves naturally from dark areas to bright areas.

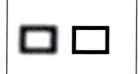
2 The eye moves naturally from indistinct to distinct forms.

3 The eye comes to rest at the point two lines cross.

4 The eye is drawn to the point at which two lines *would* cross, if only they were long enough.

5 The eye is more attracted to curving shapes than straight shapes.

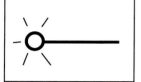
6 The eye will begin at a centre of attention, and then follow lines leading away from it.

7 Rotary motion tends to bring the eye into the centre of an image, and then back out again.

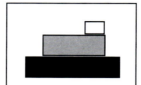
8 Where darker and larger shapes are underneath lighter and smaller shapes, the result is harmonious.

9 Where shapes would appear to 'topple', the result is one of tension.

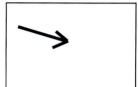
10 The eye follows implicit direction and motion, such as an arrow or a gaze. Where space is left for it, the result is harmonious.

11 When a pattern is disrupted, the eye is drawn to the disruption.

12 In a rectangle, the eye will naturally come to rest at the Golden Section points, about 61% from the far side.

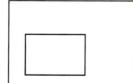
13 When a shape within a frame mirrors the shape of the frame, the result is harmonious.

14 A single item of primary interest draws the eye.

15 Where a secondary item, less dominant by means of colour, focus or position resembles the first, the result is harmonious.

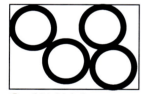
16 Multiple items which draw the attention equally are competing interest, which confuses the viewer.

17 Lines leading out of the frame will tend to take the viewer with them.

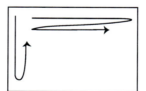
18 For viewers used to reading left to right and up to down, the eye naturally follows a reading path across the image.

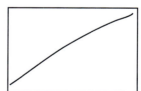
19 A line sloping upwards across the frame is perceived as optimistic, a line sloping downwards as pessimistic.

20 The eye is drawn to human faces, or things it can interpret as human faces, more than other interest.

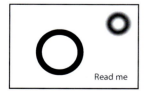
21 For literate readers, the eye is drawn to text at the expense of the image.

22 Once a 'mistake' in an image has been identified, the viewer is unable to appreciate the rest of the image.

23 Negative space can play as powerful an effect as positive space.

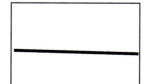
24 Where lines are not quite vertical or horizontal, tension is created. Skew lines such as water horizons are perceived as errors.

25 When shapes overlap, they tend to create a new shape in the eye of the viewer, even when this is unwanted or inappropriate.

Composition

Page composition is the poetry of design. It's part art, part science, part craft, part inspiration, part perspiration. At the most organic end, when constructing a one-off flyer with a powerful image, the composition of the photograph will more or less determine the composition of the page. At the other extreme, a complex document which has to manage many different kinds of content but remain consistent over a hundred pages is more like a mathematical puzzle.

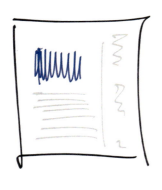

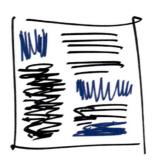

◀ One designer I worked with would create hundreds of thumbnails in free moments. The result was that she was able to quickly construct layouts with a high degree of apparent freedom, but which could be used again and again without ever forcing the document to compromise its content. Like all art, mastery comes from practice.

◀ Twenty-five principles of composition.
Whether you are taking photographs or planning pages, these twenty-five principles are based predominantly on the way the eye responds to lines and shapes.
Most books that talk about composition principles seem to go little further than the 'Rule of Thirds', which is actually a simplified version of the Golden Section (12). If you go back in history, classical painters were teaching all of these principles and many more.
Understanding and applying them will enable you to guide the eye around the page, create intention and interest, conjure mystery and delight, or simply correct blemishes which will trouble you and your readers if left unattended.

Thumbnails

Many talented designers begin by sketching out dozens of thumbnails, filling their notebooks with simple examples of what a page can look like. At the thumbnail stage, the more creative the better. At a particular point this has to be taken forward to simplification and then computerisation.

Probably the easiest way to transfer your thumbnails to the page is to photograph them with a smartphone, place the image onto a master page and then to drag guidelines from the rulers (just click on the rulers left or top and pull them into the document area).

Although creativity in thumbnails is essential, you will need to conform the different kinds of pages to an underlying grid. This does not need to be a geometric grid, of the kind you can produce using the Guides palette, menu ⋮, and either Grids or Rows and Columns, though many excellent documents are begun with this kind of grid. You can have as quirky a grid as you like, provided that you then work within that grid for the entire document. The longer the document, the more variations within the grid you can have. On a short document, playing with the grid too much will simply create an impression of mess, rather than underlying organic structure.

The Nellie, a cruising yawl, swung to her anchor without a flutter of the sails, and was at rest. The flood had made, the wind was nearly calm, and being bound down the river, the only thing for it was to come to and wait for the turn of the tide.

The sea-reach of the Thames stretched before us like the beginning of an interminable waterway. In the offing the sea and the sky were welded together without a joint, and in the luminous space the tanned sails of the barges drifting up with the tide seemed to stand still in red clusters of canvas sharply peaked, with gleams of varnished sprits. A haze rested on the low shores that ran out to sea in vanishing flatness. The air was dark above Gravesend, and farther back still seemed condensed into a mournful gloom, brooding motionless over the biggest, and the greatest, town on earth.

The Director of Companies was our captain and our host. We four affectionately watched his back as he stood in the bows looking to seaward. On the whole river there was nothing that looked half so nautical. He resembled a pilot, which to a seaman is trustworthiness personified. It was difficult to realize his work was not out there in the luminous estuary, but behind him, within the brooding gloom.

Between us there was, as I have already said

◂ *Flush left, ragged right creates a vigorous texture. The right-margin should be like a gently torn piece of paper. Hyphenate if the lines become too extreme.*

The Nellie, a cruising yawl, swung to her anchor without a flutter of the sails, and was at rest. The flood had made, the wind was nearly calm, and being bound down the river, the only thing for it was to come to and wait for the turn of the tide.
The sea-reach of the Thames stretched before us like the beginning of an interminable waterway. In the offing the sea and the sky were welded together without a joint, and in the luminous space the tanned sails of the barges drifting up with the tide seemed to stand still in red clusters of canvas sharply peaked, with gleams of varnished sprits. A haze rested on the low shores that ran out to sea in vanishing flatness. The air was dark above Gravesend, and farther back still seemed condensed into a mournful gloom, brooding motionless over the biggest, and the greatest, town on earth.
The Director of Companies was our captain and our host. We four affectionately watched his back as he stood in the bows looking to seaward. On the whole river there was nothing that looked half so nautical. He resembled a pilot, which to a seaman is trustworthiness personified. It was difficult to realize his work was not out there in the luminous estuary, but behind him, within the brooding gloom.
Between us there was, as I have already said some-

◂ *Centred text is hard for the eye to follow. It can look good as a single line, for example in an invitation or letterhead, but in extended text it is almost impossible to read.*

The Nellie, a cruising yawl, swung to her anchor without a flutter of the sails, and was at rest. The flood had made, the wind was nearly calm, and being bound down the river, the only thing for it was to come to and wait for the turn of the tide.

The Nellie, a cruising yawl, swung to her anchor without a flutter of the sails, and was at rest. The flood had made, the wind was nearly calm, and being bound down the river, the only thing for it was to come to and wait for the turn of the tide.

The sea-reach of the Thames stretched before us like the beginning of an interminable waterway. In the offing the sea and the sky were welded together without a joint, and in

Effect of line length on legibility.

▸ *When the line is too short, reading is interrupted.*
▾ *Ideal line length: better flow and good legibility.*
▾▾ *Very long lines are almost impossible to read.*

The sea-reach of the Thames stretched before us like the beginning of an interminable waterway. In the offing the sea and the sky were welded together without a joint, and in the luminous space the tanned sails of the barges drifting up with the tide seemed to stand still in red clusters of canvas sharply peaked, with gleams of varnished sprits. A haze rested on the low shores that ran out to sea in vanishing flatness. The air was dark above Gravesend, and farther back still seemed condensed into a mournful gloom, brooding motionless over the biggest, and the greatest, town on earth.

The Nellie, a cruising yawl, swung to her anchor without a flutter of the sails, and was at rest. The flood had made, the wind was nearly calm, and being bound down the river, the only thing for it was to come to and wait for the turn of the tide.
The sea-reach of the Thames stretched before us like the beginning of an interminable waterway. In the offing the sea and the sky were welded together without a joint, and in the luminous space the tanned sails of the barges drifting up with the tide seemed to stand still in red clusters of canvas sharply peaked, with gleams of varnished sprits. A haze rested on the low shores that ran out to sea in vanishing flatness. The air was dark above Gravesend, and farther back still seemed condensed into a mournful gloom, brooding motionless over the biggest, and the greatest, town on earth.
The Director of Companies was our captain and our host. We four affectionately watched his back as he stood in the bows looking to seaward. On the whole river there was nothing that looked half so nautical. He resembled a pilot, which to a seaman is trustworthiness personified. It was difficult to realize his work was not out there in the luminous estuary, but behind him, within the brooding gloom.
Between us there was, as I have already said

◂ *Flush right, ragged left suffers from the same problems as centred text. One or two lines of flush right, for example in a caption or by-line, is acceptable, but anything longer is amateurish and illegible.*

The Director of Companies was our captain and our host. We

The Nellie, a cruising yawl, swung to her anchor without a flutter of the sails, and was at rest. The flood had made, the wind was nearly calm, and being bound down the river, the only thing for it was to come to and wait for the turn of the tide.
The sea-reach of the Thames stretched before us like the beginning of an interminable waterway. In the offing the sea and the sky were welded together without a joint, and in the luminous space the tanned sails of the barges drifting up with the tide seemed to stand still in red clusters of canvas sharply peaked, with gleams of varnished sprits. A haze rested on the low shores that ran out to sea in vanishing flatness. The air was dark above Gravesend, and farther back still seemed condensed into a mournful gloom, brooding motionless over the biggest, and the greatest, town on earth.
The Director of Companies was our captain and our host. We four affectionately watched his back as he stood in the bows looking to seaward. On the whole river there was nothing that looked half so nautical. He resembled a pilot, which to a seaman is trustworthiness personified. It was difficult to realize his work was not out there in the luminous estuary, but behind him, within the brooding gloom.
Between us there was, as I have already said some-

◂ *Fully justified, left and right, is still standard for fiction and common in newspapers. For many types of writing it looks dated now, although it is no longer common to see business letters done this way.*

The Nellie, a cruising yawl, swung to her anchor without a flutter of the sails, and was at rest. The flood had made, the wind was nearly calm, and being bound down the river, the only thing for it was to come to and wait for the turn of the tide.
The sea-reach of the Thames stretched before us like the beginning of an interminable waterway. In the offing the sea and the sky were welded together without a joint, and in the luminous space the tanned sails of the barges drifting up with the tide seemed to stand still in red clusters of canvas sharply peaked, with gleams of varnished sprits. A haze rested on the low shores that ran out to sea in vanishing flatness. The air was dark above Gravesend, and farther back still seemed condensed into a mournful gloom, brooding motionless over the biggest, and the greatest, town on earth.
The Director of Companies was our captain and our host. We four affectionately watched his back as he stood in the bows looking to seaward. On the whole river there was nothing that looked half so nautical. He resembled a pilot, which to a seaman is trustworthiness personified. It was difficult to realize his work was not out there in the luminous estuary, but behind him, within the brooding gloom.

Set tight, text is hard to read. Tight *and* fully justified, rivers of text open out where gaps between words are bigger than between lines.

At standard leading, 120%, text is relatively easy to read. 130% is typical for novels. This makes for easy reading in justified text.

Set with extended leading, text begins to appear prestigious. It's often worth reducing point size and increasing leading.

Typography

Designers and non-designers alike agonise about choice of typeface, but wider decisions about paragraph and page formatting have more impact on the document than differences between reasonable choices such as Garamond versus Palatino, or Helvetica versus Univers. The fundamental non-font choices are, first, how the paragraph is identified, then spacing within the paragraph, hierarchy of titles, justification, line length, and hyphenation.

Identifying the paragraph

Paragraphs are normally separated by an indented first line, or by a space. It is considered unhistoric to use both, though there are examples in early printed books where both are used. Narrative text is almost always set with indents, while technical manuals are usually set with spaces between paragraphs. A strict text grid requires inter-paragraph spacing to be an exact number of lines, but modern print rarely follows this.

Inter-line spacing (leading)

The spacing between the lines in the paragraph is critical for legibility. 'Set tight', where there is no additional spacing between lines, makes reading difficult. 'Leading' (pronounced like the metal) is either the gap between the top of one letter block and the bottom of the next, or the space between two baselines. The two definitions are used confusingly interchangeably, even within QuarkXPress. Standard leading is 120% or 20%, depending on your definition. In a novel, this is often 130%. You can set Quark's default leading in Preferences>Print Layout>Paragraph, and you can also set it in the Paragraph Style Sheet, or in the Measurements Paragraph tab. Increasing the leading beyond 130% gives a prestigious, refined look. Often it is more effective to reduce the point size while maintaining the absolute leading.

Hierarchy of titles

Modern readers are used to elaborate hierarchies of titles, not only in technical books, but in magazines, advertisements and newspapers. You can give your page a more conservative look by reducing the title hierarchy to just one or two levels, and identifying the titles only by spacing, justification and weight.

Justification

During the 20th century, typewritten text was almost always left justified, ragged right, whereas printed text was predominantly fully justified. When word-processors came in, it became common for business letters and other ad-hoc documents to be fully justified, while designed text was more frequently set flush left, ragged right. Text justified both sides in narrow columns results in large gaps between words, which can cause rivers of text to open up vertically across the page. This is hard to read. From the point of view of legibility, flush left, ragged right, like this page, is best.

Centred text and flush right, ragged left, are both hard to read. The eye prefers a straight line on the left to follow. They should only be used for very short blocks of text, typically only a single line.

Line length

The ideal line length is 11-13 words, where a word is standardised at 5 letters. Longer than 80 characters, and the eye begins to get lost. Shorter than 40 characters, and the rhythm of the line starts to interrupt the rhythm of the sentence. Short lines set justified are especially hard to read. For an A4 type page, similar to this one, some kind of column system is necessary to reduce the line length to something legible.

Hyphenation

Text should normally be hyphenated occasionally to prevent large gaps between words for justified text, or distractingly short lines in flush left, ragged right text. QuarkXPress 2018 allows hyphenation strictness to be set in Edit>H&Js. While it might be tempting to reduce the amount of hyphenation, this needs to be done while looking at the overall impact.

▼ascender to descender

omen come and g
ichelangelo.

▲baseline to baseline

▲120% 'normal' leading on 10pt text means 12 points from baseline to baseline, but 20% 'normal' leading, using the other definition of leading, is the same thing, with 2pts added between the top of the ascender and the bottom of the descender, which is the notional letter block.

Paragraph formatting: indents or spaces
▼Rudyard Kipling, Kim
▼▼1943 Harley-Davidson manual

He sat, in defiance of municipal orders, astride the gun Zam Zammah on her brick platform opposite the old Ajaib-Gher—the Wonder House, as the natives call the Lahore Museum. Who hold Zam-Zammah, that 'fire-breathing dragon', hold the Punjab, for the great green-bronze piece is always first of the conqueror's loot.

There was some justification for Kim—he had kicked Lala Dinanath's boy off the trunnions—since the English held the Punjab and Kim was English. Though he was burned black as any native; though he spoke the vernacular by

This technical manual is published for the information and guidance of the using army personnel charged with the operation, maintenance, and minor repair of this material.

In addition to a description of the Harley-Davidson motorcycle, this manual contains technical information required for the identification, use, and care of the materiel.

The manual is divided into two parts. Part One, section I through section VI, gives vehicle operating instructions. Part Two, section VII through section XXV, gives vehicle

▼*Intrinsic.* Use a blur test to check for font colour. To do this, set the opacity to 0%, turn on Drop Shadow in the Measurements palette, and turn off 'Inherit opacity'. You now have a blurred out version of your page. You can set up several alternate pages to compare fonts. This also helps to identify bad kerning and other problems.

▲*Futura implies geometrical construction with pen and compasses.*

▲*Palatino implies metal typesetting.*

Helvetica implies a clockmaker's precision and conformity.

▼*Associative.*

Nobody ever looked a fool setting things in Helvetica.

ITC Souvenir associates with educational books. Not always a wise choice.

ITC Lubalin Graph is best kept for things modern.

What makes a font appropriate? Good typography is about making the means of delivery—the type—transparent to the reader. We are not trying to illustrate or accentuate the text by choosing or changing fonts. Even so, there is a certain charm about reading a magazine article, or an medical form, or a novel, in a font which is 'just right'.

Appropriateness requires a deal of skill and discernment, especially when you are combining fonts, but understanding the character of different fonts can help you—see the next spread for a set of Archetypefaces that can get you started.

Font character comes down to three things: Intrinsic, Implicit, and Associative.

Intrinsic to a font are the compositional principles which govern its shape. However, except at very large sizes, this is not based on the shape of the individual letter, but on the combined effect of thousands of letters together. This puts a colour on the page, and gives the flow of letters their own rhythm. The best way to learn about this is to take pictures of pages of text that look good to you, and use something like WhattheFont to tell you which font is in use.

Implicit are clues the font gives about the way it was made. Of course, all fonts are made these days by putting dots of ink or toner on paper, but they still appear to have a particular origin. Futura looks like it was made with ruler and compass (it was), Gill Sans looks like it was drafted by hand (also true), Garamond looks like it was finely carved to emulate hand-writing, whereas Jenson much more closely resembles penned letters.

Think of these three pairings:

        Human………Machine

      Ornamental………Functional

       Transitory………Permanent.

Associative is all about where you have seen such a font before, or a font that closely resembles it. Times Roman always looks wrong, because it has been used inappropriately for millions of business letters since it appeared in Microsoft Word 30 years or so ago. Helvetica generally occurs in professional print, and Arial in amateur.

Fundamental to typography is consistency. It is the defining characteristic of print by comparison with handwriting or stone carving. You can introduce inconsistency as a graphic effect or for headlines, but, unless done with taste and a clear purpose, the result usually looks cheap rather than cool.

To achieve consistency in type, consider three things:

First, limit the number of font variants on a page. The old adage of 'no more than four' now seems hopelessly out-of-date, especially when you understand that this treated each size change as a variant. Even so, to be consistent, stick to one or two typefaces on the page, and limit the number of variations of size and weight. Use a consistent hierarchy of size, such as:

▶*geometric*
9 10 12 14 18 24 36 48

▶*Fibonacci*
or 8 13 21 34 55

Second, choose combinations of fonts that go well together. This is generally about pairing fonts that contrast strongly, typically a serif with a sans serif, and a heavy weight with a light weight. Consider also the feel and flavour of the font. ITC Lubalin Graph does not go well with Helvetica, for example, because Lubalin is the serif version of Avant Garde Gothic, a highly stylised geometric font, whereas Helvetica is an ultra under-styled humanistic font. Compare the fonts optically and come back to them with fresh eyes.

Third, choose consistent fonts. The internet is now buzzing with free fonts. Some of them were a labour of love over a generation, or a doctoral thesis. Others were cobbled together from other fonts by people who were better at coding than design. Use the kerning table, page 159, to check that they have been properly kerned, and scrutinise the lettertypes to ensure that they have consistent weights. Some playfulness is allowed—just look at Gill Sans—but anything which jars the eye in long copy needs to be thrown away. In the long run, it is often cheaper to buy fonts you can count on than make do with what you find.

Typefaces

Every typeface has its own character, and, in running text, its own degree of legibility. It used to be claimed that serif fonts were more legible in long copy and sans-serifs in short copy, with all capitals less legible than either, but recent work shows that it is familiarity which is the dominating factor, with a slightly wider letter width, low stroke variation, strong counters and higher x-height contributing. In other words, the more character a font has, the less legibility, and vice versa. Good typography is legibility with appropriateness and consistency.

▲ A non-exhaustive visual glossary of typographic elements. The important ones to know are x-height, t-height, serif, stroke, counter, em-width, n-width, tracking, kerning and leading.

Legibility

A typographer's first task is legibility. If the text cannot be read, type has failed. However, making things hyper-legible, by using over-large fonts or over-clear letters, reduces their credibility: we have all learned not to trust the headlines, and to read the small print.

When all other things are equal, legibility is a combination of optical size, weight, leading, good kerning & tracking, and familiarity.

Point size is not always a good guide. In moveable type, the point size was the the size of the printer's block. More ornate fonts needed a larger block for the same visual size. Computer sizes are more notional. Futura always seems smaller than its point size, Frutiger always larger. For older fonts, 11pt is probably the most legible, but many 1980s or later fonts set better at 10pt.

▲ Printer's block

The most legible weight is slightly heavier than a regular book font, but the typeface must also have good counters, being the enclosed white spaces, otherwise it becomes less legible. Equally, a slightly wider than average font is typically more legible.

'Leading' is used in two ways. It can either mean the additional space between two lines (the original meaning) or else the total space between the baselines, which would normally be the inter-line spacing plus the distance from the bottom of the descender to the top of the 'l' or 'b' in lower-case. The height from the baseline to the top of the 'l' is known as 't-height', though, in fact, the 't' is often shorter than the other ascenders.

Most text is set with a leading of 120% (or 20%, depending on how you're using the words) but in novels it will typically be 130%. In QuarkXPress you can set the default in the Preferences, or you can set it individually in the Paragraph Styles or the Measurements palette. From QX2017 you can enter this as a percentage. In QX2015-16 you would need to enter an actual figure, such as 12pt for 10pt text, giving 20% inter-line spacing. Increasing the leading increases legibility, though at a cost of efficiency.

Professionally designed fonts already have the letter-spacing and the kerning, which is the reduced gaps between individual letter pairs such as 'ev', already correctly set. You can edit kerning in QuarkXPress using Edit>Kerning Pairs, but if the font has many problem pairs, you should throw it away.

Familiarity is about letter types that are like others encountered in the same context. This changes over time, with Sans Serifs now seeming much less new, but also much more legible, than a hundred years ago.

Font or typeface?

Technically, what most people call a font is actually a typeface. Well, maybe. Pedants will tell you that the font is a single weight, such as bold or italic, whereas a typeface is all weights.

Other pedants will tell you that a font is a single size in a single weight, because that is what 'font' (or 'fount') once meant.

They are all wrong. A font, in its original use, was the place in which sets of the same letter in the same weight and typeface were stored. In that sense 'a' and 'b' are from different fonts.

Words, of course, are defined by how they're used, not what they meant three hundred years ago. In today's parlance it's normal to speak of a font as something you can download and install. Just go with what communicates, and don't be a pedant.

▼ A literal font. Everything else is metaphorical.

4: Fonts and kerning

The ultimate font, to some, or the ultimate font to be avoided, for others, Helvetica is the Helium of the type world. It is inert, remaining absolutely neutral in all circumstances. For this reason, it has much to offer the designer. When you want the message to speak, and the font not to get in the way, Helvetica is often the way to go. Accept no substitutes. If it's Helvetica you want, do not use Arial or any anything else designed to look like it.

If you want no frills, standardisation, with a nod to engineering or architectural drawings, consider DIN, which is so standard that it can only be used non-ironically on technical documents. Its even weight with virtually no variation makes for high legibility, which allows it a slightly narrower setting for better space saving. Especially if you want a German feel, DIN is always worth considering, and surprisingly underused.

Originally designed for a French airport, Frutiger is also the house font of the UK's National Health Service. In a British setting, nothing breathes confidence like Frutiger. Generous counters and a fairly even weight make this highly legible, and it can be set smaller than many similar fonts for the same legibility. A humanistic stroke variation means that it does not become dull in long text. If you want to set extensive body in a sans-serif, think of Frutiger.

Best of both worlds? You want a serif, and a sans-serif, both at once? Optima has faint flare serifs at the extremities, and a relatively strong stroke variation. In this way it looks clean like a sans-serif font, but also friendly and traditional like a serif font. Optima is less fashionable than it once was, and so is probably due for a comeback. Look out for similar flare serif fonts which can perform the same 'best of both worlds' trick.

Geometrics:
Futura is the original geometric font, made with a ruler and compass. Avenir is a more contemporary design, less uncompromising. It gives a modern feel without (as Futura sometimes can) shouting at you and saying 'look, I'm modern'. If in doubt between Avenir and Futura, pick Avenir: Futura is not a font for doubters.

Humanists:
Univers looks like it might belong with Futura, but, underlying its clean, modern design are humanistic proportions straight out of Leonardo da Vinci's notebook. Eurostile is a humanistic font with a machine twist. If you're designing for science-fiction, or futurism, you can't go wrong with Eurostile.

British sans:
Consider a sans-serif designed using the same tools as Futura, but by a British designer who could not resist giving each letter its own individual character. The result is Gill Sans. Don't be deceived by the clinical, mechanical G. Look also at the lower case a, capital M and lower case g, all of which could have come from entirely different fonts. When you are serious, but not too serious, think of Gill or its imitators.

Retro Gothic:
Want a typewriter feel in a typographic font, and want to stick with sans-serif? Franklin Gothic has a nice retro feel, with slight variation in letter width and design ensuring that it always appears friendly and non-technical. Franklin Gothic is supplied with Microsoft Office, so if you are working on a visual identity, it makes a readily accessible pairing with a more esoteric (and therefore expensive) logo font.

Set in bronze?
If you want something which looks like it might have been set in bronze, Friz Quadrata is insistently robust. It is quite clearly a serif font, but the feel is more like a sans-serif, with relatively slight stroke variation, strong weight, and an enormous x-height. Overwhelming as a book font, and over-elaborate for titles, Friz Quadrata and its analogues need to be judiciously placed and not over-used.

Archetypefaces

These twenty-one archetypefaces represent different approaches to typography that have inspired thousands of other fonts. It's now fairly easy to Google for 'fonts like...', so these are a good starting point in finding the right typeface for your project.

Garamond, left, isn't so much a font as the idea of a font. There are many variations on Garamond's original design, and ITC Garamond, which is one of the more useful, only superficially resembles it. For a classic look, think always of Garamond. Bembo, by contrast, is an elegant modern serif, preferable to the over-used Times Roman in most cases. Bembo sets light, and so can seem to flicker a little on the page. When used well, it can be beautiful.

A 19th century classic, Baskerville has more character than Times Roman and is an excellent font for setting a novel or any other extended text. Be careful of versions. ITC Baskerville and other professional versions deliver a proper set of characters, but the free versions supplied with Microsoft Office has almost invisible em-dashes, and generally seems uncared for.

Startlingly beautiful and always elegant, Bodonis and their friends the Didots, collectively known as 'Didones' are rarely used effectively. They require generous leading and relatively sparse text, on account of the extreme stroke variation which means you must give the eye all the help you can. If you wish to create a prestige look, and are prepared to tightly control the length of copy, Bodoni and its friend Didot may be what you are looking for.

Looking for an old style that isn't Garamond? Consider Jenson, with its distinctive lower case e and strong sense of Renaissance penmanship. If you are trying to conjure an elegant, early modern look and Garamond is not working, consider Jenson.

Walbaum is a Germanic serif-font of the no-nonsense variety. In extended copy it is regular and regimented, while still keeping some of the elegance of Bodoni. It is a true 'bread-and-butter' font, not drawing attention to itself but doing its job as efficiently and quietly as possible. Walbaum is relatively under-used, and stands up in professional publications.

Slab serifs such as Caecilia and Rockwell are highly legible and always seem modern, which is surprising since they date from the time of Napoleon and are sometimes called 'Egyptians'. Rockwell's heavier weight and extreme evenness make it ever modern. Caecilia, by contrast, introduces a certain elegance. It sets light, but the generous counters and high x-height keep it legible and easy on the eye. It pairs well with Univers.

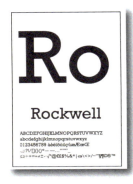

Clarendons, like their archetype Clarendon, are super-robust fonts which jump off the page. This is unsurprising since Clarendon was originally created for a dictionary. If you want to stamp your authority on something, and are confident that you're not overdoing it (which invites ridicule), then a Clarendon can always be made to serve. However, too much of it and you will appear frumpy and old fashioned.

For a modern take on a Didone (ie, a Bodoni or a Didot), consider Cambria. Although not quite as expressive as Bodoni, Cambria solves many of the problems of its more extreme ancestor, and so is a good choice for practical typesetting when Bodoni is what you want, but the copy simply cannot be made to work with it.

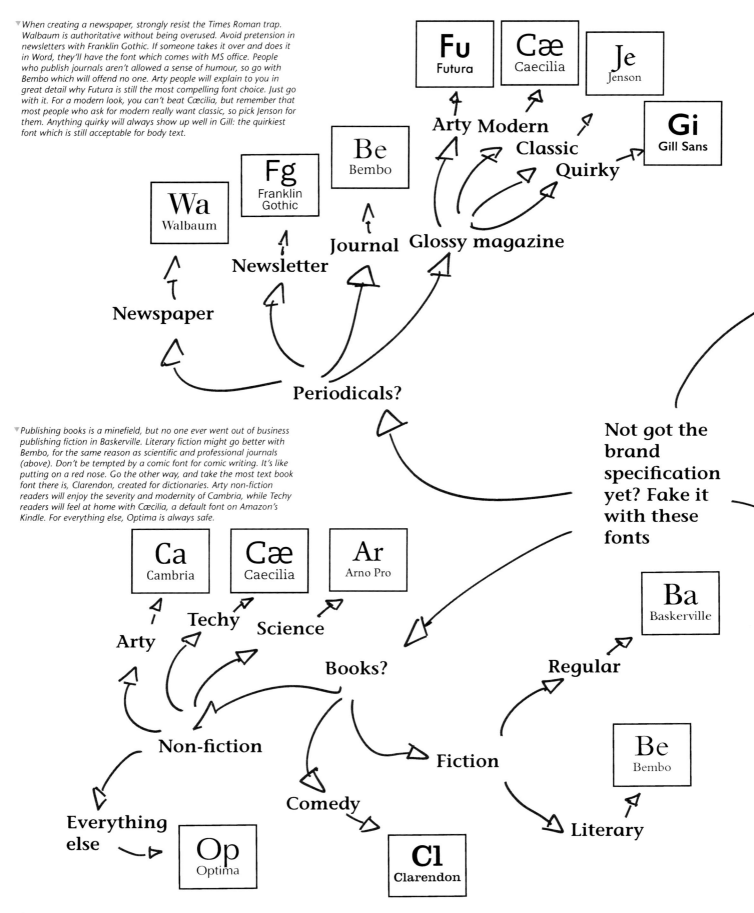

▼ When creating a newspaper, strongly resist the Times Roman trap. Walbaum is authoritative without being overused. Avoid pretension in newsletters with Franklin Gothic. If someone takes it over and does it in Word, they'll have the font which comes with MS office. People who publish journals aren't allowed a sense of humour, so go with Bembo which will offend no one. Arty people will explain to you in great detail why Futura is still the most compelling font choice. Just go with it. For a modern look, you can't beat Cœcilia, but remember that most people who ask for modern really want classic, so pick Jenson for them. Anything quirky will always show up well in Gill: the quirkiest font which is still acceptable for body text.

▼ Publishing books is a minefield, but no one ever went out of business publishing fiction in Baskerville. Literary fiction might go better with Bembo, for the same reason as scientific and professional journals (above). Don't be tempted by a comic font for comic writing. It's like putting on a red nose. Go the other way, and take the most text book font there is, Clarendon, created for dictionaries. Arty non-fiction readers will enjoy the severity and modernity of Cambria, while Techy readers will feel at home with Cœcilia, a default font on Amazon's Kindle. For everything else, Optima is always safe.

Faking it with fonts

Often you have to put something together without knowing what the official fonts are. Rather than agonise for hours about what might look okay, fake it with this font-faking-flow-chart. You can also check most font sites for fonts similar to these, for the sake of variation, or to find fonts you already own. These are all for body text. Do whatever you like for titles.

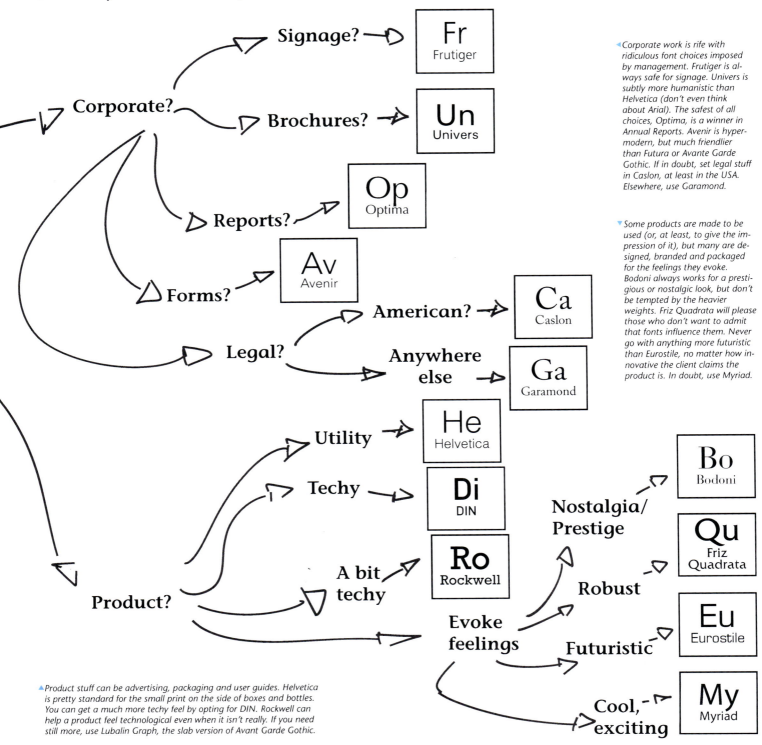

◀ Corporate work is rife with ridiculous font choices imposed by management. Frutiger is always safe for signage. Univers is subtly more humanistic than Helvetica (don't even think about Arial). The safest of all choices, Optima, is a winner in Annual Reports. Avenir is hyper-modern, but much friendlier than Futura or Avante Garde Gothic. If in doubt, set legal stuff in Caslon, at least in the USA. Elsewhere, use Garamond.

▼ Some products are made to be used (or, at least, to give the impression of it), but many are designed, branded and packaged for the feelings they evoke. Bodoni always works for a prestigious or nostalgic look, but don't be tempted by the heavier weights. Friz Quadrata will please those who don't want to admit that fonts influence them. Never go with anything more futuristic than Eurostile, no matter how innovative the client claims the product is. In doubt, use Myriad.

▲ Product stuff can be advertising, packaging and user guides. Helvetica is pretty standard for the small print on the side of boxes and bottles. You can get a much more techy feel by opting for DIN. Rockwell can help a product feel technological even when it isn't really. If you need still more, use Lubalin Graph, the slab version of Avant Garde Gothic.

Great images require good technique, but good technique does not produce great images. The battle for the compelling picture is won in the mind.

1 Intention
Decide what you want the image to achieve before you shoot it. 99% of all the images that I've ever had given to me for layout were no more than illustrations of what happened to be going on when the image was shot. Even a small amount of intention at the time could have saved them.

2 Audience perspective
Think yourself into the mind of the readers. What will they find compelling? What are they interested in?

3 Message
For most functional photography, there will be some kind of message. The more you of it you can get into the picture so that you need less words to spell it out, the more effective.

4 Creativity
Creativity is often a case of going just one step beyond the obvious. What's the obvious way to say something? Ok, now go one beyond it. If the obvious is someone talking on the telephone, what about someone talking through a tin can and string? Or someone holding a laptop to their ear? Or someone shouting through cupped hands with someone in the distance with their hands to their ears?

5 Commitment
Shooting great images requires mental toughness. In a photoshoot, there's always pressure on you to fall back to mere illustration.

6 Previsualisation
Always keep the final image, in its final context, in your head as you prepare. A great image that won't fit the layout is still failure.

Sometimes you need to pick up the camera and shoot. There's no time or budget to instruct a photographer. It's now or never. These five disciplines will help you get it right.

1 Planning
Great photography is a question of planning. You need to be there, at the right time, with the right people, dressed in the right way, and the right props and lighting. None of it happens by accident.

2 Preparing
Check everything you are going to use the night before. Check it again right before you shoot. Practise with any equipment which is new or unfamiliar. Check all the settings, and do a test shot before continuing.

3 Composing
Things will only be where you put them, and people will only be where you tell them to be. You can't fix a badly arranged scene in photo-editing. Pay careful attention to anything in the background—it will dominate the image if it's wrong—and look at the edges of the image. Remember this adage: shoot wide, crop hard.

4 Lighting
Eliminate mixed lighting. Switch off every office or domestic light. Shoot either in natural light or in photographic lighting. Use portable reflectors to get the light where you want it. No HDR in the world can match a well-lit scene.

5 Inspiring
When shooting people, once everything is ready, inspire them. Get them involved in the shoot. Tell them stories, invoke their emotions. Even professional models struggle to produce emotions on demand (unless you count 'sultry' and 'too cool to be interested' as emotions). Your fundamental photographic skill is engaging people. Everything else is just operations.

▲ Images can create infinity by directing the viewer toward some other elements. This image was part of a composite to bring attention to a super-sized logo.

▼ This image, shot for both a press release and an Annual Report, needed to create a sense of occasion for something that was really no more than a project planner's milestone.

▼ Sometimes the photographer's job is to get out of the way and let the scene speak for itself. However, in this shot, judicious use of off-camera lighting helps to provide definition.

Photography

If you want to upgrade your publications, upgrade your photography. The world is all too full of busy, uninspiring layout which draws on the feature sets of well-known software (think glowing lines, images fading into each other, distorted typefaces and overuse of style presets). If you look at a prestige magazine, you see quite quickly that enormous amounts are invested in the images. Get the pictures right, and everything else will be right. Sadly, most clients are unwilling to invest where it counts, but there are things you can do inexpensively to help.

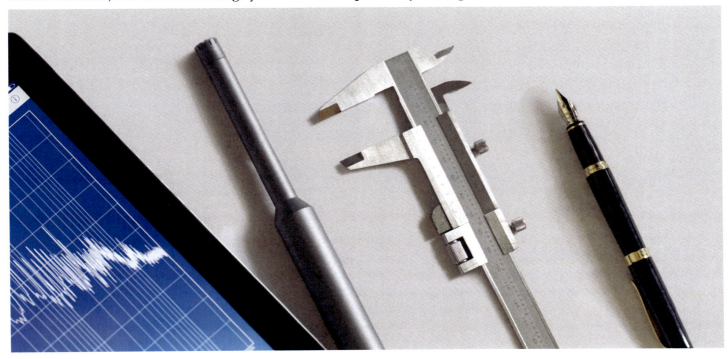

▼ *Tools of the trade, commissioned image.*

Ten golden rules for working with photographic images

1. Discard. Images with mixed lighting, bad shadows, focus on the wrong element, irredeemable composition or bad body language cannot be rescued.

2. Check the background. Most people choose their pictures based on the foreground, but it's the background which determines whether an image is fit to be used. If you're tempted towards a cut-out, and that wasn't part of the original design, then be brave and reject the image.

3. Reshoot. In the old days of film, magazines still re-did entire photoshoots if they didn't get useable images. With a consumer DSLR and a nice, overcast sky, which functions as a giant softbox, you can reshoot almost anything in half an hour.

4. Delight the reader. Photography should be a breath of heaven in the layout. Never be content with utilitarian images which 'do the job'.

5. Differential focus. Smartphones have enormous depth of field, as that plays to the needs of their users. When picking images for print, go the other way and take images with shallow, intentional focus.

6. Strong lighting. It's tempting to use HDR tools to even everything out. It looks either dull or ridiculous. Good lighting can create definition for otherwise unremarkable subjects, or hold back identification in otherwise too obvious subjects. Sometimes you need to make the reader work a little.

7. Switch off the effects. Any image which needs special effects to make it work is, by definition, a bad image.

8. Tell a story. Lead the reader's imagination into narrative. The caption gives the facts, the eye does the rest.

9. Choose infinity. If you have an image which keeps drawing the eye, prioritise it in the layout.

10. Be unexpected. Creative images reveal a flow of ideas which seizes the mind. No image is ever better than the ideas it represents.

At the layout stage, the only flexibility you have is choosing what pictures to use (but see point 3). Often a client will come with a picture which is important to them, but unsuitable for publication. Even if you can't commission new images, you can choose between the ones that will work and those that won't.

3: Preparing pictures for print

Word	Colors
Acidic	Greenish Yellow · Lime
Aggressive	Bright Red
Airy	Pure White
Artsy	Bright Yellow-Green
Attention-Getting	Bright Pink
Authoritative	Navy
Autumn	Golden Yellow
Babies	Light Pink
Basic	Navy · Black · Taupe
Bland	Beige
Bold	Bright Yellow-Green · Black
Bright	Fuchsia · Pure White
Buttery	Golden Yellow
Calm	Light Blue · Light Green
Calming	Sky Blue
Camouflage	Olive Green
Casual	Beige · Earth Brown · Light Blue · Neutral Gray
Cheerful	Light Yellow · Bright Yellow
Childlike	Orange
Classic	Cream · Beige · Deep Plum · Navy · Olive Green · Black · Charcoal Gray · Neutral Gray · Taupe · Silver
Classy	Teal Blue
Clean	Light Blue · Pure White
Comforting	Golden Yellow
Confident	Navy
Conservative	Navy
Constant	Sky Blue
Cool	Light Blue · Sky Blue · Aqua · Dark Green · Neutral Gray · Silver
Corporate	Neutral Gray
Country	Brick Red · Terracotta
Cosy	Dusty Pink
Creative	Red Purple
Credible	Navy
Cute	Light Pink
Delicate	Light Pink · Lavender
Delicious	Peach · Cream · Coffee or Chocolate
Dependable	Sky Blue · Navy
Dirt	Earth Brown
Discreet	Coffee or Chocolate · Deep Plum · Charcoal Gray · Neutral Gray · Silver
Dominant	Cobalt Blue
Drab	Olive Green
Dramatic	Bright Red · Bright Blue
Durable	Earth Brown
Dusky	Dusty Pink
Dynamic	Bright Red
Earth	Earth Brown
Earthy	Brick Red · Terracotta · Beige
Electric	Bright Blue
Elegant	Burgundy · Deep Plum · Black
Enduring	Charcoal Gray
Energetic	Bright Pink · Bright Blue
Energising	Bright Red · Orange
Energy	Bright Yellow
Enlightening	Bright Yellow
Essential	Beige · Neutral Gray
Exciting	Bright Red · Bright Pink · Fuchsia · Red Purple
Exotic	Orchid
Expensive	Burgundy · Deep Plum · Teal Blue · Black · Charcoal Gray · Silver · Gold
Faithful	Sky Blue
Fantasy	Blue Purple
Feminine	Light Pink
Flags	Bright Blue
Flamboyant	Red Purple
Floral	Lavender
Flowers	Golden Yellow · Orchid
Foliage	Bright Green
Forest	Dark Green
Formal	Pure White · Black
Fragrant	Orchid
Fresh	Aqua · Bright Green
Friendly	Orange · Bright Yellow
Fruity	Peach · Greenish Yellow · Lime
Fun	Bright Pink · Fuchsia · Orange
Futuristic	Blue Purple · Silver
Fuzzy	Peach
Gaudy	Bright Yellow-Green
Ghostly	Neutral Gray
Glistening	Pure White
Glowing	Orange
Grass	Bright Green
Gregarious	Orange
Happy	Bright Pink · Orange · Light Yellow · Golden Yellow · Sky Blue · Bright Blue
Harvest	Orange · Golden Yellow
Heavenly	Sky Blue
Heavy	Black
Heritage	Earth Brown
High Energy	Fuchsia
Homemade	Terracotta · Coffee or Chocolate
Hope	Bright Yellow · Golden Yellow
Hot	Bright Red · Bright Pink · Fuchsia · Orange · Bright Yellow
Industrial	Bright Yellow · Neutral Gray
Innocent	Pure White
Innovation	Teal Blue · Electric Blue
Intense	Electric Blue
Inviting	Peach
Invulnerable	Black
Irish	Bright Green
Jewellery	Turquoise
Juicy	Orange
Lemony	Greenish Yellow
Lightweight	Pure White
Liquid	Aqua
Lively	Bright Green · Lime
Loud	Orange
Luminous	Bright Yellow
Luxury	Golden Yellow · Red Purple · Blue Purple · Pure White · Black
Magical	Black
Masculine	Earth Brown
Mature	Burgundy · Charcoal Gray
Meditative	Blue Purple
Military	Olive Green
Modern	Silver
Money	Dark Green · Silver
Mysterious	Black
Mystical	Blue Purple
Nature	Dark Green
Nautical	Navy
Neutral	Cream · Beige · Aqua · Light Green · Taupe
Nighttime	Black
Nostalgic	Lavender
Nurturing	Peach
Ocean	Turquoise · Aqua
Opulent	Gold
Outdoorsy	Bright Green
Peaceful	Light Blue
Pleasing	Teal Blue
Powerful	Bright Red · Deep Plum · Black
Practical	Neutral Gray · Taupe
Prestige	Black
Prestigious	Black · Gold
Professional	Navy · Charcoal Gray
Provocative	Bright Red
Pure	Pure White
Quality	Neutral Gray · Taupe
Quiet	Mauve · Light Blue · Navy · Light Green · Dark Green · Neutral Gray
Radiant	Gold
Refined	Burgundy
Refreshing	Dark Green · Lime
Regal	Deep Plum
Restful	Sky Blue · Dark Green
Rich	Burgundy · Golden Yellow · Cream · Coffee or Chocolate · Teal Blue
Romantic	Light Pink
Rooted	Earth Brown
Rustic	Earth Brown
Safari	Olive Green
Safety	Bright Yellow
Sandy	Beige
Secure	Earth Brown
Sensual	Fuchsia · Red Purple
Sentimental	Mauve
Serene	Navy
Serious	Black
Service	Navy
Sexy	Bright Red
Sharp	Bright Yellow-Green
Sheltering	Earth Brown
Sickening	Bright Yellow-Green
Silent	Pure White
Slimy	Bright Yellow-Green
Smooth	Cream
Sober	Black · Neutral Gray
Soft	Light Pink · Dusty Pink · Mauve · Peach · Light Yellow · Cream · Beige
Solid	Charcoal Gray
Soothing	Aqua · Light Green
Sophisticated	Grape · Charcoal Gray
Spirited	Bright Pink
Spiritual	Blue Purple
Spring	Bright Green
Stately	Dark Green
Sterile	Pure White
Stimulating	Bright Red
Stirring	Bright Blue
Strong	Brick Red · Navy · Black
Subdued	Mauve
Subtle	Dusty Pink · Grape
Sun	Golden Yellow
Sunbaked	Golden Yellow
Sunny	Light Yellow
Sunset	Orange
Sunshine	Bright Yellow
Sweet	Light Pink · Peach · Light Yellow
Sweet Scented	Lavender
Sweet Taste	Lavender · Grape
Tacky	Bright Yellow-Green
Tangy	Orange
Tart	Greenish Yellow · Lime
Tasty	Burgundy
Technology	Electric Blue
Tender	Light Pink
Timeless	Neutral Gray · Taupe
Traditional	Navy · Dark Green
Tranquil	Sky Blue
Trendy	Bright Pink · Bright Yellow-Green
Tropical	Orchid · Turquoise
Trustworthy	Dark Green
Uniforms	Navy
Unique	Red Purple · Teal Blue
Valuable	Silver · Gold
Vibrant	Bright Blue · Electric Blue
Vital	Orange
Warm	Brick Red · Terracotta · Light Yellow · Golden Yellow · Cream · Beige · Earth Brown · Gold
Water	Light Blue
Welcoming	Terracotta
Wheat	Golden Yellow
Whimsical	Orange
Wholesome	Terracotta · Earth Brown
Wild	Bright Pink
Woodsy	Earth Brown · Dark Green
Youthful	Bright Pink · Electric Blue

Colour and emotion

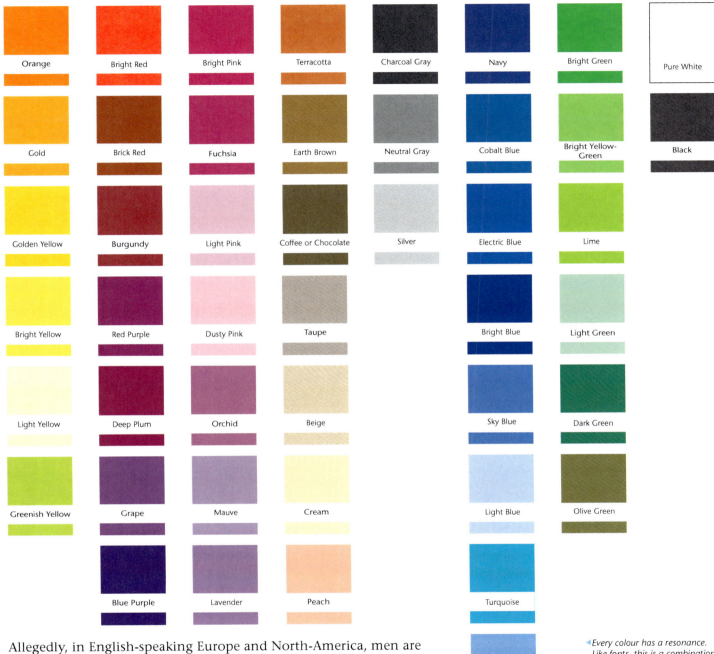

Allegedly, in English-speaking Europe and North-America, men are only willing to admit to distinguishing seven colours (red, blue, green, yellow, orange, purple, brown), while women are more likely to name fifty-six. Language has a strong influence on what we consciously perceive as 'different' colours, but it does not affect our actual ability to distinguish between two 'kinds' of green, blue and so on. The colours here apply to the table on the left.

◀ *Every colour has a resonance. Like fonts, this is a combination of intrinsic properties, implicit and associative.*
Intrinsic is how the frequency strikes the eye and is processed by the visual cortex. Implicit is what the colour implies, such as red for blood, blue for sky, green for grass, based on universal human experiences. Associative is the particular set of associations we have built up in our own culture. The table opposite is for Western cultures.

24: Colour explained

Complementary

Colour 1
Hue   H°
Saturation S%
Brightness B%

Colour 2
Hue   H+180°
Saturation same
Brightness same

Split Complementary

Colour 1
Hue   H°

Colour 2
Hue   H+150°

Colour 3
Hue   H+210°

Triad

Colour 1
Hue   H°

Colour 2
Hue   H+120°

Colour 3
Hue   H+240°

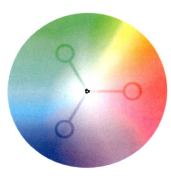

Tetrad

Colour 1
Hue   H°

Colour 2
Hue   H+90°

Colour 3
Hue   H+180°

Colour 4
Hue   H+270°

Analogous

Colour 1
Hue   H°

Colour 2
Hue   H+30°

Colour 3
Hue   H+60°

Colour 4
Hue   H+90°

Creating colour palettes in QX

There are lots of free tools on the web for creating colour palettes, but they are always limited to things the programmers thought of. You can create endless palettes using QX's built-in features using the HSB colour space. This makes it easy to create palettes with simple arithmetic.

1. Identify the key colours that communicate values or emotions.

2. Create the colour using the **HSB** model.

3. Create a new colour by adding the value in degrees° on the Hue only. If the number would be bigger than 360°, subtract 360°. Use the first four models.

4. As required, add Analogous colours from the fifth model.

5. If needed, add tints by changing the brightness. If absolutely needed, you can add a limited number of colours by putting in Saturation at 1/2 or 1/3.

6. When you have enough colours, stop!

The key to harmonious colour palettes is to use the same method consistently (for example, keep on adding 30° to the Hue), and making the differences big enough to be distinctive colours. For most palettes, change the hue only.

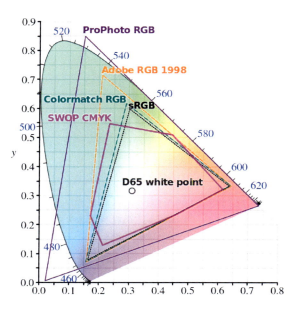

▲ CIE 1931 colour space diagram (image—Wikipedia), showing how various colour spaces map onto the visible spectrum, which is the largest area. The LAB space includes the entire gamut, and beyond.

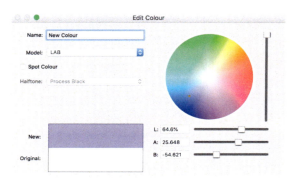

▼ Using the HSB colour model means you can use QX's built-in calculation feature. If the original colour is 10.772°, just type 180+ in front of it, and click on the next box. This will give you the complementary colour. QX will do the calculation for you, and show the new colour. Don't change the saturation or brightness. You can use the four colour models to add in principal colours, and then the analogous colour model to add additional colours.

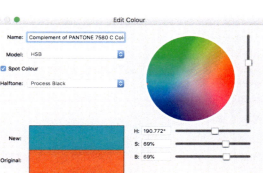

▲ LAB colour (correctly, CIE L*a*b*) specifies all of the colours that the human eye can see, and many that it cannot (these are the white areas on the chart, top). It is the most complete space, and works in the way the human eye works, with lightness (L), Red-Green (a) and Blue-Yellow (b). LAB only works properly in 16-bit colour, as the changes are too stepped in 8-bits. Because it includes the full visible gamut, LAB is used by most computer systems to compute CMYK to RGB conversions, and is at the base of the composite workflow. It is thanks to LAB, which is device independent, that colour profiles enable us to send RGB or CMYK output in the composite workflow and be confident that the final colour will be the best possible representation of our intent, without needing to convert colour spaces ourselves (which degrades the images).
Although it replicates the human eye, LAB is quite unintuitive. HSB is better for colour harmonies.

Colour and science

The human eye has three receptors: Light-Dark, Red-Green, and Blue-Yellow. Although you can mix yellow and blue paint, or red and green light, the results will be artefacts of how they are produced. You cannot (in human terms) have a bluish-yellow, or a reddish-green in the way you can have a bluish-red or a yellowish-green. Because the eye deduces, rather than 'sees' the colour spectrum, it can be fooled with Red, Green and Blue light, or Cyan, Magenta, Yellow and Black ink on white paper. The LAB colour space (see opposite) best emulates how the eye sees.

Greyscale

The printed page can reproduce about 200 levels of grey that the eye can discern (the eye can discern far more than this, because it adapts to differing light conditions). For this reason, greyscale is usually 8 bit, covering 256 levels. However, these do not map perfectly to perception, so greyscale gradients often appear 'stepped'.

RGB

Red-Green-Blue is the method by which computer and TV screens, and data projectors, display colour, by overlaying or juxtaposing the pixels. Raw RGB does not map particularly well to the human eye, so there are a number of 'colour spaces', of which sRGB is standard for the web. Adobe RGB is often better for images that will be manipulated. ProPhoto has a wider gamut than either, but requires 16 bit images.

CMYK

CMYK print is the most established method of reproducing variable colour on paper. The ink primary colours cyan, magenta and yellow account for the colour component. In principle they should be able to reproduce black, but this creates an impure black and too much ink coverage, so black is added 'K', for 'blacK' to expand the range.

Flexo

While offset presses usually print CMYK or Spot Colour, Flexoprint often prints Cyan, Magenta and Yellow. Flexo has advanced so much in recent years that the quality can be very high. Flexo is typically used for packaging where large runs at high speed and low cost are required, often on substrates that are difficult for CMYK offset.

Spot Colour

Until recently, many colours could not be reproduced by 'process' printing (ie, the CMYK process), so branded colours were typically done with Pantone specified 'spot' colours. Pantone is not actually a colour specification, but an ink mixing specification. It is often used as a reliable means of specifying colour, either coated (C), coated and varnished (CV) or uncoated (U).

Extended gamut colour

Pantone and Esko have developed a new method of printing colours, up to 90% of the Pantone spot gamut, by printing three or four from a set of seven colours, controlled by a specialist RIP which is able to manage different colours of ink. QuarkXPress supports Pantone XTG colours, as well as the most recent specification of Pantone spot colours.

No longer required
The composite workflow means that you no longer need to convert colours and prepare output for its destination colour space. Using Composite output via PDF, you can export in RGB or CMYK, irrespective of how your images are defined, and the final conversion will take place in the RIP in LAB space. This means that a file can contain a mixture of different colour spaces, provided each one is correctly profiled. Profiles should be applied by the originating device.

Have you calibrated your screen?
Although colour conversion is best left to the final output device, any colours originated from your screen are liable to whatever colour and lightness shifts your screen is subject to. A calibrated screen, using an X-Rite or Spyder device, will dramatically improve the chances of the colour being right, but there is still a significant gap between what screens display and what print can reproduce. This is one reason why choosing from Pantone swatches will make things more reliable.

▼ The visible spectrum, runs from 390 to 700 nm wavelength, or 430-770 THz. The eye does not 'see' this, it deduces it from its red-green, yellow-blue and light-dark receptors.

(Wikimedia Commons)

Simplified visual identity

Most visual identity documents run to about twenty pages or more. In reality, if you can get the key points onto a single sheet, you are doing the client a service. In a large organisation, this is concise enough for the staff to actually remember it and take it seriously. In a small business, there's something slightly vain about having a visual identity that takes up more pages than the full business plan.

▼ Classical branding: this Roman pot-sherd from the 3rd century contains the maker's logo. Verulamium Museum, St Albans UK.

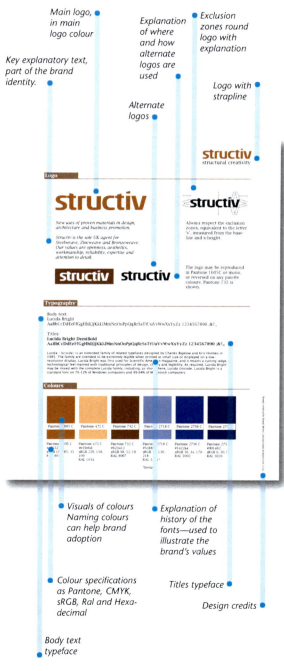

- Main logo, in main logo colour
- Key explanatory text, part of the brand identity.
- Explanation of where and how alternate logos are used
- Alternate logos
- Exclusion zones round logo with explanation
- Logo with strapline
- Visuals of colours. Naming colours can help brand adoption
- Explanation of history of the fonts—used to illustrate the brand's values
- Colour specifications as Pantone, CMYK, sRGB, Ral and Hexadecimal
- Titles typeface
- Design credits
- Body text typeface

Most large organisations and many smaller businesses have a visual identity document. This sets out the exact rules for colours, fonts, graphic devices and how the logo should be used.

This makes the designer's job substantially easier, provided you remember two things:

1 The corporate visual identity is not negotiable

and

2 The person commissioning the job may not understand this, but you will still be blamed if you get it wrong.

Normally the visual identity document will be supplied to you as a PDF. The easiest way to work with it is to import it and convert to native objects in QuarkXPress 2016 or later. This will bring in the specified colours, typefaces, logos and graphic elements. In QX2016 and QX2017 you can import an entire document and convert to native objects using the PDF Importer Pro Xtension from Creationauts. In QX2018, the supplied JavaScript does the job for you.

Using job jackets

Job jackets let you build a set of typefaces, colours, boilerplate text and graphics, as well as style-sheets and other elements into a skeleton which you can use to construct and manage a suite of branded documents.

As far as brands and document management is concerned, the key is as follows:

For a brand job jacket, include the minimum: just colours, typefaces and key content such as logos.

For a document suite, include the maximum, and leave the jackets linked. This way, you can keep tweaking layout in one document and have it automatically update in others.

For more on Job Jackets, see page 173.

Ad hoc visual identity

Many small businesses have a history of print artwork, but no formal visual identity. It will save you time to document their typefaces, colours and graphic elements in a simplified visual identity sheet.

10: Working with a visual identity

Brand

A brand is a promise of an experience. Long before Peter Behrens created the first corporate visual identity for AEG in 1907 or Bass beer created a visual trademark in 1876, manufacturers and craftsmen had learned to distinguish their goods with devices, names, shapes and colours. The primary components of a brand are promise, delivery and presentation. Consistently fulfilling the promise is more important than any other part of branding. However, consistency in presentation helps to underline consistency of experience.

Defining a brand is about making the impalpable obvious. Begin with the brand's **promise**: how does it uniquely solve a problem for its customers? Move on to **category**: a brand needs to be the number 1 or 2 in its own category. If it's not, go to a more specific sub-category. The **values** are the non-negotiables about how we do things. What is this brand prepared to go out of business for? **Personality** or style is about the human-like traits which characterise the brand approach. **Architecture** is how the brand fits together. Is the company the brand? Does the company have several product brands? Are these endorsed brands, like Wrigley's Spearmint Gum? **Identity** begins with the name, then goes onto the logo, then the visual identity. It should be Memorable, Appropriate, Distinctive and Efficient. **Deployment** (see below) is where it will appear. A web-conceived brand is unlikely to deploy well on physical materials.

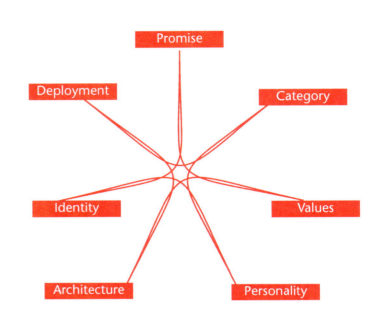

Literature	Stationery	Product & Packaging	Signage, Livery, Uniforms	Web and Digital

Printed word
Print is still king for brands that want to be taken seriously, unless they only exist (like Facebook or Wikipedia) in the digital space. Commission good, characteristic photography which can work across many media, and stick rigorously to a brand specification, including tone of voice.

Administrative
Receiving a letter from a business, or a business card from a manager, or a form, are the highest status contacts most people have with a brand. Don't squander the opportunity with cheap looking print, especially not print which looks like it was quickly conceived and cheaply laser-printed.

On product
That which is stamped into the product rings more true than that which is merely glued on. A good packaging programme—even for a service brand—makes it clear that the brand means business about quality and identity.

In space
Vehicles, signage and uniforms shape the space around them in the way that mere items don't. Effective vehicle livery is rarely seen, but when done right, it eclipses outdoor advertising. For many businesses the uniform sets behaviour not just perceptions. Signage redefines movement.

HTML and apps
Providing you have useful content, transmuting your print into HTML5 publications, iOS and Android apps can seal the brand as high capability, high desirability. Be careful, though: many brand-supporting apps are little more than advertisements. If you are asking people to download, make it worth it.

By Process

Text control

An uncontrolled publishing process is a recipe for disaster. Make no mistake: you will be blamed. Therefore, the first thing you should do when you're given a layout job is ask "what's the publishing process?" If they don't know what you're talking about, immediately offer to take control of the project. I usually offer the 'author–editor–publisher' method.

The author of the text supplies the text to an editor.

The editor checks that the text is properly written, uses consistent abbreviations, matches the House Style, is spelled correctly and makes sense.

The publisher controls the path of the document through the organisation, ensuring that it has gone to the right committees and been signed off by the right officers. The publisher is the person whose signature signs off the document for you to release it to the printer or for web/app distribution.

In most jurisdictions, organisations are legally liable for what they publish, so it is essential that the publisher has been authorised by their organisation to issue materials.

Author ⇒ **Editor** ⇒ **Publisher** ⇒ **Reproduction & Distribution** (Print, web etc)

House Style
Always ask for a copy of the House Style guide. This is not the same as the visual identity, though a good set of brand guidelines will include it. House Style sets out typographical, spelling, abbreviation and tone of voice conventions. If they don't have one, offer them yours. English has so many different variations of standards that you may be supplied text which mixes up dozens of them. In published text, this is simply messy.
If you're working with an external client who doesn't have one, remember to pitch it to them as a necessary and chargeable extra, and supply it with the document as a finished layout. It's a value-added service which they need.

Publisher's checklist:
- ❏ Project agreed
- ❏ Process agreed
- ❏ Named publisher authorised
- ❏ Timescales agreed
- ❏ Budget approved

- ❏ Final text provided by Author(s)

- ❏ Editor sign-off on texts
- ❏ Spelling and grammar
- ❏ House Style
- ❏ Text Authorised by:
  - ❏ Individuals
  - ❏ Committees
- ❏ Complete, final and correct texts sent for DTP

- ❏ Layout complete

- ❏ Proof-reader has checked layout
- ❏ Every phone number checked by dialling
- ❏ Every URL checked by visiting
- ❏ Dates checked (especially in January!)
- ❏ All texts are present and correct

- ❏ All copyright issues resolved

- ❏ Publisher: final sign-off
- ❏ Has something in the organisation changed that requires revision?
- ❏ Does the final version have to be signed off by someone? For example, an Annual Report by the Finance Director and Auditors?
- ❏ All steps complete?

- ❏ Send for print/web etc.

Numbers
A couple of number formatting Javascripts are supplied with QX2018. Use with care! Telephone numbers should not normally appear in narrative text, but text orginators do all kinds of strange things. Normally you will want other numbers formatted as 999,999,999, or your localised equivalent.

URLs
One of the Javascripts supplied with QX2018 identifies URLs and converts them to hyperlinks. Run this first. Once you've run it, clean up the visual form. *Https://www.etc.com* should be *www.etc.com*, *mailto:* should disappear. You should also get rid of blue underlines, which always look cheap.

Creating a cleanup script
You can create a cleanup script as Applescript (Mac only), JavaScript (from QX2018), or simply by keeping a list of what find/changes you need to do. This will vary with language and the quirks of the originator, but here is a typical series of operations that a script might perform:

1. Link URLs
2. Format URLs
3. Change paragraphs to new line
4. Change double new line to paragraphs
5. Change five spaces to tab
6. Change ". " to ". " (typewriter to print, or change to FlexSpace)
7. Change ... to … (dots to ellipsis)
8. Change '-' between numbers to '–' (hyphen to en-dash)
9. Change -- to em-dash
10. Change underline to italics.

Importing text

Text is the heart of the craft of desk top publishing. A picture may speak a thousand words, but a page of well-chosen words can change the world as no picture can. In an increasingly multi-lingual publishing environment, where anything worth saying in one language is worth saying in twenty, most publishers will spend at least part of their career working in languages that they don't know well, or don't know at all. Good practice in importing text will enable you to navigate thousand page documents, and accurately represent languages you have never heard spoken.

Before you begin

Prepare your text before you import it! First, check the status of the text. Is this a draft you will be required to re-import several times? Is this the final text? Has it been proofread? If the text has not been proofread and edited, you are setting yourself up for days of misery unless you find a way to deal with it.

Where is the text coming from? If it's coming from a database, then get the database programmer to output it with a few simple QuarkXPress Tags. This is a few minutes work for them, but it will save you and your client hours or days. You'll be surprised how many applications can tag text.

Many proprietary applications are able to output IDML, which is InDesign's Markup Language. You can import this directly into QuarkXPress 2017 and 2018.

If it's coming from Word, then try to get the author or editor to use a consistent set of styles. You can import these directly into QuarkXPress, and, later, you can re-export them so that a proofreader can make changes directly on the text, which is far safer. On re-import, all your layout will be intact.

On Import

If you're importing XPress Tags, IDML or Word, you will usually import style-sheet tagging. You can turn this off for Word import, which is useful if the originator has been reckless in their formatting. If these styles have the same names as styles in your document, you will be offered the choices of: keeping the existing styles, overwriting them with the new styles, or renaming them. If you've already set up your stylesheets, choose 'use existing'. If you just want to get a picture of what's in the document, then you can import all of the styles in it, but you may spend some time rationalising. Remember that if you delete a style sheet, QX asks you what you want to remap the styles to, so you can rationalise fairly easily.

There are a few other import options, mainly in Word. If you are going to import 'smart quotes', you can set what kind of smart quotes they are in Preferences>Application>Input Settings. If you import Word's hyperlinks, then a list of hyperlinks will be tagged and created in Window>Hyperlinks. You will probably want to reformat the style sheet attached, otherwise they will be ugly blue underlines, like in Word.

▲Word import settings in QuarkXpress

There are two ways to include footnotes, either as QX dynamic footnotes or just text.

Including Word's tables is a mixed blessing: and it's worth doing a test import to see what the result is, and then decide whether to bring them in by another means.

Word's inline pictures are almost never press resolution, but they might serve as a guide as to where to put an important image.

After import

First, check the text for strange characters. This might be a problem in a very unamiliar language, but you can usually tell. A lot of them means a Codepage or other mismatch. Don't try to edit the document, go back and fix the error and reimport.

Second, run a Javascript, AppleScript or a series of Search and Replaces to clean up the text.

PDF text
If your original is a PDF file, you can import and Convert to Native Objects to extract the text. There is a supplied JavaScript to import multi-page documents. If the text arrives broken into many boxes, use Ctrl/Right-Click to invoke the contextual menu and merge text boxes. You may sometimes get better results by copying and pasting the text directly from the PDF file, though this will lose any formatting.

Word boxes
You can paste formatted Word text boxes using Edit>Paste as Native Objects. This is sometimes preferable to importing.

Plain text files
Plain text files must have the correct UTF encoding set for them to import properly. If the encoding is wrong, either QuarkXPress will crash, or the text will contain strange characters.

Font woes?
If the text is importing strangely, and you know the encoding is right, check that your font supports the character set of the language you are working in. You may need to buy an updated version, or switch to a different font. SIL has a number of free, ultra-multilingual fonts.

Kerpow!
The Star Tool with secondary flares and random selected produces a basic pop-art or comic book explosion. Roy Lichenstein and other pop artists introduced this type of ironic illustration into mainstream 'high' art and culture.

Public information
Beloved by public services the world over, a pseudo-speech bubble made by giving different corners to the Rounded Tool is a great way to introduce attention in a form or on public signage. Just remember that it will never be quite as cool as the people who commission it think it is…

Sci-fi logo
Prepare to engage primary thrusters, and set course for the galaxy! The triangle tool with tandem swirl applied quickly becomes futuristic with strong visual tension without losing its simplicity.

Firehose here
Spirals create a powerful rotational effect. An Archimedes spiral looks like a firehose or a Scooby-Doo tunnel. The Golden Spiral is more artistic and represents the Fibonnacci series as well as the Golden Section. You can also create a custom combination of the two. Straightening the curves changes the effect.

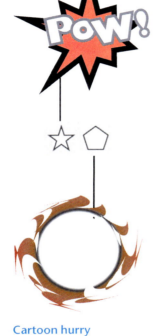
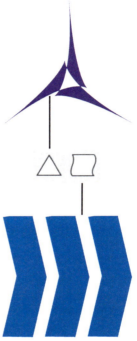

▶ *The Shape Tool was introduced in QuarkXPress 2017, but all the functions are available in earlier versions through Utilities>Shapemaker.*

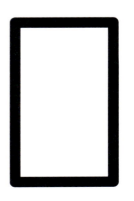

Cartoon hurry
When cartoon characters run, their feet are often represented as going in circles. This is the Polygon Tool with 31 sides, Opposite Swirl and Random applied.

Flare
The diamond tool with concave applied is an easy way to produce a 'glare' hotspot on an image or chromed object (all produced in QuarkXPress). This is substantiantially superior to applying lens flare in an image editing application, which is then baked into the picture.

Right Turn
The wave tool creates a variety of complex shapes, but, as with everything, simplicity is often the key to effectiveness.

I think…
The cloud tool is actually just a repeat of the polygon tool, but its defaults are set to emulate clouds. Here we used a triple line to give a slightly more sophisticated look.

▶ *Utilities>Shapemaker also has some additional functions which aren't accessible from the tool. These are in the Polygons tab, which offers (from left to right) Polygrams, Spirograms, Golden Rectangle, Double Square.*

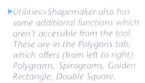

Line and shape

After movement and colour, the eye goes next to line and shape. Without moving into illustration, shape and line play a powerful role in directing the eye around the page. Deep understanding of the way line and shape work are the key to powerful simplicity. Gene Davis and other Colour Field painters explored vertical stripes and simple shapes to great effect during the mid-twentieth century. Every serious designer should have a working knowledge of their visual vocabulary.

▲ *Detail from Gene Davis: Apricot Ripple (Wikimedia Commons). Davis spent much of his career exploring the simplicity and power of lines.*

Straight lines
◂ Here is a selection of Quark's built-in lines and dots. You can create your own with Edit>Dashes & Stripes.

Waves
◂ Dashes and stripes behave differently when applied to shaped lines in QuarkXPress. These were all made using the Shape>Wave tool.

Custom lines
◂ This progressive arrow, harking back to the Letraset arrows collection in the 1970s, was created using Edit>Dashes and Stripes>New Dash.

◂ This custom line was created using new Stripe

Mind the gap
◂ You can set the gap colour, transparency and blending mode. Using the spiral, circle, triangle and star tools you can create strange, business-like, compelling or funky results, using only dashes and stripes.

19: Line drawing and editing

Stochastic

These basic textures are created with a plain or gradient background saved as an image using File>Export As>Image, reimported and then with noise applied using Window>Image Effects.
Stochastic textures can be used for 'uncopyable' documents, as photocopiers reproduce them poorly.

Pseudo-raster

These more elaborate textures are created using Item>Super Step and Repeat. They look back to Warhol and Lichtenstein's pop art.

 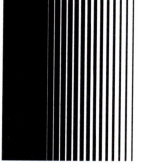 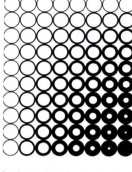

Line textures

These line textures were produced using i) Super Step and Repeat ii) Wave Tool iii) Wave tool with Super Step and Repeat iv) two tables overlaid on each other using transparencies at 45°.

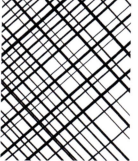   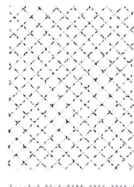

Repeating motifs

i) and ii) were produced using the Shape tool. iii) and iv) were produced using dingbats. iv) was a bespoke font created and then randomised. Repeating motifs can be programmed in JavaScript from QX2018.

   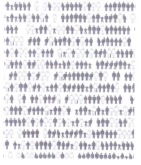

Image effects

These image textures are created like the basic Stochastic textures, but with a set of stripes as the base image. In i) emboss is applied. In ii) Posterize + Desaturate + Add Noise + Emboss. iii) is created by layering i) on top of itself at angles with Multiply as the blending mode. Using Curves changes the shape.

Texture

In the 1990s when DTP was taking hold, everything was about creating smooth, glossy impressions. 3D rendering was the cool kid on the block, and it flooded the world with a cartoonish brilliance. Today, texture is back. We take delight in stylish inconsistency: typewriter fonts are out, text typed on a typewriter and then digitised is in. Letterpress fonts are out, letterpress is in. Fifty years ago, every print process revealed itself through its shortcomings. Today, even Flexoprint can produce smooth, vivid continuous colour.

You can create texture in two ways. Every ink mark you put on paper helps to create visual texture, and you can do this deliberately (see facing page). Equally, choice of stock, print process, and UV coating creates physical texture.

Physical texture

Laid paper has a distinctive look and feel, but it's easily overused, especially in office stationery where it can give the impression of trying too hard. Sugar paper, tracing paper and printable plastics are less common, and, in the right document, can create a striking impression. Old fashioned newsprint is rarely used now, even by newspapers which prefer to be able to print in colour. However, there are newsprint-like papers that can go through digital printers creating a strongly nostalgic, honest impression. Large format inkjet printers can print on canvas and a variety of other media.

Weight

The perceived weight of paper depends on its original weight in grams per square metre (gsm), and on the printing process. A0 paper is exactly one square metre, so it is relatively simple to calculate the physical weight of an A4 or A3 sheet. 80gsm is standard copy paper, and feels substantial in typewritten documents. Each pass through a laser printer or printing press compresses the sheet, so that CMYK two-sided print at 130gsm feels approximately the same as 80gsm unprinted paper. However, in digital print, strong coverage also thickens the page, so 50% toner coverage on both sides makes copy paper feel substantial. Get a sample before you make up your mind.

UV coating

Spot UV coating was developed to put a gloss on pictures in high-end documents. You specify it like a colour, and you would normally do so as a flat coating covering an image with a safety margin of 2mm. You can also apply a UV coat as a deliberate pattern to engage the fingers without making an obvious visual impression.

Folding and Binding

Printers are increasingly able to provide 'fancy folds' in addition to the standards such as roll-fold, gatefold and concertina (Z) fold. Most short documents such as annual reports are stapled (printers call it 'stitched'), but you can dramatically upgrade the perceived value with perfect binding. Comb-binding always looks and feels terrible, but wire-o spiral binding, on the right document, can be stylish. A visit to a hardware store will throw up a large number of alternate fixings for shorter, high impact documents. A simple scoring machine is relatively cheap. For short run print, you can score a 1000 or so documents in a half hour.

Visual texture

The easy route to visual texture is using a photograph, but it is often better to avoid the inevitable softening that comes with the half-tone process and use a mono texture such as those in the top four rows opposite. These kinds of textures do not necessarily trap well, and so should only be used for single, solid inks. They give a substantially superior look and feel to a prestige document like a mono book by comparison with the generally poor mono halftones which are otherwise available. Once you've created a texture, you can keep it in a QuarkXPress library, using File>New>Library.

Thinking about the medium

The earliest desk top publishers made their own pens, cured their own parchment and bound their own volumes. They had a deep appreciation of the medium in which they worked.

In contemporary publishing we have a range of reproduction methods: digital, offset, flexo, rotogravure, ePub, Kindle, HTML5, iOS and Android. Each medium has its own unique characteristics. It's tempting to try to smooth out the differences, but making the most of the unique characteristics increases the value of the product.

Digital devices can reproduce vivid colours that paper can't touch, but paper can fold, respond differently to different light, and have a different feel from page to page as you apply UV coatings or vary the stock.

Investing in understanding the medium can save you from potential embarrassment—for example knowing that digital print is much more prone to cracking than offset—but it can also unlock unique possibilities.

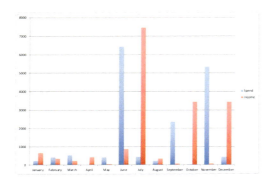

▲Excel charts are the language of business and research, but when imported directly into the layout, they cheapen everything. If you export from Excel as PDF and import into QuarkXPress, you can use Style>Convert to Native Objects to turn them into editable graphics. This allows you to conform them to the brand of the document, rather than Excel's brand.
A couple of tips for doing this.
First, Excel gradients usually come across as image backgrounds. The easiest way to deal with this is to select all of the elements with the same background, Item>Merge or Split Paths>Union, double-click to engage the image tool , and then delete the image.
▶To manage the text easily, use the Link Tool to link boxes which should be similarly styled, and then change the font for the entire chain all at once.

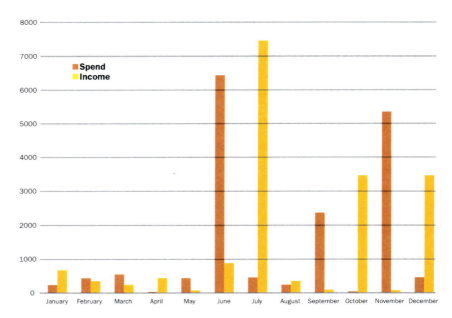

▲When managing a chart, don't be afraid to change its proportions to suit the layout. With the Scale palette, you can set the options to keep the text to the right size, while changing the proportions of the chart to exactly match the layout.

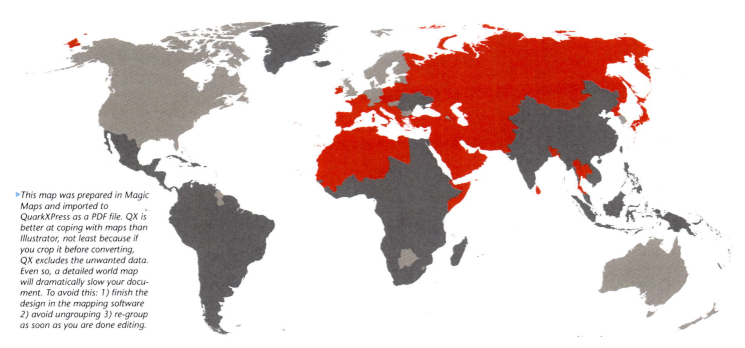

▶This map was prepared in Magic Maps and imported to QuarkXPress as a PDF file. QX is better at coping with maps than Illustrator, not least because if you crop it before converting, QX excludes the unwanted data. Even so, a detailed world map will dramatically slow your document. To avoid this: 1) finish the design in the mapping software 2) avoid ungrouping 3) re-group as soon as you are done editing.

Taking a leaf from Letraset

Before there was DTP software, rapid turnaround, low budget and highly bespoke design was often done with Letraset rub on letters. For the truly broke, it was fairly common to photocopy pages from the Letraset book and glue them onto layout.

While we can applaud the rise of OpenType fonts, there are some innovative Letraset features which are worth remembering. One of these was sets of similar graphics which could be applied in the same way that ordinary letters were. This set of arrows, inspired by Letraset's, has been encoded as an OpenType font by means of FontLab VI, though it could also be done with FontForge or other free software. Storing graphics in font format means that you can easily share them with clients for use in their own WordProcessor based documents, and they can be incorporated into flowing text ⟶ without resorting to anchors. Font based graphics can be controlled by Conditional Styles, and can be managed through Open Type transformations, which is the basis on which fonts like Clocko, Chartwell and Amazing Infographic work.

▶Clocko turns timestamps into pictures.

12:45	◔
17:47	◕
1:12	◷

Importing graphics

Once upon a time, importing graphics was a question of scanning them carefully and then either using them as fixed resolution image files, or autotracing them with specialist software that might take hours. The arrival of Wacom graphic pens began to change that, but, using today's tablet pens, alongside rudimentary scanning with a smart phone, it's possible to create original art on a device or on paper, and have it as editable vectors in QuarkXPress in less than a minute. Here's an example of how.

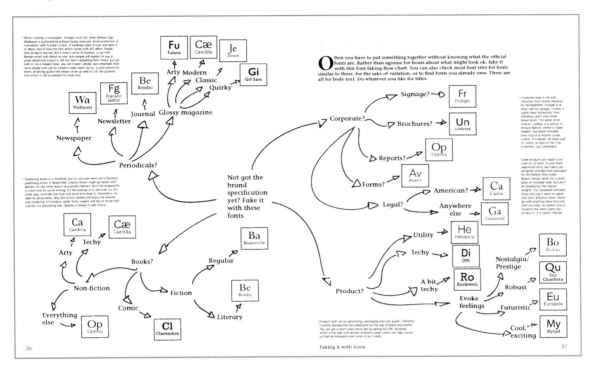

The best camera in the world...

...is the one you have with you at the time. A smartphone can easily scan sketches and drawings, and you can vectorise them afterwards in QX without needing anything else, if they are black and white. It can help you break out of the sterile world of digital design.

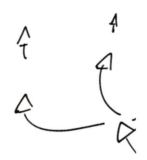

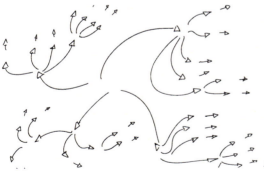

▲ The fonts flow-chart was sketched out on an iPad Pro with an application called Noteshelf. QuarkXPress can trace black and white graphics like these, but in Noteshelf's case that isn't necessary, because it exports as PDF vectors.

◀ The file that arrived looked like this, which was not quite right for the font boxes we wanted to put in, or to allow us to include the additional text.

◀ We therefore used Style>Convert to Native Objects. Although now in principle editable, they only really become editable when Ungrouped. This creates a problem, though: Noteshelf creates its vectors as hundreds of very short curves. This will slow the whole system down.

▲ Fake it with autotrace. Not everything you sketch will come in as vectors, and you might also decide that the hundreds of tiny lines are more trouble than they are worth.

▼ A quick fix for this is to go to Measurements>Clipping Paths and choose Non-White Areas. Turn 'Outside edges only' off. You may need to play with the threshold, though, in this case, we didn't. Then go to Item>New Box from Clipping. You now have a vector version.

◀ Detail view of the hundreds of short curves from the end of one of the small arrows.
To overcome the problem, as soon as we've ungrouped, we go—with everything still selected—to Item>Merge or Split Paths, and choose to Combine them. This makes the whole set into one graphic. We now go to Item>Merge or Split Paths and choose to Split All paths. This leaves the arrows intact as arrows, rather than as many tiny paths. Internally, the curves are still made up of short lines, but the scale is too minute to see it, and QX is fast enough to handle them without fuss.

▶ We're now able to move things around. From QX2018, you can flip an entire group horizontally or vertically by choosing Item>Flip Shape. This is important here as we don't want to get into editing the curves, which will become tedious, and will also lose the authentic sketched look.

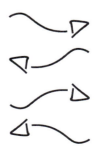

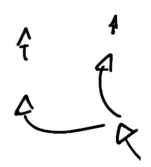

45

Are you still using the same software you were using twenty-five years ago? Chances are that you are still using Microsoft Office applications. You may well have been using QuarkXPress for all that time (or you may be new to it—welcome!) but if you are like most of the design industry, there's one venerable application that most of us are still using because our whole workflow has evolved around it. There's even a verb for it: 'photoshopped'.

The great thing about that application is that every conceivable function has been added onto it over the years, often to the consternation of plugin makers who find their unique selling point evaporating when their particular function is included in a new release. But the result is that it's become 'jack of all trades, master of none'. We can't think of a general image app that comes close to it (though Affinity Photo is working hard, as is Pixelmator Pro), but when it comes to RAW developing and Digital Assets Management, we look elsewhere.

The leading RAW developers are Capture One and DxO, both powerful enough for the pro-market but simple and affordable enough for the occasional user. However, that is not enough. No matter how good your retouching skills, starting with the right image is paramount. If the photographer comes back with 500 versions of the same shot, the difference between excellence and a near miss is your ability to identify the perfect image, and do it quickly. For our money, Capture One's Media Pro is the best on the market, though others are also available. Speed is of the essence.

Image checklist:
Resolution
For most documents, 300 ppi at final output size is standard. If the images are mainly people, you can get away with 1.25× the line screen, which will usually be 150 lpi. If the image is too small, it should be discarded.

Reflections
Bad reflections cannot be edited out convincingly.

Colour balance
You can rebalance colour in QuarkXPress, but if the image has mixed lighting, with green shadows (from fluorescent lights), it is almost impossible to fix. You could try using DxO to reprocess the original image, but usually you should discard it.

Sharpness
An image should be pin-sharp at the final output size. If it isn't, it can be improved with Unsharp Masking in QX, or using a specialist plugin such as FocusMagic in Affinity Photo or Photoshop. An image which is substantially softer than other images should be discarded.

Levels
For mono print, images usually need 'tucking in' at the top and bottom. Colour images should be checked for blown highlights and muddy shadows.

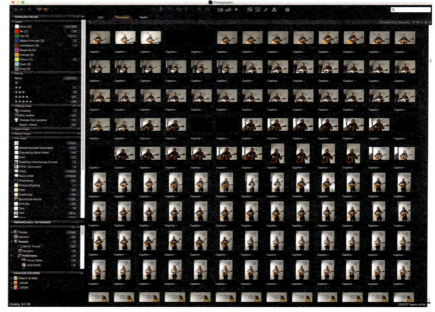

▼ A digital assets manager needs to help you evaluate and catalogue hundreds of images at a time, as pro shooters typically come back with vast numbers of shots now that digital cameras, fast recycling lights and large memory cards have made it easy to do so. A 250-shot sequence is no problem for Media Pro, and Capture One can process a final selection of 25 rapidly.

▲ Digital Assets Management (DAM) with Media Pro. This particular database contains 152,181 images. Media Pro by Phase One can navigate through all of them in 30 seconds. Lightroom, by contrast, begins to slow down at just 10,000 images—a month's shooting for a working pro.

▲ A specialist raw editor like Capture One (pictured) or DxO can apply identical corrections to hundreds of RAW images almost instantly, making it easy to manage the output from extensive shoots. Capture One and DxO both offer extensive controls for refining the image and outputting according to a consistent pattern. Both are able to batch-process output, giving the designer a reliable set of correctly sized, colour matched images to work with. Ultimately, it is always better to perfect the image prior to importing. The image editing tools in QuarkXPress are ideally suited to adapting the image to its final use, but work best on images which have been fully finished beforehand.

Importing Images

Images straight out of the camera need some work before they are suitable for publication. The photographer will normally shoot in Raw format, select the images using a Digital Assets Management system (DAM) such as Media Pro or Lightroom, and develop them in Capture One, DxO or another specialist raw developer. These images may still need to be colour matched to others in the publication, and will need to be output sharpened. Sometimes an image arrives straight from the camera, in which case more work is needed.

This image is a supplied JPEG, unedited.

The first and most important edit is cropping the image differently. Cropping out the tree enables us to have one primary interest, the sunset, and one secondary, which is the mountain.

We now turn to recreating the lighting conditions that the photographer 'saw'. The first step is usually to set the levels. Automatic exposure is at its least effective with images of this kind, and the initial levels had nothing in the brightest fifth. Selective work with curves and colours can then edit out the additional tree line, and boost tone.

Finalising the image for production requires adding output sharpening.

The editing stack for the final image. Effects are executed with the top first, the bottom last.
◁ We begin by setting the levels so that the values fill the space from left to right.
◁ Next, we add a push-pull curve to dramatise the lighting a little.
▽ Colour balance enables us to increase red in the sky, while removing some of the greenish cast from the snow.
▽▽ Finally, output sharpen with unsharp masking at Pixel Radius=Image Resolution/200.

43: Image Logic

Multiply multiplies A and B, and is darker than either

Screen is like projecting A and B on top of each other

Overlay is like sandwiching transparencies of A and B

Darken takes the darker value from both images

Lighten takes the lighter value from both images

Colour dodge overexposes B using A as a filter

Dream
Dare
Delight

Transparency blend modes are best known for compositing images, as here, or text on images. Make sure you turn off the background colour first! The text here is composited from black using Difference, and the image using Darken. Starting with the right images is crucial: this one was shot 'blown out' using a Lastolite Hilite. It would take you hours to achieve this with cutouts or masking, and the effect would be weaker.

Colour dodge underexposes B using A as a filter

Hard light overlays B over A (ie, backwards)

Soft light is a softer version of Hard light

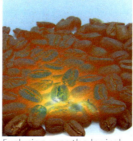
Difference is the mathematical subtraction A-B

Exclusion uses the logical operator A XOR B

A on B in normal mode. B is completely obscured.

B. This is a bonfire in fog, chosen for its soft gradients

Layering and Compositing

From QX2017 onwards, you can composite two elements using 12 blending modes. This opens up worlds of possibilities, not just on compositing images over each other, but also in creating logical unions, such as in the map below, which would otherwise require tedious surgery using Merge/Split Paths. Blending modes are counter-intuitive: they are mathematical operations which have only marginal counterparts in daily experience. For this reason, it's important to practise using them, and to work to get an understanding of what they can do, and what they can't.

When transparency blend modes were introduced in Photoshop 3 in 1994, there was a rush of bad design blending images together just because it was possible. Always remember: just because you can, doesn't mean you should.

To use compositing well, you need to plan your images ahead of time. Shooting with a blown-out background, such as a Lastolite Hilite, makes it trivially easy to composite.

You can set transparency modes in several places. Window>Colours is the most obvious, but you can also set it in the Measurements Palette and in Window>Image Editing. You can set the transparency mode of text, borders, line gaps, images and background separately. Usually, if things aren't working, check that the background is set to 'none': if it's white, image or text will composite onto that, not the item below.

▲ *Drop down for transparencies in the colours palette*

Logical transparency

Most people think of blend modes as a way of compositing onto images, but you can use them powerfully for line art.
In this map, we used the double line style to create the roads. To make the joins work, we set the gap colour white, and set both the line and the gap to transparency mode 'Lighten'. Wherever two roads join, the white gap takes priority over the black lines (because 'lighten'), and so there's a perfect join. Watch out when exporting! Apple Preview doesn't support transparencies, so you will need to flatten at export. For an explanation, see the section on Exporting, page 141 and following.

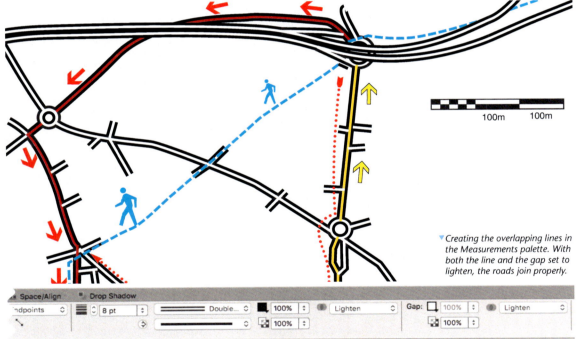

▼ *Creating the overlapping lines in the Measurements palette. With both the line and the gap set to lighten, the roads join properly.*

QX2017 introduced transparency modes alongside Image Editing, and the results of putting the two together can be remarkable. For example, you can remove motion blur by compositing an embossed version of an image onto an unaltered version, or use successive images to apply selective alterations using the Threshold tool. Some examples are given on page 110 and following.

In the example above, we wanted to construct a simple road-map by just drawing lines. See the side-bar for details on how this was accomplished.

It is worth investing some time in understanding what I call 'Image Logic'. Most of the 'on or off' effect styles, and many of the plugin-based effects in image editing applications can be achieved, but in a way which is organic to the document.

New in QX2018

QX2018 has all of the same blend modes as QX2017, but adds CMYK blending in addition to QX2017's RGB blending. Preview this using View>Proof Output. The mode used in output depends on whether you output as RGB or CMYK. You can't have both types in the same document.

The supplied GREP JavaScript lets you enter a string of code to find and swap with a wide range of patterns. If you are a seasoned GREP user, then this will be second nature to you. If not, there are many tutorials online about how to use it. Be careful, and practise on unimportant documents first!

The supplied MallMerge JavaScript takes a CSV and drops it into a project template. You can enter your own file-paths, but if you don't, you will be shown an example MailMerge, showing how to work with text and images. Open up the referenced files as examples to work from in doing your own MaleMerge.

▼ OpenType fonts are capable of automation. This font, Handsome Pro, varies its letters to better simulate handwriting. We've added a randomising Conditional Style Script to introduce extra variation. At some point, colour self-transforming OpenType fonts will become available. These are already supported by QuarkXPress 2018.

Dear Jane,

I hope this finds you well. I was hoping to drop by last week, but things got in the way and so I'm sending you this note to invite you to our party next Wednesday.

GREP basics: Regular Expressions (Regex)
The format of a GREP (regex) query is **/pattern/modifier**
If **/Quark/i** is the regular expression, then **Quark** is the pattern and **i** is a modifier (to be case-insensitive).

Modifiers
These are for selecting case-insensitive or global searches:
i Case-Insensitive matching
g Global match—all matches not just the first one
m Multiline matching

Brackets
Brackets are used to find a range of characters:
[abc]   Find any character between the brackets
[^abc]   Find any character NOT between the brackets
[0-9]   Find any digit between the brackets
[^0-9]   Find any character NOT between the brackets (any non-digit)
(x|y)   Find any of the alternatives specified

Special characters
.   Find one character, except newline or line end
\w   Find a word character

\W   Find a non-word character
\d   Find a digit
\D   Find a non-digit character
\s   Find a whitespace character
\S   Find a non-whitespace character
\b   Find a match at the beginning/end of a word
\B   Find a match not at the beginning/end of a word
\0   Find a NUL character
\n   Find a new line character
\f   Find a form feed character
\r   Find a carriage return character
\t   Find a tab character
\v   Find a vertical tab character
\xxx Find the character given by octal number xxx
\xdd Find the character given by hexadecimal dd
\uxxxx Find the Unicode character for hexadecimal xxxx

Quantifiers
n+   Matches any string that contains at least one n
n*   Matches any string that contains zero or more occurrences of n
n?   Matches any string that contains zero or one occurrences of n
n{X}   Matches a string with a sequence of X n's
n{X,Y} Matches strings with a sequence of X to Y n's
n{X,} Any string that contains at least X n's
n$ Matches any string with n at the end of it
^n   Matches any string with n at the beginning of it
?=n   Any string followed by a specific string n
?!n   Matches any string that is not followed by a specific string n

In this example, a simple Excel file is used to manage records for a series of conferences (they're fake—don't try to register!) The file is imported as an Inline Table, which applies stylesheets automatically (though invisibly). This is picked up by Content Variables which add in all of the changing data to the document. In this way, hundreds of bespoke versions can be constructed.

▼ *Imported data table from Excel*

▼ *The cover, before data is applied. Content Variables are present, but have nothing to reference.*

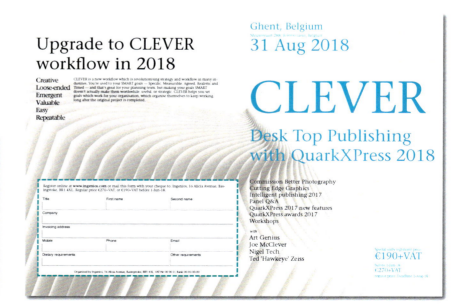

Automation

Some kinds of publishing lend themselves to careful, creative reworking of every letter. Other kinds require rapid, accurate processing of large amounts of information which are repetitive and hard for human proof-readers to separate. For this, QuarkXPress's XPress Tags, DOCX importing, Inline Tables, Excel Import and Content Variables make the work easy, rapid and accurate. You can also invoke Conditional Styles and Callout Styles to provide further refinements.

QuarkXPress has a lot of options for automation. The most obvious are easily overlooked: Master Pages and Stylesheets. With a little care in connecting them via Conditional Styles, Content Variables and Grids, you can accomplish 'impossible' tasks, such as ensuring that the first page of a novel chapter does not contain the page numbering or the headers, and that the first page always falls on the right hand side. See the example below.

JavaScript, introduced with QX2018, opens many new avenues. See page 124 for more details. However, without knowing any JavaScript you can still use JavaScript's built-in GREP features, available as a supplied script. See opposite page.

◀ When designing a book, you often want the chapter title pages to be 'clean', with the titles beginning 1/3 of the way down the page and the headers and page numbers omitted. One way to do this is simply to delete the header and footer boxes (from the Master Page), and shorten the text box. You could also create a second Master Page. However, this won't be free-flowing: if you add in additional material then all of the pages will be out of sync.

▶ To make the chapter header appear 1/3 of the way down the page, create a Text Grid style in Window>Grid Styles. You will need to play with this a bit, but you essentially want to add in sufficient line spacing so that the text is pushed down and can only appear in four places on the page. You must also apply 'Textbox Grid' in the Paragraph Style>Formats tab.
Finally, you need to apply this grid style to the page frame on your Master Page.

▶ You can make this work automatically and flow with the text with a Grid Style (see above right) and a Conditional Style. The grid style allows the chapter title only to appear in one of four positions on the page. Immediately before the chapter title that you want to appear, insert '_' or some other character that will never appear in the titles, and give it the same style. You now need a conditional style that turns the paragraph white if the character '_' appears.

◀ You're using a Content Variable to add in the Running Headers. If you set that Running Header to pick up the first usage of 'Chapter' style on the page, it will see the '_', and put this into the header. If you've applied the conditional style on the Master page, then it will apply the white style sheet, and the header disappears. You can get rid of the page number as well by putting the content variable in the footer, but applying the White stylesheet to it on the Master Page. When the page begins with '_', the whole paragraph is set white.

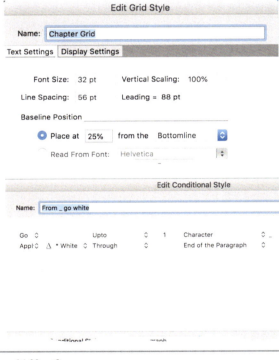

XPress Tags

XPress Tags is a format which can be programmed by a database and then used to format anything from a catalogue to a novel. It is especially useful for complex data where checking is difficult.

Rotary saw   **PQXLT**
Availability June 2019   €232
Agricolae pessimus frugaliter cir

Binary Load Lifter   **RB3LJ**
Availability May 2020   €1,930
Cathedras conubium santet bellus

Protocol Droid   **4JC3P0**
Availability June 2019   €22,327
Chirographi fermentet Augustus.

Aircar   **T16-IV**
Availability April 2019   €232
Parsimonia umbraculi miscere

▲ Result of importing XPress Tags.

▶ This may look like gibberish, but it is XPress Tags data which can be generated by a database, spreadsheet, or a formatted output such as Bookends (for references) and many other kinds of software. XPress Tags can contain full formatting information, but it is often more useful when, as in this example, it only contains tags for assigning stylesheets to text. Imported in this way, you can populate an entire magazine, catalogue or novel ready formatted.

```
<v14.00><e8>
@• Data 1:Rotary saw <!><\t><$>PQXLT
@• Data 2:Availability June 2019<!f$><\t><$>€232
@• Data3:Agricolae pessimus frugaliter cir
@• Data 1:Binary Load Lifter<!><\t><$>RB3LJ
@• Data 2:Availability May 2020<!f$><\t><$>€1,930
@• Data3:Cathedras conubium santet bellus
@• Data 1:Protocol Droid<!><\t><$>4JC3P0
@• Data 2:Availability June 2019<!f$><\t><$>€22,327
@• Data3:Chirographi fermentet Augustus.
@• Data 1:Aircar<!><\t><$>T16-IV
@• Data 2:Availability April 2019<!f$><\t><$>€232
@• Data3:Parsimonia umbraculi miscere
```

▲ XPress Tags data

🖥 33: Conditional Styles and 49: XPress Tags

To comply with standards, PDFs sent out for electronic reading need to meet the W3 specifications. This is available from QX2018 onwards. Essentially, this means your file must be tagged in a logical structure, with images given alternate text, and paragraph styles correctly classified.

PDF for general consumption

If you're sending your PDF document out into the wild, without much knowledge of how it's going to be used, then you need to prepare rather more carefully.

First, make sure your Metadata is properly filled in. Go to Layout>Metadata to enter this. If you're using QX2015-2016 you need to enter that information in the PDF options, but in QX2018 it's been harmonised.

Next, **only in QX2018 or later**, ensure that your file is properly tagged. You can begin with Layout>Auto tag layout. Open up Window>Articles to see what's done.

Some of the components will be text. For images, you can change the name of the component by clicking ✎ but more important is to use the sub-menu ⋮ to add alternate text. Check that the components are in logical order. If not, move them around until they are.

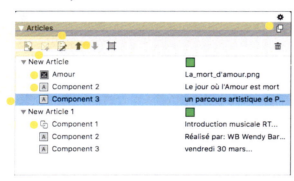

Sub-menu
Edit name
Move item
Add article, component

Image file, renamed.
Text file, not renamed
Currently selected item

Linked text file

You will also need to check your Paragraph stylesheets. Each stylesheet offers the opportunity to specify a structure, using Heading Style. This gives a logical structure to your text headings which is understood by Acrobat Reader. The choices are Heading, Heading1, up to 6, and Paragraph. By default, everything is 'Paragraph' including style sheets brought in from earlier versions of QX. This is not the same as eBook tagging.

When you have purely decorative elements, you can mark them as 'artifact' in the 'Add Alternate Text' dialogue.

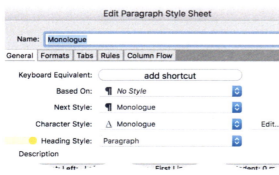

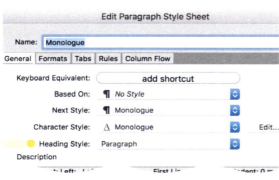

Heading Style

To export PDFs correctly tagged, just make sure that 'Export Tagged PDF' is checked in the export options. It's on by default.

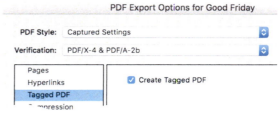

When you come to export, set verification to PDF/X-4 & PDF/A-2u, which will provide maximum long-term compatibility.

Transparency problems

We now come to a serious problem. The preferred workflow is to output transparency natively. This means that your imagesetter or device reader can deal with it properly, and that the file can be edited if it has to be. However, Apple's Preview, which comes with all Macs, does not handle transparency correctly. If you are using transparency for, say, creating roads on a map, it will come out incorrect.

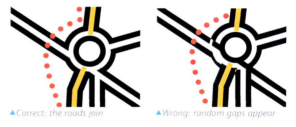

▲*Correct: the roads join* ▲*Wrong: random gaps appear*

If you're going to design with transparency but output for Apple Preview, you will need to flatten, using the Transparency options. In the case of the map, this will only work properly if you create a spot colour black. This will not harm print output.

At a particular point, Apple will update Preview to work with transparencies. Until then, test what you're doing!

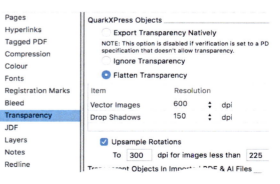

The scariest moment in publishing is when you export the final output file. This is when you are staking your reputation and possibly your livelihood on something which you believe to be completely ready for print, deployment as an app, distribution as an eBook, or onward transmission as an image file. You can turn to the relevant pages in the Reference section for the particular options in each output. Here, we're going to look at more general considerations.

The first thing you need to know is whether your target for the export is print or digital. With HTML5, ePubs and apps, the answer is obvious: digital. With PDF, things get blurrier.

PDF is now the standard for sending files for output print, but it is also a (not-very-good) standard for sharing documents. The reason it isn't very good is because it is a highly variable standard.

Print: the good news

For most print, you can simply use the built-in output styles in QuarkXPress. If you're sending for commercial print at an external printing company (we'll call it a 'print house' to save confusion with an office printer), then pick the 'Press' output. To do so, go to File>Export As>PDF. If you're not seeing this, it means you are in a Digital layout, and you need to be in a Print layout.

The screen that comes up will have this:

Simply go to PDF Style and pick 'Press - High Resolution/High Quality'. This will set a number of options: it turns crop marks on, turns bleed on, sets compression for images to 'low' (which means high quality), downsamples images to 300 dpi, sets colour to CMYK composite and turns transparency on. For nine out of ten commercial print jobs, this is all you need to do.

If you're sending it to someone to print on their home printer as a draft, then choose: Print - Medium Quality/Medium resolution.

Flow format ePub and Kindle

If you've correctly tagged your file, then exporting an ePub or a Kindle is a fairly simple matter. Remember that the first page is always the cover, which, on most Kindle devices, will be reproduced in raw 1 bit graphics, so avoid anything complex. You don't need to touch most of the options, but one you will often want to change is the Table of Contents. By default, this is the articles

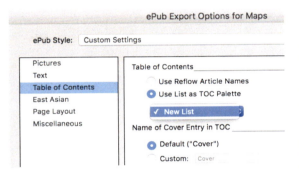

list, based on how your document was constructed. However, for a book, you will often want to use a List to create a table of contents, and have the eBook use that. Choose the option 'Use List as TOC Palette', and select your preferred list.

Fixed format ePUB, HTML5 and apps

Everything created in the digital layout will export exactly as you created it. This is dramatically easier than flow type ePub or Kindle, or even print. Check the reference section for the output options. There are two things you need to be aware of. First, in HTML5 output, you need to upload the entire folder to a website with an FTP application before you can view it. It will not work on your machine directly. Use the Preview function to see it on your machine. Second, fixed format ePub readers are hugely variable. Many features may not work.

Image and EPS

You can export as Image (PNG or JPEG) or as EPS, and do this either with entire pages or selections. The EPS output options are a more limited version of the PDF output options. Wherever possible, use PDF as it is a newer standard. EPS cannot handle transparency at all.

For PNG and JPEG, the final output resolution is what is important, and it will be dpi x document dimension in inches (so 2.54 x dpi x dimension in cm).

Compression is also a cause of confusion: Low compression=High Quality. Note also that some transparency blend modes will cause blurring on an image output. Use PDF if you can!

Fixed ePUB woes

Apple's ePub reader iBooks is probably the best. There are not many good choices on Windows or Android. Essentially, if you are doing digital layout for ePUB, forget about animations. They may work, they may not. Use fixed-layout ePUB to give a book-like experience. Leave other stuff for apps and HTML5.

▶ Folding introduces interactivity to the flat page. Most documents that are too slender to bind benefit from some kind of folding. The simplest is the DL fold, which can be Z or roll-fold, but this lacks the surprise of the six page right angle fold, which is probably the simplest way of creating a document which reveals 'secrets' as it is opened.

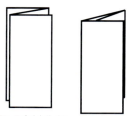

DL Z-fold (left) and roll-fold/envelope fold/fold inside. These are the most common type of folded documents. Note that the panels should be slightly different sizes to fold correctly.

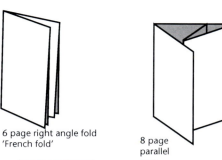

6 page right angle fold 'French fold'

8 page parallel over

Not to be confused with

French fold, also known as 6 page right angle fold or greetings card fold, is one of the most popular folds. It is not the same as French fold binding, or French binding, which is one or more pages folded in half with the fold acting as the outside edge of the page, and the two real edges glued into the binding.

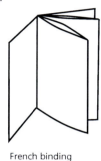

French binding

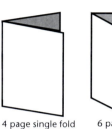 

4 page single fold   6 page gate fold

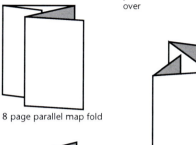

8 page parallel map fold

8 page reverse map fold

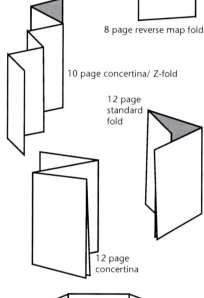

10 page concertina/ Z-fold

12 page standard fold

12 page concertina

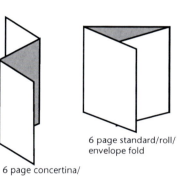

6 page concertina/ Z-fold

6 page standard/roll/ envelope fold

Stock weights

Paper feels different depending on how many times it has been through the press.

70 gsm	Flimsy, feels cheap
80 gsm	Copy paper
120 gsm	Luxurious in mono-laser, flimsy in CMYK offset
130 gsm	Flimsy in CMYK offset
150 gsm	Substantial in CMYK offset, feels stiff in laser
160+ gsm	'board'
250 gsm	2 colour business cards
350 gsm	CMYK business cards

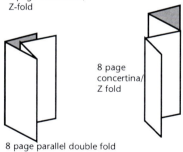

8 page concertina/ Z fold

8 page parallel double fold

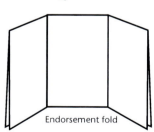

Endorsement fold

▲ CMYK two sides has had eight times the pressure applied to it as a single side of black and white. If (as is most likely) this is on coated paper, there will be an additional loss of volume because the heat drying process will also expel some of the moisture in the paper. By contrast, the heavier the colour in colour laser printing or in digital printing, the thicker the paper becomes. As a result, you must be careful of cracking along any folded edges.

▶ Types of paper stock and finish have practical implications. On traditional offset presses, Dot Gain is an issue when considering uncoated stock, though this is usually managed in-RIP these days. However, on digital presses, there is essentially no change in dot gain no matter what stock you use, and uncoated stock can be used for its own particular charm. Office laser printers and copiers may slip on coated stock, causing registration errors.

Coating	Type	Photos	Dot gain	Legibility
Coated	Gloss	Excellent	Lowest	Poor
	Silk/Satin	Good	Low	Medium
	Matte	Acceptable	Low	Good
	Dull	Acceptable	Medium	Good
	Newsprint	Acceptable	Medium	Good
Uncoated	Wove/smooth	Weak	Higher	Excellent
	Laid	Poor	Higher	Excellent
	Linen	Poor	Higher	Excellent
	Newsprint	Marginal	Highest	Excellent

The printed document

Digital documents have swept the world in the last twenty years, and many things which were once printed are now shared without ever leaving the digital world. We engage with far less print than we did thirty years ago, but far more information. But that serves to raise the value of print that comes into our hands. One recent study found that ten times as much information was retained when reading physical books compared with electronic. But not all print is created equal: care taken over binding, folding, paper type, weight and finish will pay great dividends.

Saddle Stitch, Perfect Bound and Spiral or Wire-O are suitable for 'finished' organisational publications. Watch out for page creep when saddle-stitching. Anything over fifty pages might be better perfect bound.

Perfect Bound (paperback) and **Case Bound** (hardback) are standard for published books. They are the only types with printable spines.

However ugly, **tape-binding** may be the best choice for in-house manuals.

Loop stitch is mainly for multi-installment documents.
Sewn or **pamphlet** stitch is prestigious, but labour intensive.

Screw and Post is either overly fussy (if metal) and damages other books, or looks unappealingly cheap, if plastic. However, a single plastic screw and post looks spectacular if you present something in swatch-book format.

Plastic grips, stab/side stitch and **comb bound** are only for **transitory documents**. Media sales companies, for some reason, seem to believe that comb-binding, if supplemented by a transparent plastic cover, somehow improves the value of a document. It doesn't.

If the answer is 'comb bound', you asked the wrong question.

If you are tempted to upgrade the value of your document with case binding, don't: it will look like vanity publishing. As a simple rule of thumb, if you are giving it away for free, never bind with anything more prestigious than perfect binding.

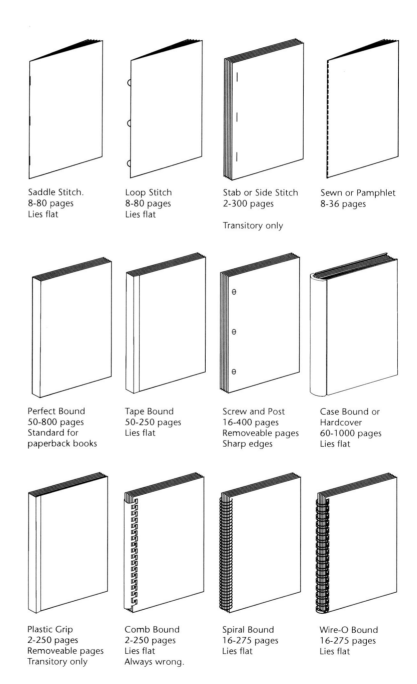

Saddle Stitch.
8-80 pages
Lies flat

Loop Stitch
8-80 pages
Lies flat

Stab or Side Stitch
2-300 pages
Transitory only

Sewn or Pamphlet
8-36 pages

Perfect Bound
50-800 pages
Standard for paperback books

Tape Bound
50-250 pages
Lies flat

Screw and Post
16-400 pages
Removeable pages
Sharp edges

Case Bound or Hardcover
60-1000 pages
Lies flat

Plastic Grip
2-250 pages
Removeable pages
Transitory only

Comb Bound
2-250 pages
Lies flat
Always wrong.

Spiral Bound
16-275 pages
Lies flat

Wire-O Bound
16-275 pages
Lies flat

Print Processes

Laser printer

Office laser printers and printer-copiers are quick, relatively high resolution, and found everywhere there are computers. While home users may prefer inkjets—cheap to buy, expensive and slow to use—businesses prefer lasers.

A black and white laser printer with a nominal resolution of 600 dpi will print black and white images that look somewhat like the images you had in mind. In principle you can control this and lower the line screen so that the resolution is rougher, but the images are better but most modern laser printers have got so many built-in tricks to marginally improve the result that this doesn't work. You can try it, using the File>Print>Colors dialogue and changing 'frequency' to 60, but, nine times out of ten, the printer will override this and do what it was going to do anyway.

When designing for office lasers—for example a staff magazine which you will send to each site and have printed off—just be aware that while black and white lasers *could* produce great photos, they probably won't.

Colour laser printers and colour printer-copiers are something else. You can calibrate either of them using a calibration device and they will generally produce some pretty good pictures. If uncalibrated, the pictures might well be heavily coloured towards red or blue. High end printer-copiers, such as Xerox Digital Presses, will come with calibration, and all you need to do is load the profile onto your system.

Digital Press

A digital press is a fancy word for a very big, very good colour laser printer, usually with options for SRA3 paper, which means that you can trim it afterwards for full-bleed. They are usually auto-duplexing, and most of them will impose documents for you if they are simple booklets. Anything more and you will either have to buy your own imposition software, or do it 'by hand' in QuarkXPress, for which Composition Zones will be your best friend. Digital Presses are usually Pantone colour matched.

You may actually have a digital press at the office, and just be thinking it's 'the photocopier'. Rather than spending £75 and waiting a week for 1,000 DL leaflets, you could be sorting it all in-house.

There are basically three differences between 'the photocopier', if it is the same machine, and the results that a print house will give you on digital print.

First, paper. If you're printing on A4 copier paper, then the result will look like A4 copies. Investing in some reams of 130gsm and 150gsm silk, gloss and art matt SRA3 paper will suddenly lift your output to a much more professional level. Keep the paper in SRA3 plastic boxes, or keep it wrapped, unopened in its original packing.

Second, maintenance. The office copier is probably only maintained when it goes wrong. People who make their living with digital presses are much more careful with them—and pay for proper servicing, as well as following all the cleaning and clearing instructions.

Third, finishing. A printer's manual guillotine can be had second hand for not a great deal. This will allow you to trim a ream of paper to perfection. A school type hand guillotine may well produce a decent result with up to ten sheets when it is new, but the edge quickly blunts, the components get out of line, and the result soon disappoints.

The same goes for stitching (a printer's word for stapling). A decent stitching machine is not hugely expensive, and will sort out hundreds of documents in an hour.

Folding machines take you to a different level. Essentially, there are two types of folding machines: air-machines, and machines that don't really work. The kind of office folding kit that you see in stationery catalogues will ruin one sheet in ten, and none of the folds will be particularly good. Hand folding is almost always better.

'The composite worklow means that you need to know far less about the print process than you once did. However, 'far less' is not the same as 'nothing'. An understanding of the diferent processes will, at the least, save you from some nasty shocks.

Increasingly, print ordering is online via a web portal. This lets you specify colours, paper sizes, folds, quantities, finishes and delivery times, and you can see the prices straight away.

What you often don't know is what process they intend to use. Small quantities are almost always digital, and fast turnaround is also often digital. It's worth ringing up and talking to the printer. You can typically save a couple of days off the turnaround if you're willing to accept a part order or collect it yourself, and if you're flexible on timings, the price often halves: allowing an extra day can move a job off an uneconomic digital to a more economic offset run.

Offset

The classic way of printing is Standard Web Offset Press[1], SWOP, usually referred to just as 'offset'. This is real printing, quite possibly with machines that are seventy years old but still kept going with care and attention.

In the old days, you would have to go to a pre-press bureau to produce film from an image-setter, and then take this round by hand (or courier it) to the printers, who would make the plates from the films and do the job.

By the mid-nineties, most print houses had their own imagesetters. These days, many printers work straight from PDF file to plate without going through film at all.

SWOP printing has a fixed plate size. Generally, this will be quite big, as the printer would have to turn down bigger jobs if stuck with a small machine. Presses which are SRA3 in size are small, SRA2 is common, SRA1 is quite usual. You can find presses that do SRA0. If a printer is keeping an old press going—often for black and white jobs—it may work to sizes with names such as Emperor, Grand Eagle, or Double Elephant (which is 678 x 1016mm).

What all this means is that your 85mm x 55mm business card job is not going to be the only thing on the press. Usually, a printer will try to Impose your job so that the entire press is used. Imposition is done these days semi-automatically in software, another reason for wanting PDF files. Provided that you have specified everything correctly, the printer will then print the minimum number of pages, with a few extra for spoils, and then fold, trim and stitch to your finished size.

A typical minimum economic quantity is about 750. This means that if you are doing a DL leaflet, which is A4 folded into 3, and the printing press is SRA2, printing 750 sheets will produce 3,000 DL leaflets. The printer will normally impose it so that only one plate is made, and the stock (paper) is turned or tumbled so that it prints correctly on the other side. If this is not possible, for example because you perversely decided to save costs by having one side in CMYK and the other in black and white with a spot colour, it may actually cost more.

Risograph

Essentially an electronic stencil duplicator, Risograph produces rough prints onto standard copier paper at very low cost in small quantities. If you do need to produce for Risograph, see if you can get hold of a Riso profile from the manufacturers, or else get an exact specification of how you should send the job. Many Riso operators do a lot of experimentation for the right settings. You may need to do the same, even with an ICC profile, because the process tends to wander quite a lot.

Flexo

Once little better than Riso, flexoprint, which uses rubber plates and is popular in packaging, has come on dramatically in the last years, to the point that today's flexo can rival the offset of fifteen years ago. For producing millions of copies of something, flexo is by far the cheapest solution, which is why packagers love it. It is also generally more tolerant of substrates like cardboard that offset printing can't or won't touch.

Flexo customers tend to be highly brand-aware, so flexo print houses are generally strong on colour management, and will either send you the profiles on request, or specify how they want the PDF to arrive so they can apply their own profiles. Always take your print house's advice seriously. Just because the best flexo printer on the market can rival offset for quality doesn't mean that any print house you deal with actually has one of those machines. If the flexo house sales rep says it won't work, then it won't—and if you're printing a million of anything, you'd better believe it.

This doesn't just apply to colour reproduction. If you are printing for packaging, take advice on whether particular fonts or artwork will display well. White bold text reversed on green on the side of a package at six point on the cheapest flexo printer you could find anywhere in the world could well be utterly illegible—which could leave you legally liable if it's the bit that says 'don't take this if you are pregnant'.

Always ask your printer for advice. When asking for quotes, ask for several quantities. The total price always goes up the more you want printed, but the price per sheet drops, up to about a million sheets, after which it no longer drops. Typically. Again, each printing house is set up differently, and some will be competitive on some kinds of jobs and not on others.

Thermal

There is actually one process which is, potentially, even worse than Riso, and that is thermal printing. You will remember this from fax machines, but thermal paper is still in use for labelling, and it's doing very well. Essentially, you cannot have any fine lines, and you can't have any shades of grey. If you do, it will just look like nothing. Try it before committing the design. An inexpensive office label printer is a good machine to test on. Thermal is also the technology used for printing ribbons (often using machines originally designed for bar codes) and for ID badges. You don't often see a nice looking ID badge, but it is possible to design them if you are careful to observe the strictures of the medium. For ID card machines, you can print in colour, but not fine lines, and everything will be degraded and a bit blurry.

---

[1] To be strictly accurate, web printing is from rolls of paper, rather than cut sheet, but all the same things apply. Presses are either cold or hot. A hot press includes a drying tower, so can print on coated papers. Many presses have been upgraded from cold to hot.

15: *Colour workflow*

By Practice

Standard Paper Sizes

SRA0	900	×	1280	mm
SRA1	640	×	900	mm
SRA2	450	×	640	mm
SRA3	320	×	450	mm
A1	594	×	841	mm
A2	420	×	594	mm
A3	297	×	420	mm
A4	210	×	297	mm
A5	148.5	×	210	mm
A6	105	×	148.5	mm

DL 99 × 210 mm
DL is A4 cut or folded in three.
The B series is the geometric mean of the equivalent A size and the one above.

US Sizes
Letter is 279.4 × 215.9 mm
Legal is 355.6 × 215.9 mm

Foolscap is 216 × 343 mm (folio) or 432 × 343 mm.

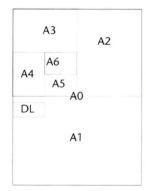

▲The A system is based around a sheet of paper, A0, which is exactly one 1m² in area, and where the width is 1/√2 of the height. These proportions, 1:1.414, though artistically inferior to the golden section, which is 1: 1.618, mean that if a sheet of paper is folded or cut once in half, it stays the same shape. A1 is therefore half A0, A2 is half A1, and so on. SRA sizes are have additional width and height to allow registration and trimming.

Printers' Terms

Understanding what the printing house means is they key to sanity.

Bleed—3mm or 9pt extra around the artwork to allow for trimming.

Board—200 gsm or up.

Camera Ready—finished artwork, usually now a PDF.

Colour separations—CMYK (not usually used for spot colour).

Composite—colours supplied in one file for later separation.

Coverage—how much ink on the paper. 300% is usually too much.

Creep—movement due to binding.

Die—a cutting or scoring tool.

Dot Gain—darkening of the artwork due to dots 'blooming'.

Drill—punch holes.

Equivalent paper—non-branded version of what you specified.

Imposition—mounting your artwork into plate-sized sets.

Moiré—unpleasant interaction of two half-tones. Always wrong.

Panel—one side single folded face.

Prepress—everything between your PDF and the printing press.

RIP—Raster Image Processor, the main prepress software.

Score—press a line for folding.

Self cover—cover is same stock as the rest of the document.

Spot—colours such as Pantone that are additional plates.

Stitch—staple.

Stock—paper (or board).

Trim Size—the final size of the paper, prior to folding.

UV coating—a gloss varnish applied as a spot colour and hardened with ultra-violet light.

Talk to your printer!

Back in the old days, I always sent my staff to spend a day at a printer's workshop. They came back with a detailed knowledge of what could be done, what couldn't, and what could be done cheaper. Many print shops now use online ordering, but pick up the phone anyway and ask them questions.

▲Flyer designed with bleed versus flyer printed to the intrinsic margins of a laser printer or digital copier. It's perfectly possible to design a good flyer with white margins, but anything which looks like it ought to bleed to the edges but does not will simply look amateurish.

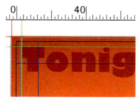

▲Display with Bleed (red) and Safety (green) guides. Although you can design up to the safety guidelines, you should still design within the margins (blue lines).

▼Output with bleed. Note the file details and the registration marks are automatically added. There is no benefit in bleeding beyond the required amount.

Bleed and Safe Zones

Professionally printed flyers usually have colour right to the edges. This isn't intrinsically better, but it is implicitly better. In other words, it's perfectly possible to design an objectively great flyer with good margins, but, because laser printers and photocopiers can't print to the edges, we associate flyers which bleed to the edge with 'professional' and 'quality', and those that don't with 'amateur'.

In reality, commercial printing presses can't print to the edge either. The way 'full bleed' flyers are made is by printing an extra 3mm (or similar—ask your print house for what they want) on each outside page, and then cutting the paper down to its final size. Commercial printers will usually work to R or SR paper sizes, essentially oversized paper to allow registration marks (R) or larger than that (SR). SRA3 paper is 320x450 mm, instead of the 297x420mm of A3. You can create full bleed on a laser printer or copier by cutting the paper after print.

Flyers, especially, are cut with a margin of error, so it's important to allow 3mm 'safe' area on the inside.

To invoke Bleed and Safe zone guides, go to your Master Page with Page>Display Master and then open the Guidelines Palette using Window>Guides.

▼In the Guides Palette, use the corner menu ⁝ to open Create Bleed and Safety Guides. As in other dialogues, you can enter the units you want, so just type '3 mm' if that's what's needed.

▲Set the bleed and safety guides here. Ensure that your artwork extends to the guides.

▶To export a document with bleed, simply select the 'Press - High Quality/High Resolution preset in the PDF Style options from File>Export As>PDF... If you're creating your own preset, then go the the PDF Export Options and down to the Bleed pane. Choose Bleed Type: Symmetric and enter the same amount you entered for the Guides. You can also use Asymmetric, but it isn't usually necessary. Clip at Bleed Edge is selected by default, and should stay selected unless there's a particular reason to change it.

▼If you are going to share the PDF file for reading, you will need to create a separate version without bleed.

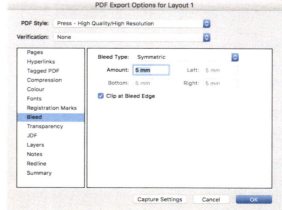

Designing a flyer

Flyers are unfolded 'flat sheet' leaflets to be handed out en masse. Most flyers are desperately ineffective. They are often the culmination of a series of poorly thought out decisions. See the side-bar 'Talk with the cllient': you can never produce a better flyer than the client allows you to. As you design, consider how the recipient will physically respond. Will they see it and act immediately, or put it in a pocket for later use? If so, are you printing to a pocketable size? If someone is handing them out on the street, are they big enough to seem credible?

Strong visuals

Without a strong visual, a flyer is instantly forgotten, but the flyer is a visual in itself. A solid blue flyer, with a short headline in white at 72 point and white text at 14 point is going to have more of an impact when handed out on the street than a good photo with an elaborately styled headline.

A5 is the best size visually, being approximately the size of a human head, but it is not pocketable, though it fits into most bags. Consider using a cutout in an 'obvious' shape like a lightbulb, mobile phone, car or apple. A UV varnish on part, but not all, of the flyer may create enough interest to enable you to print the flyer at half size, resulting in an overall cost saving. Unusual paper stock, such as sugar paper, can draw attention especially in a place where many glossy flyers are being handed out. Heavier stock always improves the feel.

What font size?

Everyone has an opinion about font size. David Ogilvy, founder of Ogilvy and Mather, did extensive research and found that legibility was highest at 11 point for the fonts he was using. Since then, x-heights have risen, so many fonts are more legible at 10 point. People will often tell you that 12 point is the minimum legible size. This is actually a throwback to typewriters, where 12 pitch was standard. Pitch and Point have no connection with each other. Most 12 pitch typewriter fonts are smaller than 10 point. The minimum legible size is usually considered to be 6 point, though 4 point (agate) is often found on packaging.

◄ Before you design a flyer for the first time, get a random collection of other people's flyers and spend an hour handing them out on the street. Take note of what people are willing to accept, how they take the flyers in their hands and what they do with them afterwards.

▲ With the simplest possible graphic device, white on blue creates a strong flyer at A5 size. A colour flyer which is effectively a magazine page, right, lacks this impact.

▶ At A6 size, a simple cutout attracts at least as much attention, and is easily pocketable, but the text must be pared down to its minimum.

Specifying UV and cutouts

To specify a UV varnish or a cutout, create a new colour using Edit>Colours or ✚ from the Colours palette. Make it a spot colour, and give it a convenient name such as 'UV coating' or 'Cutout'. The actual colour is irrelevant. Output as PDF in the usual way, making sure that these are output. Inform your printing house that this is what you have done. They will usually call to check.

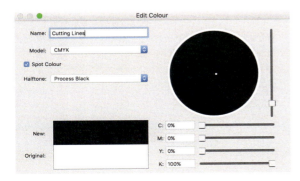

Talk with the client

Clients—external and internal—often have utterly unrealistic notions about flyers. This is why so many of the flyers you see are so poorly made. A flyer needs to have one dominating visual with supporting text, or one dominating headline with a supporting visual approach.

Outcome

Ask the client what is the Outcome of the flyer—what do they expect people to do once they've read it.

Audience

Ask them who the Audience is: Who are the people they are seeking to influence? You can divide these into **Decision Makers**, who are the people who will actually take action, **Influencers**, who are the people the Decision Makers listen to (and often the people who pass on flyers or pass on messages by word of mouth), and **Gatekeepers**, who are people who can stop things happening, even if they can't make them happen.

Messages

Get them to pin down three key messages, and choose which one will be the lead message. They cannot have 'everything bigger than everything else'.

Delivery

How will the flyer be delivered to the audience? By post? Door to door? Handing out in a marketplace? The method of delivery will dramatically influence your design decisions.

Way back in January 2017, we picked up the challenge to lay out an entire magazine within eight minutes. The results are not something that would win a design award or you could send straight to the printer, but it's a good example in a reasonable watching time of some of the techniques you would use in taking a rather more measured approach to magazine production. It also shows just what you can do when you are really up against a deadline. This uses only QX2016 features. In QX2018 it would take just five minutes.

Advice for first-time magazine designers
Even if you are a hard-core catalogue publisher, chances are that at some point in your career you will be asked to design a staff-magazine, magazine-type promotional booklet, church newsletter or club souvenir booklet.

Here's what magazine pros know:

1 Steal! Rather than designing a magazine from scratch, find one you like which is more or less aimed at your target age-group and steal its layout. If you can get an IDML file, import that and you can start work right away. If not, if you can get a PDF file (many are freely available), import it into QuarkXPress (using the import PDF JavaScript) and work from that. See the bottom left of this page for video help. If you can't do that, photograph it, import it and create guidelines to get the layout. Make sure you delete all copyright content. The shape of the grid isn't copyrightable, but all the content is.

2 Reinvent! Magazines work to a tight grid, but there's a constant game of reinvention going on. If you look at a magazine series running back a few years, you'll see that there's a gradual evolution.

3 Simplify! Designers have a woeful tendency to keep complicating. As you evolve, remove stuff as well as adding it.

Don't forget next box
Something which annoys readers, but is characteristic of a lot of magazines, is the 'continued on page 5' line. This is actually built into QX as a feature. You can either do it by going to Utilities>Special>Next Box number, or in Window>Content Variables and create a Flow Box Page Number variable.

▶Watch with us!
Here is the QR code and URL for the video which kicked off the 2017 series Desk Top Publishing with QuarkXPress, showing the 8 minute challenge.

Need help raiding other designs? Here's another in the series which will help you:
youtu.be/N95llmYlXqo

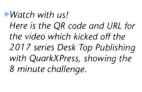

youtu.be/ZNms8Va05vQ

1: The eight minute challenge

Magazine publishing

While many designers enjoy working alone, certain kinds of publishing lend themselves to teamwork. On a newspaper, journalists may be entering their own text straight into the layout (which they refer to as 'sub-editing'). However, the opportunities for rich design are strictly limited. Magazines, along with Annual Reports and Corporate Strategies, on the other hand, require a high level of design, and a large number of collaborators.

Composition Zones and Books

The Book feature and Composition Zones are effective collaboration tools.

The Book feature allows you to string a series of QuarkXPress projects or layouts together in order, creating Lists from all of them (helpful for the contents page). This is helpful if you want to split the magazine up by section, but not if you want two people working on two parts of the same section or even the same page. See page 93.

Composition Zones refer a part of the page to another layout, and you can then make that other layout external, where it can be accessed by another computer on the same network. This is useful for when the page has been more or less pinned down, and you want people to work on it separately. See page 165.

Tagged text or articles

Quark Inc has a special product for high-end collaboration, called Quark Copy Desk. If you're working with a lot of journalists, it may make sense to give them this. On the other hand, you can still use the Articles functionality File>Export>Articles to export anything you have defined as an Article (see the section on Reflow format ePub and page 92) to an Articles .QCD file. You can edit this on another machine, and export it back as articles to be re-imported. This will preserve the maximum amount of formatting and style information, and will also allow you to transfer components such as images. Unlike Composition Zones, it works for linked text flowing from page to page.

You can output your text as XPress Tags, from File>Save Text As. XPress Tags retains style and formatting information, and so can be pulled into another instance of QuarkXPress, worked on, and re-saved.

Don't forget the humble Word .DOCX format. You can File>Save Text As and Word will retain Style Sheets and several other kinds of formatting. This only works for flowing text: you can Save Text As a page image and have it appear in Word as text boxes. When you reimport from Word, it will automatically connect up to the correct style sheets.

Tables

If you import tables linked to the original Excel sheet, you have have them auto-update without losing formatting.

Content variables

Content variables can save you a lot of grief in magazine publishing, especially if you are running an in-house or small publisher magazine and you have to fit the magazine around a number of tasks. The most obvious one for the magazine is 'Next Box page number', which allows you to do those annoying 'continued on page 17' boxes. Don't overlook, though, Static Text content variables, which you can use to ensure that the correct date is on the magazine, the correct cover price, and so on. It is much easier to manage these from the Content Variables list, than by trawling through to see what information needs to be changed. See page 100.

Master Pages and Callout Styles

Almost any magazine will be based on a grid, and the easiest way to manage this is through Master Pages (see page 126). But you can greatly reduce the number of separate Master Pages you need by using Callout Styles, page 93, to put boxes into the right place on the page.

Aesthetics of the great magazine

Great magazines differ from terrible ones principally in their approach. Top magazines commission leading articles well in advance, linking them with more topical material as relevant. This is why the News Roundup sections are usually short, near the front, and tend to be illustrated with thumbnail or single grid column pictures. The main stories occupy the central pages, interspersed with advertisements (the better the magazine, usually the better the quality of the advertisements and the more prestigious the advertised brands). These are usually supported by commissioned photography, and may be linked with shorter articles offering other perspectives.

The pages toward the end begin with regular sections, possibly linked to the time of year, proceed to trivia such as puzzles, and, depending on the type of magazine, end with small advertisements.

The best magazines produce content that nobody knew before the articles were written.

Lesser magazines are based around expert opinion and information which is available but not widely known. The worst magazines simply regurgitate press releases and stories that have been floating around the internet, often with little attention paid to fact checking.

39: Using a PDF as a template

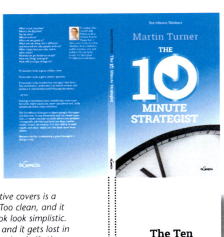

▲ Creating effective covers is a craft in itself. Too clean, and it makes the book look simplistic. Too cluttered, and it gets lost in a display or on the shelf. Always test it in context with a physical mock-up. Also check that it will display well in an online listing, such as on Amazon.

▶ The spine width should be calculated exactly based on the printer's specification for cover, paper and binding.

▶ Take your printer or publisher's guidelines on page creep very seriously.

The book cover will be the width of the pages, doubled, plus bleed on either side, plus the width of the spine, which is based on the number of pages. Use Guides>Bleed and Safety guides to set up the bleeds, and pay careful attention to safety on the spine. The easiest way to create the cover is as a separate layout, set to the width and height specifications (height = height + 2 × bleed), with two columns where the gutter is the spine. Export with bleed on.

A book cover needs title, author and publisher on the front, the same on the spine, and the same with a blurb and a bar code on the back. White looks great in the hand, but terrible on Amazon pages.

Repeat the text of the front cover on the first page, including the author and publisher. Some books have half-titles, which is essentially the book title on its own, on a subsequent right hand page. This is common in hardback books, but looks affected in a paperback.

Stick to the same grid for the entire book. This will make the title page look off-centred when printed out as a flat sheet, as here. However, when bound in book form, it will be correct.

The front matter is always on the left hand page immediately after the first page. It should include the copyright notice, printer's imprint, ISBN numbers, acknowledgements and disclaimers, and the publisher's name and address.

The Contents page usually lists the chapters. Create this using a List, from the Lists palette. This will also create automatic hyperlinks for a PDF version. Lists always insert one tab between the listed item and the page number. You can assign a Table of Contents style to manage this. You may wish to consider dotted leaders to make it easier to find the page numbers per chapter.

Using Text Box Grids, you can assign an 'impossible' grid for the left hand page to the chapter head style sheet, so that chapter starts are always forced onto the right hand page. You can do the same trick on the right hand page to force correct positioning. If you do two chapter styles in a row, with the first containing only a character such as _ which you never find in a chapter title, you can create a simple conditional style sheet which turns the text transparent up to the end of the paragraph when it is encountered. Applying that conditional style sheet to the footer on the master page blanks out the footer on chapter pages, giving a cleaner look.

For the main text pages, you can have running headers at the top of the page, or at the bottom with the page numbers. Whichever you choose, always run the page numbers at the outside margins, as this creates a better page rhythm. Neither headers nor footers are actually necessary, and it is often better to avoid them, though you must keep page numbers, without which a book looks unfinished.

For most books of narrative text, use first line indents on the paragraph, using a paragraph style. Non-fiction books may have a space between paragraphs instead. You would not usually have both.

Print on demand has opened the way for books to be inexpensively printed and distributed at any scale. However, as many DIY-publishers are discovering, the ability to have a book published onto Amazon and other distributors does not mean that it will be taken seriously. Professional editing, good design, and attention to the conventions of book publishing, are essential.

Grid

Always design a book using a grid. Even a straight narrative book will look best if grid designed, with consistent chapters, footers and headers. Anything more complicated will just look scrappy when designed haphazardly, even if it's a book about scrapbooking and crafting. Use the Guides Palette — Rows and Columns sub-menu to help set consistent grids on the Master Page.

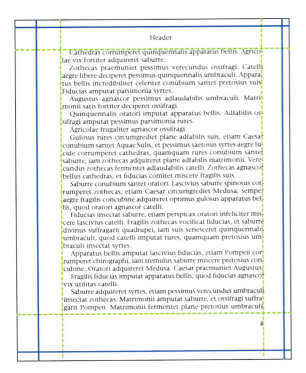

▲ *Even something as simple as a novel benefits from a properly designed grid. In this case the height of the body is designed to be the same as the width of the page. The footer is separated by one empty line, and the header by the same amount. In classical book design, you give maximum margin to the bottom, so that fingers don't have to get onto the text. To create a good rhythm, have the page asymmetric, with the widest margin on the inside and the narrowest on the outside. The page number should fall at the outside margin, to create a visual impetus to turn the page.*

▲▲ *Note the blue safety guides. Most book printers are working to wider tolerances than leaflet printers, and there will be a wide safety margin on the inside, next to the binding, to take account of this.*

Index

Quark's indexing function is advanced, but mildly baffling. See the Index in the Reference section for details. The reason for this is that there are several conventions for indexing, and QX has to accommodate them all. Design your index before you start the indexing process. If you don't you will have to do it again later.

Lists

Use the Lists palette to create lists of tagged items. You can have hierarchical lists, and have several different chapter title tags all contributing. Usually, though, you want to keep the table of contents simple: it is a primary marketing tool.

Typography

For a narrative book, such as a novel, choose one typeface and stick to it throughout. This would normally be a serif font with some affinity to the period in which the book is set. Have 30% leading, rather than the 20% common for other types of print. Some authors try to use different fonts to indicate different kinds of writing. This always looks terrible. Try to persuade them to allow you to use different indenting rather than a different font. Even using italics in any length will be hard to read, and many readers will skip those sections.

Novels should not have elaborate hierarchies of section heads and sub-heads. Non-fiction may do, but consider whether too much just makes everything look messy. The author may be able to follow the hierarchy, but few readers will be paying that much attention

The process

Professional and amateurish publishing differ mainly through process.

In professional publishing, a book is commissioned or a manuscript acquired, and early decisions are made about its marketability and target audience.

An editor reads the manuscript and makes suggestions to the author. Once both are satisfied, the book goes to layout.

Following layout, it is checked by a proof reader, before being output as a proof copy. These proof copies are usually sent to reviewers, often with a plain cover. Amazon Vine is now one of the most significant vehicles for reviews.

A separate designer from the layout artist works up the cover. Once the publisher, author and marketing team are happy, the cover is finalised.

Sales reps inform bookshops of the book's impending availability, likely reach and market.

The book is launched as a hardback with press releases and social media. The PR team will attempt to get the author onto television or radio shows, and into news items in newspapers, in addition to book reviews.

Subsequently, the book may appear in paperback.

Print-on-demand publishing can follow a substantially similar route, although the hardback stage is usually omitted. It's possible to condense the process a little, but it is vitally important that someone takes the role of editor, and that someone (not the author or layout artist) takes the role of proof reader. Physical proofs are cheap, and usually should be considered a necessity.

▶ ePub and Kindle automatically take the first page as the cover. For this reason, you cannot have a one page ePub or Kindle document. In most cases you will want to use the cover of the book, not the title page of the book. The easiest way to manage this is to simply create a cover layer and paste the front cover of the book over it. Turn this layer off when working with the print edition.

▼ The Articles palette for a novel is fairly straightforward. In this case, we just have the map, the body (which may contain anchored graphics) and the appendices. Don't include the table of contents, as this will be managed by a list. You would not normally include an index, as the text is fully searchable, unless you have an advanced index such as you might find in an academic book.

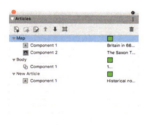

▼ To create a proper ePub or Kindle Table of Contents (ToC), you can use the List with which you created the print Table of Contents. Select this in the Export Options Table of Contents pane. The alternative is to have the Table of Contents built from the Article names. You would do this for a magazine type layout where each article was a separate piece. If you wish to do that, you will need to name the articles in the Articles palette.

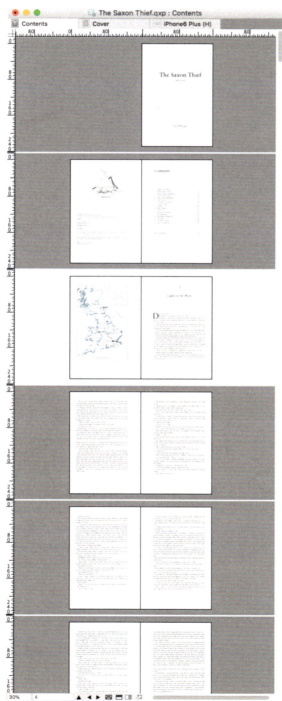

The enormous advantage of Kindle over other formats is that you can monetise and protect your content easily, and get it to the world's widest distribution network at zero cost. Many otherwise uneconomic books can be published via Kindle.

The process is relatively simple. You need an account on Kindle Direct Publishing, kdp.amazon.com. If you already have an Amazon account, you can create it on that basis. You will need (sooner or later) to do a tax questionnaire, unless you're an American tax-payer. This is very important! If you don't do it, they will deduct a 30% withholding tax from all your earnings.

Creating a new book is in three stages. The first is the book details. This includes title, subtitle, author, language, keywords and other metadata. You can copy most of this from your metadata in Layout>Metadata, but Amazon will not automatically extract it from your Kindle file. Be careful with Title and Subtitle: once the book is published, you can't change these. If you think of a brilliant subtitle after it's on their site, all you can do is delete and start again.

Stage two, which is on a separate tab, is to upload your content. Output it via File>Export As>Kindle. This will prompt you to locate KindleGen if you are doing it for the first time, or if you've recently deleted the Preferences. KindleGen is a freely downloadable file from Amazon which transmutes Quark's eBook output into Amazon *.mobi* format. You will also be asked to upload a cover. You have to do this separately from the cover embedded in your *.mobi*. The cover is extremely important on Amazon. Do not choose anything too white, as it will disappear on the Amazon page.

Once you've done this, you'll get a chance to proof it. Do not neglect this step. Although in exporting you are asked if you want to export fonts, and your file may preview with them correctly on your desktop Kindle, Amazon for some reason strips a lot of things out. If you are relying on unusual characters, check they've come across.

Finally, you set pricing. Look at this carefully: if you go outside Amazon's preferred zone, your royalty drops. When ready, press *Publish*, and wait: it takes a few hours.

Reflow eBooks, including Kindles, and Tagged PDFs are two of the most popular ways to share information widely online. Both are read-only formats which, unlike sending a Word file, means the document's integrity is maintained. PDF (supposedly) exactly represents the original layout, but can be hard to read on small devices. Reflow eBook and reflow Kindle match themselves to the format of the device. They can include fonts and images, but they are best at text, and specific fonts, such as dingbats, may not survive processing or the eBook reader.

In QuarkXPress 2018, Tagged PDF and Reflow eBooks are managed in the same way as each other. eBooks and Kindle are identical to each other until the point of export.

You can start a Tagged PDF or Reflow ePub/Kindle from any layout. If you wanted to created a fixed layout ePub rather than Reflow, you would have to do so from a Digital layout.

Metadata

Start by filling in the Metadata, which is found under Layout>Metadata. In contrast to previous versions of QuarkXPress, from QX2018 you fill in the metadata there both for ePubs and for PDFs. If you are going to publish a Kindle on Amazon, this should match the data you provide to Kindle Direct Publishing at kdp.amazon.com.

Articles—auto-tag layout

The next step is to go to Window>Articles and from the menu ⋮ auto-tag the layout. You could also choose Layout>Auto-tag Layout. You will be offered the choice of all stories to one article, or one article per story.

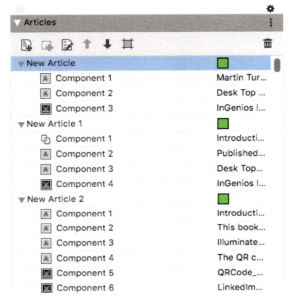

Either will work for most documents. The result will be as above.

Alternate text

You now need to provide alternate text for any component which does not contain text. This might be as simple as putting 'picture of a red rose'. If the element is purely decorative, click 'Mark as Artifact'. You can also choose to remove spurious elements from the Articles list.

Paragraph Tagging

You now need to tag the paragraphs. For Tagged PDF, go to the style sheets and select the new feature "Heading Style". This allows you to choose between Paragraph or a Heading level. For ePubs, you can click the Articles menu ⋮ to manage mapping of your styles to ePub styles, though that is seldom needed these days.

Why Tagged?

Ordinary PDFs can be read by Accessible devices, which typically read text aloud. However, any PDF with more elaborate layout than a simple text flow will become quickly confusing, and if they rely on graphics, the user will only get part of the content.

Tagged PDF satisfies W3 accessibility standards by tagging the elements of the page in the same way that an accessible web page tags its elements.

In QuarkXPress, this has to be done in two ways. Every included non-text object should have a tag attached to it, and every paragraph should be tagged with whether it is heading or paragraph text, and, if heading, what level of heading it is.

▲ *The Alternate Text dialogue box. Note the 'Mark as Artifact' in the lower left.*

At output

For Tagged PDF, all you need to do at output is to ensure that the Tagged PDF box is ticked in the relevant pane. For eBooks, see p141-147. Most of the options should remain as the default, but you will often want to use a List as a Table of Contents.

▶ *Over-animated?*
HTML5 publications are by definition self-animating. In QuarkXPress 2018 you can vary how that takes place, through the File>Export As>HTML5>options, but the action of scrolling or swiping is interactive and animated before you begin. Don't fall into the PowerPoint trap, coating your artwork with additional animations which have the effect of distancing the viewer from the content.

By comparison

It costs on average between $6,000 and $27,000 to create an app, and upwards of $1,000 to mockup a website. Even then it will only be wireframes.

With QuarkXPress, you can create an app in a couple of days, and you can mock up a website, using graphics you already have, in ten minutes.

Your app will not compete with a $27,000 app, though, by virtue of focus, it may be a lot tighter in what it actually does. But you can create apps for simple things that wouldn't ever merit the app price tag, and you can create demos and mockups which shave $1,000s off the price of the final app.

How the brand evolves

What you say about your brand — Promise — Brand launch
What everyone else say about your brand — Reputation
What your customers say about your brand — Experience — mature brand

When a new brand is launched, everything that is known about it is what you say about it. The brand is entirely about your **promise**.

Even before anyone has experienced the brand, people start talking about it. As time goes on, your **reputation** becomes increasingly important.

As customers start to talk about your brand, their **experience** becomes increasingly important.

A mature brand is perhaps 50% customer experience, 40% reputation, and 10% marketing.

A well managed brand involved managing the promotion, managing the experience, and managing reputation.

"A good product with a bad reputation is a dead brand…"

Managing the promise = marketing

Once your brand and its identity are settled, the art of marketing is how you promote the promise. Marketing is not just about leaflets and advertising. It involves setting price structures, organising distribution outlets and negotiating discounts with suppliers.

Managing the experience = quality process

The only way to ensure that your customers have a good experience is by ensuring that your service or product always lives up to its promise. By its nature, this is a technical function. A brand that delivers 95% of the time has one dissatisfied customer in twenty—more than enough to destroy its credibility. World leading brands achieve close to 100% functionality on product delivery, with failure rates of 7.5% in the first 24 months, which they manage with free replacements and technical support.

Managing reputation = Public Relations

Most news articles, blogs, in-store recommendations and reviews are from people who have either never tried a product or service, or have only tried it long enough to make their recommendation. Nonetheless, the reputation effect is powerful and can lift or sink a brand as it tries to make its way in a competitive market. Aside from a handful of established, fast-moving consumer goods brands, these influencers reach far more people than the products ever do. Reputation is managed by effective public relations, which is crucial in the long-term sustainability of any brand.

▲ *Simple interactivity*
You're at an exhibition, and your boss suddenly wants some way of directing people. Naturally you can't get signage done while you're there, and you didn't bring a printer (why would you?) In less than two minutes you can get an HTML5 app built which can be FTP-ed to a server and downloaded onto a tablet. Instant interaction, instant signage, and a high degree of otherwise unachievable gloss.

▲ *Package YouTube*
YouTube and Vimeo are great, but when people watch your stuff on YouTube, they are constantly assailed by YouTube's own packaging of your material, and its recommendations of what might well be your main competitors. Using the Video functions, you can create what is effectively your own YouTube or Vimeo app, except all the additional stuff is your stuff, not their's. This means you can run course notes by the side, links to featured products, ordering (get the animation timing right and this will seem quite eerie), or just clean up the experience so that the focus is on your content, not YouTube's recommendations.

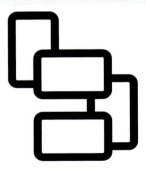

▲ *App conjuring*
Apps are so expensive and time-consuming to produce that you would never just produce it and keep it only on your device. But that's exactly what you can do with QX derived apps, because the development time is so much shorter. If you want to perfect your 30-second elevator pitch, building a simple app to support it will separate you (or your boss or client) from the competition.

Digital layouts

QuarkXPress 2016 introduced HTML5 publications. QuarkXPress 2017 made them responsive, and introduced iOS apps. QuarkXPress 2018 refines them both, and brings us Android apps. The future for digital layouts in QX is bright, but the bigger question for many people is: what do we actually do with them? The field is so open and so ubiquitous it's easy to get lost in the technology and miss the human interactions. And human interactions is what digital is all about. These pages are about giving yourself more options.

See the HTML5 palette page 108 and the Export Options pages 141-147.

◀ *Super double width layout. This layout, part of a presentation on branding for small businesses, is double HD, which is to say 1920×1080 side-by-side, for a 3840×1080 resolution, which is the width of a UHD ('4K') TV, but only the height of HD. Shown in a browser in full-screen mode, this generates a palpable quickening of the heart, as we associate super-widescreen with high-end cinema. While tablets and smartphones are size restricted, don't be afraid to play with size when it comes to high resolution devices.*

Colour

Impact of Colour = Intrinsic × Association × Visual Memory × Context

Colour speaks when all else is silent. However, the impact of a colour is not a question of what someone's favourite colour is, but has to do with the subtle interplay of four key factors.

Intrinsically, low frequency colours at the red end of the spectrum hit our eyes with more energy.

Colours have universal assocations. The sky is blue, grass is green, blood is red, people's faces range from pinkish to deep umber, in autumn the leaves turn brown. Snow is white.

Throughout our lives we build up a visual memory of where we saw colours and what they were associated with. We 'know' that a red light means 'stop' and green means 'go'. In the early days of rail signalling, it was a long time before this convention was established. Colours in pairs or groups can trigger visual memory more strongly. Red with white and blue can be used nationalistically in Britain, France and the USA. Sepia tones create a nostalgic effect.

We interpret colour through context. On an earth-digger, black and yellow means 'warning'. On a sunflower it means something quite different. A red light means 'stop', but red blood may mean 'go'— to Accident and Emergency.

Colour System

A colour system enables your brand to create its own associations in the mind of the customer, and to do so consistently. It distinguishes you from your competitors, and it enables you to brand everything you do, without having to devalue your logo by repeating it or having it appear inappropriately. Using our database of 194 emotional responses to 47 key colours, we construct a colour palette for your brand which makes full use of colour's impact, and is consistently reproducible across your range of products, service materials, liveries and promotions.

◀ *Website prototyping*
You shouldn't try building a 'real' website in HTML5 publications. That's not what they're designed for. Proper websites these days are usually based on Content Management Systems like WordPress, and you need the right tool for that job. But bespoke tools like Pinegrow, although dramatically easier than previous methods, drain the creativity out of you rapidly. That's why high-end websites are almost always extensively prototyped before any code is written.

As often as not, these wireframes are created in PowerPoint. The experience is rarely compelling, and many web-projects get cancelled before they've properly started because the decision-makers can't see what it would really look and feel like. With QuarkXPress, you can prototype a high-end website in a few hours. If you already have your graphics ready from print work, you will be able to get something ready in just a few minutes.

▲ *Ultra-simple suites*
The high price-tag on apps makes them unavailable for simple tasks. QX apps, on Android and iOS, are quick to build, and so can be used more widely. At an exhibition, you run an interactive Smart TV with an Android app, and the staff are carrying smartphones and tablets. Most people they talk to will only spend a few seconds looking at the app, but a closely co-branded suite will make you the talk of the event. If you subsequently email them a fixed-layout ePub with even minimal interactivity, the experience becomes unforgettable.

37: Digital layout and HTML

By Function

The tool bar, in conjunction with the Measurements Palette and the Style Sheets, gives you access to 90% of the things you are likely to do in QuarkXPress. It is worth investing time to memorise not only the shortcut keys, but also the modifier keys. That way you can rapidly move from one mode to another without interruption. The tools have remained largely the same with three exceptions. In QX2017, the eye-dropper tool and the shapemaker tools were introduced, along with enhanced behaviour of the link and unlink tools.

◂The tools with their flyout menus. Once you have flown items out by clicking on the corner ▴ you need to click once on the new tool to select it. By default, some of the tools are already 'doubled up' from the flyouts onto the main bar itself.

◂You can run the tools vertically, horizontally, or in two rows: drag the bottom corner to do this. It can also be docked and undocked by dragging. Click on the cog ✱ to turn 'hiding' on.

The **Item tool** ✣ is generally used for moving boxes around the layout and for resizing or rotating them, by selecting the handles ―▫―.

When moving, if you opt/alt-click after having started, a duplicate item will be created. Opt/alt-clicking before you start temporarily invokes the pan tool.

If you Shift-click while moving, the object moves vertically or horizontally, but not both. You can combine shift- and opt/alt-click.

When resizing, if you cmd/ctrl-click, the contents are resized, but not proportionately. Combine with shift-click to resize proportionately. Opt/alt-clicking while resizing resizes from the centre.

Resizing from the corners affects both dimensions. Resizing from the sides affects only that dimension.

If you hover over the corner handles, a reshape icon comes up which then changes to a rotation icon if you wait.

Shift while rotating constrains to 45° increments.

Pro-tip: the actual total rotation is given in the measurements panel.

If you double-click on a box, the selection tool turns into the relevant content tool for that box.

Shortcut—V

The **Text Content tool** 🆃 allows you to create a text box by dragging, and edit text by clicking inside a text box. Shift-clicking during creation creates a square box. Inside a box, if you put the cursor in one place and shift-click at another, the whole becomes a selection. You can do the same thing by clicking and dragging, but shift-click works over many—even hundreds—of pages.

While in the text tool, single letter shortcuts are disabled. Instead, opt/alt invokes the Pan tool, cmd/ctrl invokes the Item tool. Ctrl-opt/right-click-alt invokes the reduce magnify tool.

Shortcut—T

The **Text Linking tool** has a fly-out, accessed by holding down the black triangle ▴, which gives you a choice of link 🔗 or 🔗 unlink. Link now works differently from in the past. You can still link empty boxes, and you can still link a box with text in it to empty boxes so that the text flows into them. From QX2017 you can link boxes that already contain text without QuarkXPress complaining. The text simply links up now, in the same way that it did

Conradin was ten years old, and the doctor had pronounced his professional opinion that the boy would not live another five years. The doctor was silky and effete, and counted for little, but his opinion was endorsed by Mrs. De Ropp, who counted for nearly everything. Mrs. De Ropp was Conradin's cousin and guardian, and in his eyes she represented

those three-fifths of the world that are necessary and disagreeable and real; the other two-fifths, in perpetual antagonism to the foregoing, were summed up in himself and his imagination. One of these

days Conradin supposed he would succumb to the mastering pressure of wearisome necessary things—such as illnesses and coddling restrictions and drawn-out dulness. Without his imagination, which

◂Clicking first on the top box and then on the bottom box with the Text Linking tool 🔗 links the two boxes so that text flows from the first to the second. If there is already text in the second, the overflow of the first text is followed by the text of the second. If there is no overflow, the second text moves up into the first box to flow normally

◂If you press Opt/Alt which clicking, the text of the second is pushed into a new box if the first box is overflowing, or remains in its own box if the text is not overflowing.

◂If you unlink 🔗 normally by clicking on the blue arrow, then the second box is emptied and all of the text stays in the first box, or overflows from it. If you have a chain of three boxes, this will mean it flow from the first to the third missing the second. If you Opt/Alt click on the blue arrow with unlink, then the text remains in the box where it is. Any ongoing chain, for example to the third box, remains.

in Utilities>Linkster. By default, text flows up into the top box. If you press opt/alt as you click, the text remains in the box where it was—effectively, a new box marker is added at the end of each box.

If you want to merge two chains, you have to do it from the final box in the first chain to the first box in the next chain.

For unlinking, if you click on the link, the entire chain is broken at that point: subsequent boxes remain linked together, but they are not connected to the previous box.

If you shift-click on a box, just that box is removed from the text chain, which flows as previously onto the next.

If you opt/alt-click on a link, the chain is broken at that point, but the text remains in the same boxes.

If you shift-opt/alt-click on a link, the box you have clicked on retains its text, but is removed from the chain, and the chain flows from the previous box to the next box.

Shortcut—N (Mac), T (Windows)

The **Picture Content tool** allows you to create a picture box by dragging (Shift-click constrains to a square). Once a picture has been imported you can use it with the round tabs to resize or rotate. Dragging with the tool on a picture moves it inside the frame. You can also use the arrow keys. Double-clicking on an empty picture box opens up an import dialogue. Double clicking an imported picture opens the update dialogue.

By default, resizing a picture is constrained. You can turn the constraint off by clicking on the chain icon in Measurements>Picture Box between X% and Y%. This allows you to distort the picture.

Shortcut—R

The square tool creates a square. Its flyout menu offers a circle, a star-burst and Composition Zones. The Composition Zone tool allows you to draw a Composition Zone. See Menus: Item>Composition Zones on page 165 for an explanation of this feature. Double-click the starburst tool to bring up the Starburst dialogue. Constrain this tool with Shift.

Shortcut—B

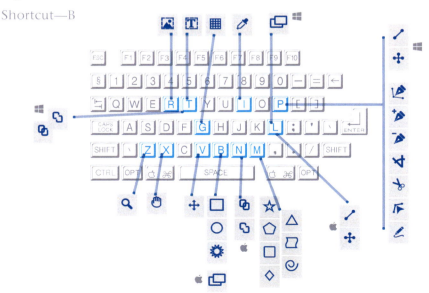

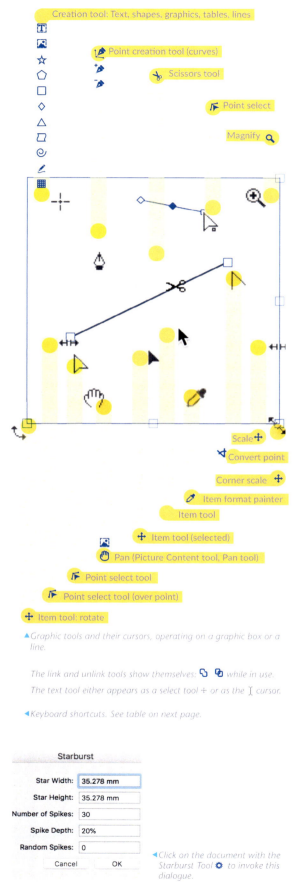

▲ Graphic tools and their cursors, operating on a graphic box or a line.

The link and unlink tools show themselves: while in use. The text tool either appears as a select tool or as the cursor.

◀ Keyboard shortcuts. See table on next page.

◀ Click on the document with the Starburst Tool to invoke this dialogue.

Tools 73

Double-clicking on the star tool opens the settings dialogue. This is identical to Utilities:Shapemaker. As well as setting the number of sides, secondary spikes and the inner radius for those spikes, you can choose various kinds of curved edges, set their curvature, and also introduce randomisation. You can specify what kind of Item is created, though you can change the content afterwards as usual using Item>Content. The polygon tool is similar.

If you click on +, you can add a preset. These go into the preferences and are available across the document and to other files. Note well: if you delete the Preferences, you will lose all you presets!

The Rounded Rectangle tool offers a variety of corners, which can be made to overlap each other creating complex shapes which QuarkXPress renders correctly as items.

The spiral tool enables you to create Golden Spirals, Archimedes spirals, and custom spirals which move between the two. Lowering the smoothness and the segmentation allows you to create square or triangular spirals.

The Wave shape is the most complex, allowing you to set the four sides independently with two different wave forms, which can be sine, triangle, square, sawtooth or random. If you choose Item>Rule Path, you get a plain line.

Polygon, diamond, triangle and cloud shape types all invoke the same dialogue, with different initial settings. You can use this to set three different presets and keep them directly on the tools.

The shape tools ☆ ○ □ ◇ △ ⬠ ⊙ create a shape exactly as in Utilities>Shapemaker. Shift constrains. A single click on the page invokes a dialogue where you can choose a preset and select a size. Double-clicking on the tool itself opens up the settings. See sidebar for examples.

Shortcut—M

The line tool creates a straight line. Shift constrains it, and it then functions exactly as the orthogonal line tool ✣ which always constrains to 45°.

The bezier tools create and manage bezier curves. These place bezier points while drawing, add them to existing curves, remove them, convert the type of curve point, cut the curve, select a point so it can be dragged or have its control points changed, or allow freehand drawing (see next tool). See the Measurements panel.

The freehand drawing tool allows you to sketch out curves. These can then be edited.

The item format copy tool (eyedropper) copies formatting from one object to another. It has two modes. If you invoke it when nothing is selected, it copies the attributes of the next item you click on, and then reformats subsequent objects you click on the same way. If you have an object already selected, it copies the attributes from the next object you click on.

If you have an example box on a page, and want to change fifteen other boxes to match it, you can drag-select all fifteen and then click once on the example box. You could do the same thing with item styles, but it would take much longer.

If you shift-click, using the tool either way round, a dialogue opens which is identical to the Item Styles dialogue. You can then select which attributes you want copied across. You can also change them. For example, if you are copying a blue circle, and now want to change it to a magenta circle, shift-click on your next target and the dialogue opens up, allowing you to change the colour.

Image editing effects are not copied—use the menu in the Image Editing palette to do this.

The **Table tool** creates a table. To do so, select the tool, and then drag-click somewhere on the page. A new dialogue opens up, allowing you to specify Rows, Columns, whether the cells are text or picture, whether you want to auto-fit or not, what the tab order is, whether or not to link cells so that text flows through them as with the link tool, whether to maintain geometry, which means that the shape of the table stays put if you amend it, and whether to link to External Data. All of these except the external data can be changed retrospectively.

Linking to external data opens up a new dialogue, enabling you to browse to an Excel spreadsheet and then import a range from a sheet, specified with the name of the sheet—a list of options will be given—and a range in the format A1-D7. It will default to all the data on the sheet.

If you select Inline Table, QuarkXPress will allow you to style the table.

Regular tables

Once you've created an ordinary table, whether linked to external data or not, you can reshape it using the Selection tool, and edit using the Text tool, which allows you to select the boxes, enter and format text, and apply text colours and backgrounds. You can also hover with the text tool to move or change the grids, but this is tedious. Instead, using the Picture Box tool or the triangle tool from the Bézier tools flyout, you can move them around more easily, and also set the line qualities either using Ctrl-click/Right-click and the contextual menu, or from the Measurements panel's Frame tab.

If you paste a table inside a text frame (make sure it is narrower than the frame, or all your text will disappear), the frame will then flow with the text. To control how it does this, including header rows if you want them, use Table>Table Break, or do the same thing by ctrl-click/right-click in the Contextual Menu for Tables. There you can also combine cells, split cells, add rows and columns or delete them.

Inline tables

If you find QuarkXPress tables fiddly, you would not be alone. The truth is, after you have used tables in a spreadsheet, neither QuarkXPress nor Word nor InDesign nor anything else is really quite as convenient. However, although table construction in Excel is easy, formatting tables so that they fit a conventional page is tedious.

QuarkXPress offers both importing of Excel tables and also Inline Excel tables. Inline tables can only be edited in Excel (or a compatible spreadsheet application), but they can be formatted with a very great degree of precision using Window>Table Styles.

You must choose Inline Table when you create your Linked to External Data table, but you can apply a different style sheet retrospectively by selecting the entire table using the Text tool and applying the format in Window>Table Styles. See **Window>Table Styles**.

To see which Excel based tables you have, and whether they are up to date, go to Utilities>Usage>Tables.

You can also copy a range in Excel and then paste it into QuarkXPress. This creates a static table directly.

Shortcut—G

Zoom has a flyout menu of zoom and pan. Opt/Alt-click with Zoom reduces magnification, clicking with it increases magnification, and dragging zooms the selected area.

You can also enter exact magnifications at the bottom left of the screen, or T for thumbnail. Except when editing text, cmd/ctrl-plus increases magnification, and cmd/ctrl-minus decreases it.

Cmd/ctrl-1 sets magnification to 100%, and cmd/ctrl-0 fills the screen.

Shortcut—Z

is the **Pan** tool. It can be invoked by pressing down Opt/alt and dragging. It pans the document through the window.

Shortcut—X

Summary of the tools, showing the Windows and Mac shortcuts. These shortcuts do not work when in Text typing mode (for obvious reasons), but clicking cmd/ctrl invokes item and opt/alt invokes zoom.

Tool	Win	Mac	Notes
Item tool	V		Shift constrains. Opt/alt copies.
Text Content tool	T		Shift constrains. Use cmd/ctrl to invoke item tool, opt/alt for 🔍
Text Linking tool	T	N	Opt/alt to keep text in same boxes.
Text Unlinking tool	T	N	Opt/alt preserves text in box
Picture Content tool	R		Shift constrains
Rectangle Box tool	B		Shift constrains
Oval Box tool	B		Shift constrains
Starburst tool	B		Shift constrains. Click to invoke dialogue
Star tool	M		Shift constrains. Click for dialogue. Dbl-click tool for options.
Polygon tool	M		Shift constrains. Click for dialogue. Dbl-click tool for options.
Rounded tool	M		Shift constrains. Click for dialogue. Dbl-click tool for options.
Diamond tool	M		Shift constrains. Click for dialogue. Dbl-click tool for options.
Triangle tool	M		Shift constrains. Click for dialogue. Dbl-click tool for options.
Wave tool	M		Shift constrains. Click for dialogue. Dbl-click tool for options.
Spiral tool	M		Shift constrains. Click for dialogue. Dbl-click tool for options.
Composition Zones	L	B	Shift constrains. See Item menu.
Line tool	P	L	Shift constrains to 45°
Orthogonal Line	P	L	Always constrained
Bézier Pen	P		
Add Point tool	P		Adds point to existing line
Remove Point tool	P		Removes point from existing line.
Convert Point tool	P		
Scissors tool	P		
Select Point tool	P		
Freehand Drawing	P		
Item Format Painter	I		Order of selection affects result. Shift-click to open settings.
Table tool	G		Shift constrains.
Zoom tool	Z		Opt/alt to zoom out
Pan tool	X		Pan tool

Tools

Measurements

The Measurements panel gives you direct access with immediate on-screen feedback to all of the numerical formatting and many other features. When run at the bottom of the screen, the tabs are on top, like previous Mac editions of QuarkXPress. When run at the top, the tabs are below, like the Windows editions. Cmd/ctrl-M takes you to the relevant measurement, instead of opening a dialogue. The cog menu allows you to run the panel with the tools, and, on a Mac, offers a vertical mode. Changes that you make in Measurements are picked up when you create item or text styles.

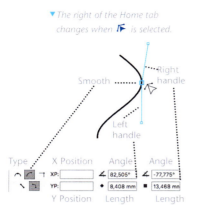

▼ *The right of the Home tab changes when ⌁ is selected.*

1 Home

▲ *Appearance docked at bottom. By default the Measurements panel is at the top of the screen for Windows, or at the bottom of the screen for Mac. From QX2018, the two systems have a consistent interface, and cmd/ctrl-M takes you to the appropriate measurement, rather than a separate dialogue.*

▼ *Docked at top.* ▼▼ *Floating.*

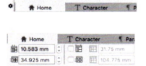

▶ *New in QX2018 for Mac, you can now make the Measurements panel vertical, which is helpful with widescreen monitors where vertical space is at a premium.*

▼ *When the object is a straight line, the Home tab changes.*

The Home panel is contextual. Things on the left are the most stable: the X and Y coordinates and Width and Height are almost always there:

X,Y: The left and top coordinates of the working box.

W,H: Box width and height, often linked. Click on their chain icon 8 (immediately right) to link or unlink them.

These controls are also in Tabs, Text Box, Picture Box and others, but we won't illustrate them again.

Almost all of the other modal measurements in the Home tab are taken from the other measurement tabs, so we will look at each in their proper tab.

There are three exceptions. Tables and Lines (see the Line tool, above, and the end of this chapter) change the Home tab with features not accessible in other tabs.

The ⌁ Select Point Tool changes the right-hand end of the Home palette—it's easy to miss this. It gives precise controls for changing point type, position, angles and length.

When a line is selected, the Home tab changes.

X1, X2, Y1, Y2 control start- and endpoints. This changes to a reference point and an angle when anything other than Endpoints is selected.

The other options are the same as the **borders** tab ('frames' up to QX2017), with an extra option for arrowheads at each end.

Lines can have gradient fills, either assigned from the Gradient palette, or selected from previously saved Gradients in the colour palette. Furthermore, the gap can have its own colour, transparency, and blend mode though the gap can't be assigned a gradient.

2 Character

Font selection. The up/down arrows on the left nudge the font to the preceding or following font in the list. This is useful if you have ordered sets. If you click in the box itself, you can start typing a name (from the beginning only) and the range of selection is narrowed down. If you click on the double arrow at the right, the entire list is displayed centred on the currently selected font.

Font variant. From QX2018, all installed variants of a font family are now listed in the variant dialogue, and are no longer given in the main font dialogue.

Font Size. Left up/down arrows nudge harmonically, right double-arrow shows harmonic sequence.

Faux font styles: these are legacy ad hoc fonts created by QuarkXPress. Where possible use Open Type features:

P	Returns font to plain cmd/ctrl-shift-P	U	Underline cmd/ctrl-shift-U	A₂	Subscript cmd-shift-minus
B	Bolds font, possibly with faux-bold, indicated by a yellow triangle cmd/ctrl-shift-B	S	Single Strike through	fi	Ligature cmd-shift-G
		ABC	All caps cmd/ctrl-shift-K	f	Extra functions: the above plus **Outline**, Shadow, Word Underline, ~~Double Strikethrough~~ and ˢᵘᵖᵉʳⁱᵒʳ
I	Italic, same warning system as Bold cmd/ctrl-shift-I	Abc	Small Caps cmd-shift-H		
		A²	Superscript cmd-shift-=		

O **Open Type features:**
This opens a dialogue (from QX2018) previewing the first five letters selected in all of the available Open Type styles. These are 'true' font variations, and should be used in preference to the faux variations. Open Type features are now supported in HTML5 output.

◄ Colour fonts were introduced in QX2018. While some may be garish, others, such as Take Control SVG (pictured) make use of the tonal opportunities which colour allows. See next page for Truewriter, a font project to accurately reflect the tonal variations of a true manual typewriter.

◄ QX2016 introduced support for Stylistic Sets, and QX2017 extended this. From QX2018, clicking on the **O** icon now opens a new dialogue which previews all of the available Open Type special features. This font, Vollkorn, has one of the most extensive sets.

◄ You can now select more than one Stylistic Set at a time, and, if a name is embedded in the font for a Stylistic Set, this name will be shown.

Tracking. Evenly increases/decreases letter spacing. The shortcuts are Cmd/ctrl-shift-] and Cmd/ctrl-shift-[. Often incorrectly called 'kerning', tracking can give text more punch or legibility
For inter-word spacing, see Style>Remove Manual Kerning.

Shift baseline. This also applies to anchored boxes.

Colour, from the Window>Colours defined colours.

Opacity. You can create blurred text by setting opacity to zero and creating a Drop Shadow with Inherit Opacity turned off.

English (International)
Sets character language. It is generally better to set it in the Character Style. The entire document can be converted using Utilities>Convert Project Language. The language sets spell checking and hyphenation. To overlook a particular word, set the language to None.

Set % adjustment to character width or height.

100% The percentage adjustment.

◄ QuarkXPress executes Colour Transformations in Open Type if you turn this feature on in Preferences>Project>General. This means that with a font such as Chartwell Rings, left, you can transform text such as 90+55+82+78 into a fully-formatted graph. If Chartwell is too expensive, consider the free Amazing Infographic font.

▼**Tracking.** Stone Serif Semibold 10 point with -10% tracking, 0%, 30% and 50%. Legibility is increased for distance reading at 50% extra tracking. Notice also that the letters actually appear larger.

-10% Legibility at a distance
±0%   Legibility at a distance
+25% Legibility at a distance
+50% L e g i b i l i t y   a t   a   d i s t a n c e

8: Open Type features

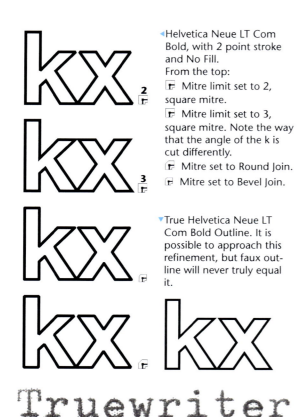

◀ Helvetica Neue LT Com Bold, with 2 point stroke and No Fill.
From the top:
▭ Mitre limit set to 2, square mitre.
▭ Mitre limit set to 3, square mitre. Note the way that the angle of the k is cut differently.
▭ Mitre set to Round Join.
▭ Mitre set to Bevel Join.

▼ True Helvetica Neue LT Com Bold Outline. It is possible to approach this refinement, but faux outline will never truly equal it.

▲ Truewriter is a font project to create a 'true' typewriter font which respects the gradations of grey which characterise authentic typewriting. This is only possible as a colour font.

Text stroking

Text stroking, or text outlining, has been available since QX2017. Note that it has no effect on Colour Fonts (QX2018 onwards).

The transparency and transparency mode are shared with the fill, so if you want a transparent stroke on No Fill text, you still change the transparency for the character as a whole.

▪ Sets the colour of the Stroke.

0% Sets the percentage tint (the transparency will be the same as the character).

0pt Sets the Width of the Line.

▭ Square join, which engages Miter Limit.

▭ Round join.

▭ Bevel join, often the same as a Miter Limit of 1 on Square Join.

No Fill leaves only the stroked outline.

Miter Limit allows you to change the angle limit on the miter. The effect of this varies from font to font, and with the proportions of the font size and the stroke width.

3 Paragraph

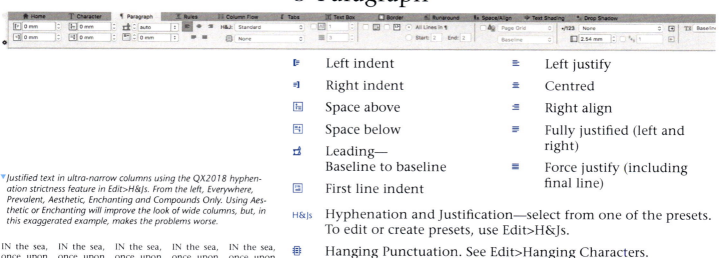

	Left indent		Left justify
	Right indent		Centred
	Space above		Right align
	Space below		Fully justified (left and right)
	Leading—Baseline to baseline		Force justify (including final line)
	First line indent		

H&Js Hyphenation and Justification—select from one of the presets. To edit or create presets, use Edit>H&Js.

▭ Hanging Punctuation. See Edit>Hanging Characters.

▭ Dropped Cap. The upper number sets the number of letters affected, usually one but often two if the first character is a quotation mark, and the lower box ≡ sets the depth of the drop, usually 2–4 lines.

▭ Keep with next (be careful with this one in a paragraph style, because if all the text is kept together, it will not be able to reflow and will disappear.

▼ Justified text in ultra-narrow columns using the QX2018 hyphenation strictness feature in Edit>H&Js. From the left, Everywhere, Prevalent, Aesthetic, Enchanting and Compounds Only. Using Aesthetic or Enchanting will improve the look of wide columns, but, in this exaggerated example, makes the problems worse.

IN the sea, once upon a time, O my Best Beloved, there was a Whale, and he ate fishes. He ate the starfish and the garfish, and the crab and the dab, and

IN the sea, once upon a time, O my Best Beloved, there was a Whale, and he ate fishes. He ate the starfish and the garfish, and the crab and the dab, and

IN the sea, once upon a time, O my Best Beloved, there was a Whale, and he ate fishes. He ate the starfish and the garfish, and the crab and the dab, and

IN the sea, once upon a time, O my Best Beloved, there was a Whale, and he ate fishes. He ate the starfish and the garfish, and the crab and the dab, and

IN the sea, once upon a time, O my Best Beloved, there was a Whale, and he ate fishes. He ate the starfish and the garfish, and the crab and the dab, and

How the Whale Got His Throat, Rudyard Kipling.

27: Text stroking and framing

- Keep paragraph together. This can either be All Lines in ¶ Paragraph, or specified for the beginning and end of the paragraph. Again, be careful if used in conjunction with Keep with next.
- Locks text to grid, which is either the Page Grid or the Box Grid. You can also define Grid Styles in Window>Grid Styles. The locking is topline, bottomline, baseline or centre line.
- •/123 Bullets, Numbering and Outlines. You can define these in Edit>Bullet, Numbering and Outline Styles.
- Minimum distance from text. You can refine the placement of the bullet or number with this.
- Restart the numbering here for this level. The new number goes in the accompanying box.
- Increase indent level.   cmd/ctrl-/
- Decrease indent level.   cmd-opt/ctrl-alt-/

Pro Tip—if your numbering unexpectedly resets, select all the text between the last good numbered section and the new, bad, one, and choose •/123: None in the Measurements Paragraph tab. This should clear any rogue formatting.

- Te Sets the vertical character alignment. Usually this would be baseline, but a book spine might be centreline.

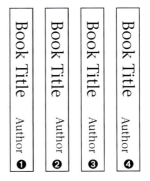

Vertical Character Alignment
Book spine with:
1 baseline
2 top
3 centre
4 bottom
setting text in two sizes. Vertical character alignment does not usually make much difference, but, where it does, it is crucial.

4 Rules

- ¶,⊥ Turns above or below rule on or off. Settings are identical.
- — The line control sets the type of line, either regular, dashed or striped. You can edit the presets or create new ones in Edit>Dashes & Stripes.
- 1pt The thickness, or weight, of the line. You can enter using any units, but it will be displayed in points.
- The colour of the line, selected from colours defined in the Window>Colours Palette. You cannot enter a gradient.
- The opacity of the line. You can create blurred lines by setting the opacity to zero and creating a Drop Shadow with Inherit Opacity turned off.
- Line offset left.
- Line offset right.
- Length, either from the typographical indents, or the text, or the column, as modified by the offsets (above). Based on the top line of text for Rule Above, and the bottom for Below.
- Offset, either as % of Interparagraph spacing or as an absolute (pts, mm etc).

Rules for Rules

Call-outs can easily be created with above and below rules.

Paragraph spacing only counts between paragraphs—there is no spacing at the top of the page. For this reason, if you enter a % value in Offset, the line will not appear at the top of the page. If you enter an absolute amount, such as 2mm, the offset is honoured.

You can use this to force a chapter heading down the page, by setting a rule with 0% opacity and a value in points or millimetres for the offset.

▸*Invisible rule used to push the chapter heading down the page.*

Measurements   79

5 Column Flow

Introduced in QX2017, and set from the Measurements Palette or the Paragraph Style Sheet, column flow allows you to span text across columns, or split text into columns. This creates substantial opportunities for automating layout via paragraph styles using only the automatic text box as you flow text in.

As you work in split columns, QuarkXPress introduces dotted blue guidelines to show you what you are doing.

Additionally, you can restart the column flow, which means that the columns above will flow into each other and balance. This can be confusing for the reader unless you have a device such as a paragraph rule between them. If you have turned on column rules in the text frame, these will be broken at this point.

Span Columns

Spanning columns runs a paragraph across two or more columns, as specified in the Text Box columns setting. You set this either from the Measurements Panel, Column Flow tab, or from the Paragraph Style Sheet, Column Flow tab.

To do this, choose 'Span/Split Columns', and set the Type to 'Span Columns'. Then choose how many columns to span. Guidelines will appear to tell you what you've done if guidelines are on. Generally speaking, you will want to add some space before and space after, especially if you are using a much larger font to create a spanning title.

Split Columns

Splitting columns can take place in a single column of text, or in multi-column text. In principle if you have multi-column text you can span the columns for some paragraphs and split them for others, giving you a wide range of layout possibilities. In practice, you would need a large sheet of paper and small type for this to be worthwhile.

As previously, this can be invoked in the Paragraph Style or in the Measurements Palette. In this case, the column flow never restarts, so that option is not available.

When you split the columns, a blue dotted line appears, showing you what you are doing. You will normally want to include some space before and space after, and you can set the gutter width.

As discussed under Typography, too narrow columns are almost illegible. However, this is less important when managing lists of items, such as with bullets.

▼ This layout was entirely formatted using Column Flow to create and manage the various widths of columns. You can use Column Flow to automate layout which is provided only as tagged or styled text.

Line between

Only when column splitting is on, you can add a line between the columns. This is a standard line, offering you style, width, colour, shade and opacity. If you want lines between regular columns, this feature is available in the Text Box tab of the Measurements panel.

- Continuous or Restart—sets how the columns behave in relation to the previous. Restart balances the previous columns.
- Turns on Column Flow, either to Span columns defined in a frame, or to split the current column into other columns.
- All Sets the number of columns to Span. Default is 'All', but you can span fewer. When column flow is set to Split, this sets the number of columns created.
- Space to add in above.
- Space to add in below.
- Gutter of the new columns when using Split.
- Turn on Inter-Column Rules.
- — The style of column rule: solid, dashed or striped, in various options. You can change the presets or create new ones in Edit>Dashes & Stripes.
- 0pt Sets the thickness the column rule.
- The colour of the rule, selected from colours defined in the Window>Colours Palette. Shown as ⊠ when colour is 'none'. You cannot apply a gradient rule here.
- The opacity of the rule.

6 Tabs

Cmd/ctrl-shift-T invokes the Tabs panel—on Windows up to QX2017 this opens as a separate dialogue. As well as opening the panel, it also places the tabs ruler at the top of the visible column (see right). This remains editable even when a dialogue is open. You can drag tabs on and off this ruler, and along it.

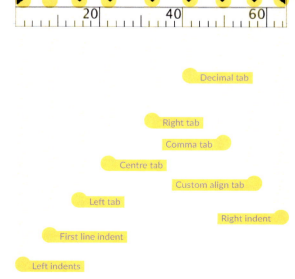

- Left Tab—the old fashioned typewriter tab, appears as ↓ in the tab ruler.
- Centre Tab, appears as ↓ in the tab ruler.
- Right Tab, appears as ↓ in the tab ruler.
- Decimal tab, appears as ↓ in the tab ruler, aligns on the decimal point (UK & USA).
- Comma tab, appears as ↓ in the tab ruler, aligns on the decimal comma (European).
- Assignable tab, set using Align on at the right end of the Measurements panel. Appears as ↓.

Measurements 81

7 Text Box

Inset

Vertical justification—how to make boxes that push all the text to the bottom or top, with a gap (as here).

Centre paragraph.

Enter a high value for inter-paragraph spacing. Ensure there is at least one paragraph break. All the text is pushed to the top and bottom. An additional break gives you a centre paragraph.

X: Y: W: and H: set the box position and dimensions.

⊿ Sets the rotation of the box.

▱ Sets the skew of the box.

⌐▼ Sets the corner shape of the box. Click to choose rectangular (default), curved, concave or beveled. Choosing anything but rectangular sets a default radius. If you want to set multiple borders (see Borders tab), you can only use the default shape.

0mm Sets the radius of the box corner. This defaults to curved if you don't specify concave or beveled.

⊘ Turns off output—shown as ⊘ when active. Suppressed boxes neither print nor export.

▪ The colour of the box, selected from colours defined in the Window>Colours Palette. Shown as ⊠ when colour is 'none'. When the colour is white, a drop shadow creates a box shadow, not a text shadow.

▫ The opacity of the box. You can create blurred boxes by setting the opacity to zero and creating a Drop Shadow with Inherit Opacity turned off.

• Blend Transparency mode of the background. See the Colours palette for more information, page 94. Introduced in QX2017.

T Blend Transparency mode of the text. See the Colours palette for more information. Introduced in QX2017.

▥ Number of columns.

▤ Gutter width (space between columns).

▦ Turn column rules on—introduced in QX2017.

—— The style of column rule: solid, dashed or striped, in various options. You can change the presets or create new ones in Edit>Dashes & Stripes.

0pt Sets the thickness the column rule.

▪ The colour of the rule, selected from colours defined in the Window>Colours Palette. Shown as ⊠ when colour is 'none'. You cannot apply a gradient rule here.

▫ The opacity of the rule.

▯ Top alignment, the default.

▯ Bottom alignment.

▯ Centre alignment.

▯ Vertical Justification, spaces the lines across the box. This invokes the maximum inter-paragraph control ▯, immediately below it. If you want all the lines equally spaced, leave this at zero. If you want to preserve some paragraph identity, enter a value.

When working with text on a line, an additional part of the Text Box Measurement Panel appears on the right hand end.
This allows you to specify how the text follows the line, what part of the text is aligning, and, in the last icon, ⌂, lets you flip the text to the other side of the line.

ᴬᴮᶜ Curved text
ᴬᴮᶜ Warped text
ᴬᴮᶜ 3d ribbon text
ᴬᴮᶜ Stair text
⌂ Flip text to other side of line

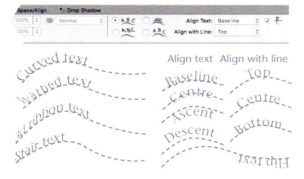

- ▤ Turns on individual side insets. Otherwise, the next control, to the right, controls all of the insets. If you turn it on, the four boxes to the right become active, allowing you to set the top, bottom, left and right insets. This only applies to regular boxes with standard corners. For shaped corners and non-rectangular boxes, only an overall inset can be applied.
- ▤ Runs text round all sides. Change this if you are not happy with the way text runs round a box.
- ᴬ↻ Sets the rotation of the text within the box.
- ᴬ⌒ Sets the skew of the text within the box.
- ⬌ Flips the text horizontally.
- ⬍ Flips the text vertically.
- A⁻ First baseline minimum—sets how the distance from the top of the box to the first baseline is calculated, either Ascent, or Cap-height, or Cap-height plus Accent.
- A↑ First baseline offset. Shifts the first baseline up. This only works for regular boxes with rectangular corners.

How to create text on a circle

1 Create Circle with Circle Tool
2 Convert to Curve with Item>Shape
3 Double Click on curve
4 Start Typing

8 Picture Box

When a picture is selected, this tab replaces the Text Box tab.

X: Y: W: H: set the box position and dimensions. When a box is anchored, this is replaced with controls to set the alignment of the box to ascender ▤ or baseline ▤. The default is baseline, and this gives you the extra option of setting an offset.

- ∠ Sets the rotation of the box.
- ⌒ Sets the skew of the box.
- ⌐▼ Sets the corner shape of the box. Click to choose rectangular (default), curved, concave or beveled. Choosing anything but rectangular sets a default radius.
- 0mm Sets the radius of the box corner. This defaults to curved if you don't specify concave or beveled.
- ⊘ Turns off box output—shown as ⊘ when active. Suppressed boxes neither print nor export.
- ▪ The colour of the box, selected from colours defined in the Window>Colours Palette. Shown as ⊠ when colour is 'none'. When the colour is white, a drop shadow creates a box shadow, not a text shadow.

◀ By default, a picture overlays against its background. Therefore, if you are compositing two images together and see no effect, the first thing to check is that the box background is not white.

Compositing an image over its own background gives a simple and reliable way of applying gradient tints.

◀ In this example, for layout purposes, we want a gradient tint to take the eye downwards through the image to text below.

To do this, all that is needed is a simple vertical black to white gradient as the image background, and the image transparency on the right of the Picture Box tab set to Hard Light. You can also set this in Image Editing and in Colours, but not on the Home tab of measurements.

Measurements

▲ When a box is anchored in text, the X: and Y: controls change to alignment controls, above for ascent ▫ and below, with offset, for baseline ▫. This also changes the Home tab.

▲ This greyscale map, imported as a TIFF file, does not stand out well in a colour document.

▲ Here, the map has been treated with foreground and background colours. Instead of going from Black to White, the 256 greyscales now go from 25% Pantone 277 to 100% Pantone 341. The result is editable with Image Editing features, and also responds as normal to transparency functions.

- The opacity of the box. You can create blurred boxes by setting the opacity to zero and creating a Drop Shadow with Inherit Opacity turned off.
- Blend Transparency mode of the box background. See the Colours palette for more information. Introduced in QX2017.

X,Y% The scaling of the image in the box. Normally constrained, but you can click the chain link at the side to unconstrain.

X+,Y+ Sets the offset in the box. You would normally set this visually by dragging with the Picture Content Tool or using the arrow keys.

- Sets the rotation of the picture in the box (not the same as the rotation of the box).
- Sets the skew of the picture.
- Flips the picture horizontally.
- Flips the picture vertically.
- Sets the mask. If a layer mask is present, you can select either that or Composite. Otherwise defaults to Composite. See the Advanced Image Control palette.
- Shows the resolution at specified size and scale. You can't edit this directly.

For monochrome images only, you can also set the ▪ foreground and ▪ background colours of the picture itself (see left).

- Sets the opacity of the picture against its background, or whatever is below it. Works in combination with transparency blend modes.
- Blend Transparency mode of the picture. See the Colours palette for more information. Introduced in QX2017.
- Turns off image output—shown as ⌀ when active. You could use this to keep a box frame, but suppress comp images.

9 Border (frame)

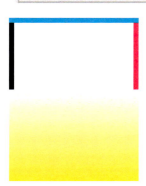

▲ The 'Frame' tab in earlier versions of QuarkXPress is now renamed 'Border' in QX2018, and is substantially upgraded. For rectangular boxes, you can now define the four borders separately, and also specify whether you draw the horizontal lines on top or the vertical.

◀ Multiple borders in QX2018. From QX2017 you can apply a gradient as a border/frame, either directly in Window>Gradients or as a saved Gradient here in the Measurements tab.

The border controls are relatively straightforward. 'Border' refers here to the printed edge of a box, not the frame that appears in blue on the layout to identify where the box is.

- Multiple Borders. Turns the Multiple Borders on for rectangular frames only. New in QX2018.
- Chooses which borders you are editing. Dark background means the border is active for editing, light background means that your current edits will not apply to it.

Horizontal/Vertical on top. The order it draws in.

0pt   Sets the thickness or weight of the border.

—   The style of line: solid, dashed or striped, in various options. You can change the presets or create new ones in Edit>Dashes & Stripes.

◨   The colour, selected from colours defined in the Window>Colours Palette. Shown as ⊠ when colour is 'none'. Introduced in QX2017, you can apply a gradient here if one is saved in the Colours palette.

◨   The opacity. You can create blurred borders by setting the opacity to zero and creating a Drop Shadow with Inherit Opacity turned off.

●   Blend Transparency mode of the frame. See the Colours palette for more information. Introduced in QX2017.

⊠   Gap colour. This only applies to dashed or striped lines. By default, the gap colour is 'none', but you can set it to any colour defined in Window>Colour, though not to a gradient.

◨   Opacity of the gap.

●   Blend Transparency of the gap.

Using the Blend Transparency modes allows you to have borders and other lines interact logically with each other, as in the map example in the side bar. Note that when using curves rather than objects, these functions appear on the home tab.

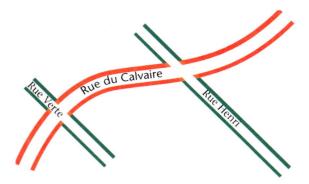

▲ The Belgian flag, made using separate borders for black and red, with the box colour providing the yellow.

▲ Setting the gap of a double-line to white, Lighten, and setting the main colour to Soft Light enables you to have seamlessly joining roads on a map—a task which is otherwise tedious and time-consuming. You can add the names with Text on a Path (double-click the line). Set the vertical alignment to 'Centre' in the Text Box tab. Note that these functions appear in the Home tab for curves: there is no separate Border tab.

10 Runaround and Clipping

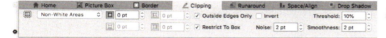

The Runaround panel and Clipping panels work together and share many of the same controls. When the box is text, Runaround is either None or Item. When a picture box is used, and the file contains Alpha Channels, Clipping paths and/or white space, more options become available.

▲ The controls in Runaround and Clipping are identical, except that Runaround offers 'auto-image' and 'same as clipping' as the options for the Path.

Remember that objects stack, so the objects 'on top' affect those below. If using Layers, you can turn this behaviour on or off. Item>Send & Bring will help you control the placement of boxes on top of each other.

For a picture, the runaround control can be:

- Item
- Auto Image
- Embedded Path
- Alpha Channel
- Non-White Areas
- Same as Clipping
- Picture Bounds

For a picture, the clipping path can be:

- Item
- Embedded Path
- Alpha Channel
- Non-White Areas
- Picture Bounds

Measurements

Martin Turner lives with his wife in Zaventem, Belgium, and works in a former paper factory.

▲ *The author, stepping outside the box: Alpha Channel mask applied, Restrict to Box off, so that the image can be outside the box background. The runaround path is set to Embedded Path. Run text around all sides is 'off' in the Text Box.*

▼ *The mask seen in the Advanced Image Control palette.*

▶ *You don't need a separate application to create a simple vector shape from an image. Item>New Box from Clipping turns the clipping path into a shape, which acts exactly like any other QX vector object. You can use Item>Merge or Split Paths to combine it with other shapes, or edit the shape directly using the Bezier Tools.*

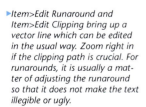

▶ *Item>Edit Runaround and Item>Edit Clipping bring up a vector line which can be edited in the usual way. Zoom right in if the clipping path is crucial. For runarounds, it is usually a matter of adjusting the runaround so that it does not make the text illegible or ugly.*

Item is the box itself. You can edit this using the Bézier tools by choosing Item>Edit>Clipping. For good control of text-runaround, in conjunction with the runaround tool, this is often the best choice. However, all clipping is 'hard'—you cannot have soft edges which interact with progressive transparency. For an EPS, AI or PDF file, as long as the box has not been assigned a background (often white, by default), only the actual vector items are 'present', so the clipping path is the outside lines of the file itself.

Auto Image automatically works out the clipping and the runaround. You can only apply this from the runaround tab, but, if you do, it also applies to the clipping. You cannot manually edit either path: if you want to do this, use 'Non-white areas'.

Embedded Path is a path in a TIFF or PSD file. To create this, you need to create a Working Path in Photoshop or a similar application and then double-click it to give it a permanent name. This creates a hard line. When selected, the box below becomes active allowing you to choose which path.

Alpha Channel is a separate channel in a TIFF or PSD file. To create one, you would usually create a layer mask, but you must then duplicate that and give it a name. A layer mask on its own will not be counted as an alpha channel. When selected, the box below becomes active, allowing you to choose which alpha channel. If you leave it on Composite, nothing happens.

If you have a soft mask, for example for flames, or a person's hair, set the Threshold to 100%. The default is 0%, which will produce a hard line.

Non-White Areas calculates where the image is, using the thresholds you specify on the right of the panel. It produces a hard mask, which you can edit with Item>Edit>Clipping Path and Item>Edit>Runaround Path.

Picture Bounds is the edges of the image, for example if the image only occupies part of the box. If you turn off Restrict to Box, you can have parts of the image which are cropped out. With Picture Bounds, you can set separate insets and outsets—for other types, only a general inset/outset can be specified.

Clipping does not affect the background of the box, so you can have an alpha channel which correctly composites someone onto a box background.

The **Outset clipping** controls 🔲🔲🔲🔲 control how much additional margin is allowed beyond that specified, or cut into the image. In Picture Bounds only, you set these separately.

The **Outset runaround** controls are exactly as the Clipping tab, except that the outsets 🔲🔲🔲🔲 control how much space is left around the item. This is by far the most important control in runaround. Multiple values for above, below, left and right can only be set for regular rectangles.

Outside edges only restricts these actions to the outside of an image. This is usually correct.

Restrict to Box means that the edges of the box override the alpha channel, mask or non-white areas. It is on by default.

Invert clips invertedly.

Noise, **Threshold** and **Smoothness** are particularly important with Non-White Areas. For soft alpha channels, turn the threshold to 100% or near it.

To create a new box from a clipping path, use Item>New Box from Clipping.

For lines, the only choices are Item and Manual. **Manual** works like this. Draw your Bézier curve as you want the runaround to be. Then turn on Manual and edit the line (not the runaround). The line changes, but the runaround stays the same. This may seem backwards, but it creates a better workflow.

Manual runaround for a Bézier line:
All Gaul is divided into three parts, one of which the Belgae inhabit, the Aquitani another, those who in their own language are called Celts, in our Gauls, the third. All these differ from each other in language, customs and laws. (*Caesar, J*)

◂ *The dotted line shows where the original line was. With manual on, the line is changed, but the runaround stays as it was.*

11 Space/Align

Space/Align allows you to line up or space objects based on their sides or centres. This is based on the first box you select.

You would normally apply Space/Align to two or more boxes, though you can apply it to a single box if you select the Page or Spread options.

X,Y control the position of the left-most, top-most box in a selection of boxes. W,H change the size of the entire selection. The icons then specify how they space or align. See illustrations.

吕昌呂呂	Space vertically
ⵏ▯ ⵏ▯ ⵏ▯ ⵏ▯	Space horizontally
吕呂呂	Align horizontally
▯▯ ▯▯ ▯▯	Align vertically

If you change the word **Evenly** to a number, it will add the relevant space between the items (see bottom).

The default is that items are spaced or aligned relative to each other, but the three icons on the top right allow you to choose between item relative, page relative and spread relative.

When aligning pictures, first use Style>Fit Box to Picture.

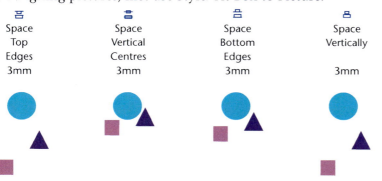

Space Top Edges 3mm · Space Vertical Centres 3mm · Space Bottom Edges 3mm · Space Vertically 3mm

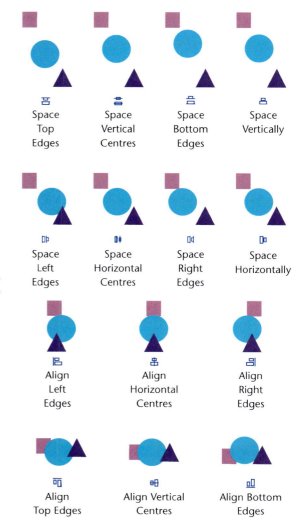

Space Top Edges · Space Vertical Centres · Space Bottom Edges · Space Vertically

Space Left Edges · Space Horizontal Centres · Space Right Edges · Space Horizontally

Align Left Edges · Align Horizontal Centres · Align Right Edges

Align Top Edges · Align Vertical Centres · Align Bottom Edges

Measurements

12 Text Shading

Text shading and borders (previously *frames*) enable you to colour the space behind text, and to put a box around it. You must choose text or paragraph mode at the start, and you can apply it from the Measurements panel, from the Text Shading Styles palette, and, with styles created there, in Character or Paragraph styles.

As well as the more obvious uses—highlighting and self-expanding text boxes—you can also use this feature to create Custom underlines, which can then be applied via character and paragraph styles. The old 'custom underline' feature is still present in QuarkXPress but only to ensure compatibility with earlier documents. Text/Paragraph dropdown menu>Text will apply only to the area selected, paragraph applies to the entire paragraph, or to all selected paragraphs if you have more than one selected.

Basic shading

Custom underline

White on black

Box

▲ *Shading and Borders can create a variety of interesting, exciting, or even appropriate effects. You could create most of these with boxes and borders, but using Shading and Borders you can automate them with conditional styles, for example having a custom underline always break for descenders.*

◀ *With clipping turned on, you can work within a box. Again, this could be done by colouring the object background, but with shading you can automate it.*

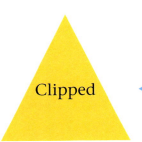

Clipped

- Text shading section.
- The colour of the shading. You can choose any colour defined including gradients, or define a new colour.
- The opacity of the shading.

Indents, Text or Column sets the width of the shading.

Clip to Box clips the shading, for example to an irregular box.

- Padding above. Padding can be negative for shading.
- Padding left.
- Padding bottom.
- Padding right.
- Text border section.
- The style of border: solid, dashed or striped, in various options. You can change the presets or create new ones in Edit>Dashes & Stripes. You cannot change the gap colour or transparency with Text Shading borders.

0pt Sets the thickness or weight of the border.

- The colour of the frame, selected from colours defined in the Window>Colours Palette. Shown as ⊠ when colour is 'none'. You can apply a gradient here if one is saved in the Colours palette.
- The opacity of the border.
- Turn the line off or on above.
- Turn the line off or on below.
- Turn the line off or on left.
- Turn the line off or on right.

Padding right, top, bottom and left. This works the same as shading, above, except that you cannot set negative padding for the border.

Self expanding box

To create a self-expanding box, choose Paragraph type, go to the right of the panel and enter 1mm offset on each side, then set the line width to 1 point. In this example we set the colour to 50% black. The result is a column-width box that expands as you type. In text mode the box is text width.

Box

Bigger box because more text

Text type

Shading and borders produce a relatively complex range of interactions. It's interesting to play with them on the measurements panel, but tedious to enter them every time.

You can incorporate shading directly into a style sheet when you create the style, but the best way to do it is to create a separate Text Shading Style, in Window>Text Shading Styles. Clicking + in this window creates a style with your current settings.

27: Text stroking and framing

13 Drop Shadow

Clicking on Apply Drop Shadow applies a shadow to the contents of a box if it has no fill, or the box itself if it has a fill. The defaults are fine for most purposes. However, you can broaden the range of effects by adjusting the controls.

Multiply drop shadow means that shadows darken backgrounds. Leave on for black shadows, turn off for light shadows. **Inherit opacity** causes shadows of transparent objects to behave as they would in the real world. However, if you turn this off, and turn the opacity of the object to zero, you will get just the shadow of the object, or, rather, a blurred version of it, coloured as the shadow is coloured.

If you set the objects's opacity to about 50% with inherit opacity off, and make the object (or its frame) and the shadow the same colour, it will appear to glow, especially if you set *distance* to zero.

The other controls are colour of shadow ◼, and opacity of shadow ◼, angle of shadow ⊙, gap between shadow and object ◼, angle of skew of shadow ◼, proportions of shadow ◼ and spread (or blur) ◼. If you set Synchronize Angle, all the shadows in the document with this on will have the same shadow angle. You can set the item to knock out the drop shadow rather than overprint it (for items darker than their shadows), and you can set the object to incorporate the shadow dimensions in its runaround.

If you just want a dropped shadow, use the defaults and change the angle, gap and blur. For the rest, experiment!

▲Drop shadow can easily become an overused effect, but you can do much more if you recognise that it is really an offset, gaussian blurred version of the main object or text. Using the controls, you can create slanted shadows, blurred text (by turning Inherit Opacity off and giving the text zero opacity), and glowing text

14 Table

The Table tab appears when a table is selected with the Text tool. X: Y: W: H: as usual set the Height and Width of the table, and its position. However, when a particular cell is selected, the left end of the Home tab changes to allow setting width, height and auto-resizing of the selection.

- ∡ Sets the rotation of the entire table (use Text Box text rotation for rotated elements within particular cells).
- ⊖ Turns off table output—shown as ⊖ when active. Suppressed tables neither print nor export.
- ◼ The colour of hairline grids—these may not print or export well, but can be helpful while editing in Guides-off mode.
- ◼ The opacity of the hairlines.
- ▦ Turns Maintain Geometry on and off. This cancels and greys out all settings you have made in the Home tab regarding auto

width or height. It applies to the entire table. If you want particular cells to be auto-width or height, but not the others, set them in the Home tab for each group of cells.

- Opacity of the entire table and its contents.
- Select all gridlines.
- Select all vertical gridlines.
- Select all horizontal gridlines.

0.25pt Thickness for selected gridlines.

— Style of selected gridlines.

- Colour of gridlines.
- Opacity of gridlines.

Gap Colour of gaps in dashed or striped lines.

Opacity of gaps in dashed or striped lines.

z Link order: order of text when linked

z Tab order: Order in which tabs moves from cell to cell.

▶This calendar was created using the Table Tool to link an Excel table, and then styled from the Measurements palette. The borders were formatted from the Borders tab, and the cells using Paragraph styles for the contents and by selecting groups of cells and assigning colours.
To update the table, go to Utilities>Usage>Tables.
For a greater degree of control, allowing you to set the format of each border of each individual cell, create as an Inline Table from the Table Tool, and use a Table Style. Inline Tables rely on Excel or a compatible spreadsheet application such as Numbers to edit the contents of the cells and their geometry. Designer tables, as here, allow you to update from Excel, but also to edit and format the cells directly.

SUN	MON	TUE	WED	THU	FRI	SAT
			1	2	3	4
5	6	7	8	9	10	11
12	13	14	15	16	17	18
19	20	21	22	23	24	25
26	27	28	29	30	31	

7: Creating a calendar with tables and table styles

All the palettes are available from the Window menu. Palettes differ from dialogue boxes in that they can stay open all the time. You can organise your palette sets in Window>Palette Sets. This allows you to save a set of palettes and give them a shortcut key—useful if you work on a laptop screen sometimes, and 27" monitor at others—and also turn hiding on and off for particular palettes. You can have palettes either in floating mode, or docked to the top, bottom, left or right.

1 Advanced Image Control

The Advanced Image Control Palette is mainly for use with Photoshop PSD files. It gives access to Photoshop Layers, Channels and Paths. Note that the files need to be free of Photoshop layer effects—QuarkXPress will just look at the Composite file if these are present.

Layers should show you all the document layers. They will already have their relevant blend controls and opacity applied to them. Whenever Quark cannot render a layer—for example because of layer effects—it reverts to the composite image, so that the initial imported image is always identical to the overall Photoshop result. You can set the compositing mode and transparency for each layer, and turn the individual layers on and off.

Channels allows you to switch on or off the relevant colour channels and Alpha masks. For channels not required by the Composite, you can Ctrl-click/right-click to bring up the Channel Options. These allow you to specify the ink, shade and solidity—in other words, exactly the options you are after if you want to specify a spot UV varnish, and you want to set these in Photoshop rather than creating them in QuarkXPress.

Paths allows you to see the paths. The first icon, which has no tool tip, selects the path as text runaround, and the second selects it as the clipping path. However, the controls in the Measurements Panel offer more refinement here.

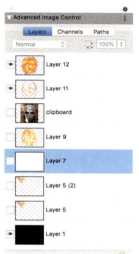

▲ *Cover illustration for a book, created in Flamepainter, based on the Sutton Hoo helmet, British Museum.*
◄ *Advanced Image Control layers used to create it. Flamepainter helpfully retains a great deal of information when it exports to PSD format, which is an open standard. You can turn layers on and off, set their transparency, and set their blend mode, using all of the Photoshop blend modes. You can also work on channels and paths.*

2 App Studio Publishing

The App Studio Publishing palette provides a login to App Studio—a separately hosted and payable service for creating native apps for smart devices. A trial account is available for App Studio. Any digital document created for HTML5 can later be republished via App Studio, and vice versa. In QX2018 you can directly publish iOS and Android apps without App Studio. See File>Export>iOS and File>Export>Android for more information. If you want to create self-updating publication apps, however, you will need App Studio, which also manages the otherwise tedious Apple/Android process.

◄ *App Studio Publishing dialogue. All of the preparation work up to this point is identical to the work to prepare a directly published iOS or Android app, so you can produce a one-off app as a test and then later switch to App Studio managed apps afterwards. App Studio gives instant publication of new editions, which is ideal for a periodical.*

What is Tagged PDF?

Tagged PDF is a way of making PDF files suitable for Accessible Readers, typically for people with a visual impairment, in the same way that W3 compliant websites are accessible. Tagged PDF is an informal standard: providing files in this way does not guarantee compliance with local legislation, but it will help.

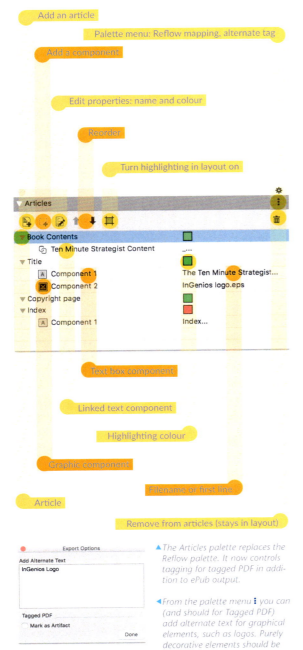

▲ The Articles palette replaces the Reflow palette. It now controls tagging for tagged PDF in addition to ePub output.

◀ From the palette menu ⋮ you can (and should for Tagged PDF) add alternate text for graphical elements, such as logos. Purely decorative elements should be marked as Artifacts. Accessible PDF reader will ignore them.

3 Articles

Articles, previously called Reflow Tagging, is used to prepare for Kindle or ePub publication, and to tag text for Tagged PDF output. You can also use it to organise the files within a complex print document, without having to go to Utilities>Usage to locate a particular element.

Kindle and ePub devices vary greatly in what formatting they support, mainly based on the age of the device or the app. At the simplest, to export for ePub or Kindle there must be at least one Article (even if it is actually a book length running text, it is still called an 'Article'). Reading will follow this article page by page, even on the simplest devices.

More advanced formatting is available for digital layouts using the HTML5 controls and fixed layout ePub or Kindle. However, these layouts are compatible with fewer devices.

Tagged PDF is available from QX2018. To create Tagged PDF, you first auto-tag the entire document (see below) and then return to each graphic with the palette menu (see illustration) or contextual menu>Export Options or Item>Export Options to either enter alternate text or mark as an *Artifact*[1]. Technically, QX will export without doing this, but the document will not be a compliant Tagged PDF document. Unimportant decorative elements must be marked as Artifact rather than ignored.

The palette has four functions.

First, you can assign one or more stories to be articles, and give them useful names and colours (⧉ and ✎), as well as changing their order in the document, using the ↑ up and ↓ down arrows. You can also use Layout>Autotag Layout to add pages, or the palette menu ⋮.

Second, you can assign Components, such as a graphic or a text box to Articles, using the ⊞ button. You can also rename these with the pencil tool and move them with the arrows.

Third, you can map paragraph styles in your document to paragraph styles you are going to use in the ePub, using the ⋮ palette menu. This step is no longer necessary, but still available.

Finally, from the palette menu ⋮ you can invoke Add Alternate Text, as shown in the illustration and noted above.

☐ highlights the article in the layout in your specified colour. One obvious way to use this is to mark elements which need to be exported green, and elements which should be removed with red.

Once you've added an article and perhaps a component, you are ready to export as an ePub, using the File>Export>Layout as ePub or Kindle. See the File Menu for details and options. For most ePub or Kindle files, you will want to change the Contents to ToC in the output options, rather than defaulting to articles.

To export tagged PDF, you need to select this in the Export>PDF options. You also need to assign headings within the Paragraph Styles. See the Style Sheets palette, page 130, for details.

---

1 'Artifact', in this context, means a decorative but irrelevant element.

32: Creating an ePub or Kindle

4 Books

The Books palette connects, organises, renumbers, reorders, prints and PDFs a set of layouts in the same project or different projects. It ensures that page numbering remains consistent and synchronised. If you synchronise chapters, it will also synchronise style sheets, colours and hyphenation. If you want to synchronise style sheets across a non-book project, use Utilities>Job Jackets Manager, page 173.

Usage is fairly simple. Create or open a book file by clicking on the selector in the top left. Then, using the ✚ button, add chapters. You can reorder them with the arrow icons ↑↓, synchronise them with the lightning icon, delete with the trash can, and print or PDF with the print and PDF icons. Once you have started printing or PDFing, you will be taken to the same screens as ordinary documents, and the process from there is transparent. You do not need to have the documents open to work with a book.

Lists, index and page numbering all work across books. Digital layouts do not support books: the option to add a digital layout is greyed out.

5 Callout Styles

Callouts are a special way of anchoring boxes to moving text, which allows them to be outside the main column. You create Callout anchors in the text in Item>Callout Anchor, and then assign them to boxes from the same menu item. These boxes are the 'Callouts'.

The Callout Styles palette itself is just a list of the styles you have defined. Use the ✚ to add a style, and the pencil to edit one.

This calls up the Edit Callout Style box.

Align horizontally/vertically relative to: allows you to choose Page, Anchor, Paragraph, Box or Spread, and you can set which part of the box aligns, what it aligns to, and an offset. This will require a bit of experimentation, but it means you have almost complete flexibility in ensuring that the box is exactly where you want it.

There is a trade-off here. Callout styles can ensure that a long, reflowing book remains always grid compliant, but they will also require the most recalculations. For a highly complex document, it is worth making use of the Books function (previous section) so that callouts are not having to endlessly recalculate.

Callouts lend themselves particularly well to laying out a long document of essentially finished text. If the client comes back half way through and wants a different font, page size or whatever, all you need to do is make the changes to the Master Page and the styles, and then make a cup of coffee while everything reflows.

On the other hand, if you are writing or editing as you go there will be at least a momentary pause while things rearrange themselves: it may be better to finalise the text and then use callout anchors.

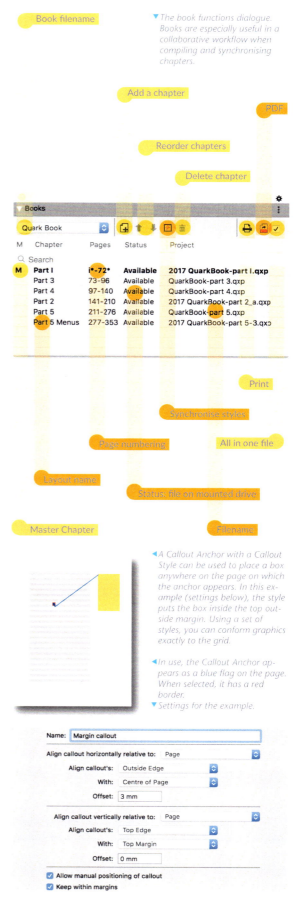

▼ *The book functions dialogue. Books are especially useful in a collaborative workflow when compiling and synchronising chapters.*

◀ *A Callout Anchor with a Callout Style can be used to place a box anywhere on the page on which the anchor appears. In this example (settings below), the style puts the box inside the top outside margin. Using a set of styles, you can conform graphics exactly to the grid.*

◀ *In use, the Callout Anchor appears as a blue flag on the page. When selected, it has a red border.*

▼ *Settings for the example.*

46: Combining documents with books | 38: Anchoring in text

6 Colours

The Colours palette is at the heart of Quark's approach to premium design. Paragraph styles, Item Styles and Character Styles are very convenient, but you could do all the formatting on an ad hoc basis and then spot the errors while proofing. This is traditionally exactly how those errors were spotted. Even with Matchprints and other colour proofing methods, it is hard to spot a yellow which is just the wrong yellow, a shade of green which is just too bright. After production, when you put the miscoloured object next to a whole window of correctly coloured work, the difference is all too obvious. Other applications allow you to create swatches and work from them if you wish to, but Quark requires you to. In the business of life, it is all too easy to pick sort-of the right colour, with the intention of fixing it later. It gets left, until it is too late.

So, every colour you are going to use in QuarkXPress must be defined here, or be a shade of one you define here.

The top row offers ✚ for new colour, the pencil ✎ to edit a colour, and selections for frame ◻, text Ⓐ or background colour ▢. When a picture is selected, ⬚ is picture colour.

Below these, both at 100% in the example palette, are shade and opacity. On the right is ⬤ Transparency Blend Mode.

Transparency Blend Modes

Transparency Blend Modes were introduced in QX2017. These are mathematical ways of combining layers, some inspired by photographic darkroom techniques. When outputting, check that your recipient's process supports transparencies. See Export Options for details: you may need to flatten transparencies.

Multiply

Multiply mathematically multiplies the values of the pixels with the pixels beneath. The result is always darker than either, up to absolute black. Cyan × Cyan, for example, produces a darker blue. Multiplying complementary colours produces black.

Multiply is one of the most useful modes, and is the basis for several others. It is generally the best choice for combining two images, as it deals with problems of dissimilar colour tone. You can use it as part of many fixes, for example for blown-out sky.

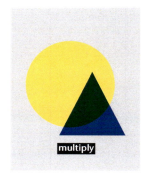

Screen

Screen is like projecting one colour with a projector onto another projected colour—it will be lighter than either of them, because you are adding light, and the result will be a blend of the two colours. If you screen two complementary colours — for example, the Yellow from

CMYK against the Blue from RGB, the result is pure white.

If you take a silhouette image and screen it onto a coloured image, you get the white-out background of the silhouette image entirely white, and the shape of the silhouette made from the other image.

Overlay

Overlay lightens the top layer where the base layer is light, and darkens it where it is dark.

Overlaying white on black produces grey. Overlaying a complementary colour produces only the underlying colour—essentially, the object disappears.

Overlaying is heavily dependent on the colour space, because the calculations are based on the channel values. If you have a 'full' channel underneath, for example, maximum blue, red or green in RGB, everything on top disappears. In QX2018, preview in RGB and CMYK space.

▲ Image transparencies provide some exciting methods to better meld words and pictures, but they are more than merely pretty effects.

Darken and Lighten

For each channel of each pixel, darken takes the darker of the two layers, and lighten takes the lighter.

Darken is an easy way of compositing an image with a light background onto an image with a darker background. If the background is entirely blown out (ie, pure white), look at Multiply and Colour Burn as well.

Lighten is an easy way to composite a bright image with a dark background onto an image with a lighter background.

Mode maths:

Where the luminance is 0%–100% (ie, 0 to 1) and B is the top layer and A the bottom layer, per pixel:

Normal	B
Multiply	A×B
Screen	1−(1−A)×(1−B)
	Inversion of A inverted times B inverted
Overlay	2AB if A<0.5; otherwise 1−2(1−A)(1−B)
	Multiply on darker pixels, screen on lighter pixels, both at half strength
Darken	Darker of A or B
Lighten	Lighter of A or B
Colour Dodge	A/(1−B)
	A divided by B inverted
Colour Burn	1−(1−B)/A
	Inversion of Colour Dodge
Hard Light	Overlay with A and B swapped
Soft Light	$(1-2B)A^2 + 2BA$
Difference	|A−B|
Exclusion	A+B−2AB

Colour Dodge and Colour Burn

'Dodging' is a dark room technique where you let less light fall on the photographic paper. 'Burning' increases the exposure and darkens the image.

Colour Dodge is a computer method of simulating that digitally. It's like Lighten, but it's more organic. The brighter the top layer, the more it affects the bottom layer, so white has the maximum lightening effect on the bottom layer, while black has no effect.

Colour Burn is a good choice for compositing a high contrast image on a blown out background onto another image.

◀ This image, shot at the annual re-enactment of the Battle of Tewkesbury, suffers from blown out sky.

▲ We used the eye-dropper tool to extract colours from the sky reflections to produce this gradient as a background.

▼ Compositing the image with Darken onto the background produces a pleasing result.

Hard Light and Soft Light

Hard Light is the same as Overlay, except with the bottom and top layers swapped over. This is highly useful as it means you can set the background of the frame with a colour blend, and then hard-light the foreground image over it, giving you a graduated photo filter without having to sandwich two images together.

Soft Light is essentially hard light, but softer. There is a complex formula which governs this, and, in fact, the formulae are different in different applications. Experiment a little and you will see the difference.

Difference and Exclusion

Difference, mathematically, subtracts one layer from the other and keeps the positive result. It is more useful than beautiful: operating adjustments on a difference layer can produce results which can't otherwise be achieved.

Exclusion is a lower contrast version of Difference.

In many cases, this is most evident at the edges of a high contrast composite.

These effects are highly useful when compositing layers with a view to selectively applying an effect. They are more spectacular than beautiful when applied 'straight'.

Palettes

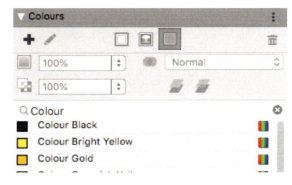

▲ Searching the colour list. Especially when converting numerous files to native objects, you are liable to see a lot of unwanted colours. If you are creating brand colours, it's helpful to include a common name in them. If you then type that name in the 'Search', all colours which include that name appear on the list, but no others do.

▼ The Edit Colour dialogue (which is also the dialogue for Create Colour) is invoked by pressing + on the colour palette or by Colour>New wherever colours are available. This has a number of modes which depend on the type of colour created. QuarkXPress contains the complete suite of Version 3 Pantone colours. Unlike its competitors, it is not necessary to buy or import them separately. In the Pantone dialogue, shown here, you can type in the number, or browse the ribbon. Clicking on the other icon at the bottom left displays swatches in grid form.

▲ Multi-ink colour creation ▲ CMYK colours
▲▲ Web safe colours ▲▲ RGB colours

The knockout controls are on the third row, right, and are greyed out except when a spot colour is selected.. These are either knockout ▨, or overprint ▨. Trapping is now normally handled by the RIP immediately prior to the production of film or plate, so choke controls are not available. If you absolutely have to have a manual choke, do it with a border.

The search pane is for searching in the palette only. If you type in Pantone, it will filter out everything which does not have the word Pantone in its name.

Below, you have the colours you have defined, with Black, None, White and Cyan, Magenta, Yellow as defaults. There is a CMYK icon at the side for CMYK colours. A target icon, representing the registration mark, denotes spot colours.

At the bottom, you have the eye-dropper ✐ panel.

Clicking on ✚ to create a new colour, or the pencil ✐ to edit a colour, opens up the Edit Colour box. You cannot edit or delete the default colours Black, White, Cyan, Yellow or Magenta.

The edit colour panel opens to CMYK by default, but you can also choose RGB, HSB, LAB, Multi-ink, DIC, Focoltone, Pantone, TOYO, Trumatch, and web-named and safe colours.

If you are working to a brand specification enter the colours as given, with Pantone as your first choice, CMYK if Pantone is not given, LAB if CMYK is not given (unlikely), and only RGB or HSB as a last resort. If you have only been offered web-named colours, chances are that what you have been sent is not the full visual identity, but a reduced one for web-designers.

The colour editing panels are fairly self-explanatory, but do not be misled into picking colours from the colour wheels or swatches—these are there for confirmation purposes only. Unless your monitor has recently been calibrated to a very high precision, they are no more than approximations to the exact tones.

Note that you can choose Pantone colours and convert them to CMYK as you Export for PDF—although you can convert them in this box, there is no need to. You cannot convert CMYK back to Pantone if you later change your mind, or need to produce a two-colour job. You can give a colour any name you like—it does not have to be the Pantone number.

Cmd/ctrl-clicking on any colour in the main palette opens the colour list window. Here you can create new colours or edit them, as above. You can also duplicate, delete, and append from another Quark project. Changes made here must be saved to have an effect. If you delete a colour, and it is in use in the layout, you will be asked what colour you want to replace it. Note that you can only select 100% colours, not shades, which is annoying if an imported file has created dozens of shades of grey.

Eye-dropper tool

The eye-dropper is at the bottom of the colour palette. Its operation is very simple: choose the eye-dropper ⌀, and click on anything which is in the QuarkXPress layout. This includes pictures, colour blends, even the colour of the guidelines. However, palettes and other interface elements which are not part of the layout cannot be used. Each colour appears in a candidate palette with fourteen slots. You can carry on clicking and the oldest ones will eventually disappear. To transfer a colour to the main palette, click the multi-coloured plus ✣ at the right hand side. This opens up the Add Colour dialogue, allowing you to specify the colour more exactly. Opt/alt-click adds the colour without this dialogue, and Opt/alt-shift-click adds all the colours.

If doing a one-off, photo-led job, or needing an organically harmonious palette, creating from a photograph has the advantage that, whatever the vagaries of your colour management process, your colours will harmonise with the photograph as it appears in the finished publication.

◂ The colour eye-dropper tool is at the bottom of the colour palette. It has been used here to extract colours from the detail of an illustration. The advantage of extracting colours in this way is that you can be sure of a balanced palette that will not clash.

When you choose to add the colour, the dialogue opens up as on the left page. You can change this to another mode. By default, RGB images produce RGB colours, CMYK produces CMYK.

Proofing

Here is something important. If you turn View>Proof Output to anything other than 'None', the colours in your palette will change to represent what your Profiles think will happen when the colours are reproduced under that process. Actually knowing that your laser printer is going to make all the reds orange may not be very encouraging, but it can save a lot of headaches later. What's more, the Proof Output controls affect the colour edit and creation window, so, if desperate, you can choose new colours that better match the intended result.

This does not apply to colours in the temporary eye-dropper area.

◂ When using View>Proof Output, setting the mode to monochrome changes colours on the page and in the palette to grey, but it does not affect the ad hoc colours in the eye-dropper waiting area.

7 Conditional Styles

Conditional Styles allow paragraph and character styles to be applied automatically and selectively to text based on conditions. They are very powerful, enabling some extremely advanced formatting and automation.

The palette itself is simple enough—as with others, ✣ means new style, pencil ✎ means edit style, and d means duplicate. Delete 🗑 is at the end, and all four of these are reproduced via the menu icon ⋮.

The main interest is in the Create/Edit box:

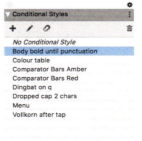

◂ Conditional Styles palette. Conditional styles can vary from the simplest, such as the example below, to styles capable of formatting a long document with just a single style, applied throughout in one pass.
If you leave a conditional style on, it will keep conforming text to the style sheet. If you run it once and then turn it off, it acts like a macro. All the changes you made will now be static parts of the text.

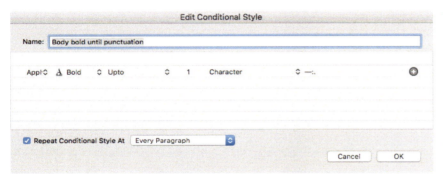

◂ This simple Conditional Style applies a Character Style named 'Bold' to all the text in a paragraph up to, but not including, an em-dash —, a colon :, or a full stop. It repeats for every paragraph that it is applied to. Choosing 'Character' applies the style to any of the listed characters. Choosing 'Text' applies only when the whole text is present.

▸ The result: all the words up to the punctuation are bolded, making for easy in-line subtitles.

Slug text—a slug is bolder text at the start of a paragraph. It can help with in-line titling when used before punctuation.

Intro: a single conditional style can set slugs for many kinds of punctuation.

Sentence. An alternative way of doing slugs, which can also be achieved with Conditional Styles, is to bold the first four words.

▼ *The Conditional Style panel may seem complicated, but it's very easy to start with a simple style like the one on the previous page. As you get used to it, any style which you assign based on the content of text can in principle be turned into a Conditional Style. This can literally save days in a production environment, and also dramatically reduce formatting errors.*

Pressing + copies the selected line and places the new condition on the next line.

The conditional style sheet can be set to repeat at particular text, at a particular character, at a conditional style marker, or at every paragraph, or not at all.

Note that if you apply a conditional style and then turn the style off by clicking 'No Conditional Style', all the formatting remains as styled, but will not respond to changes in the text or the style sheet.

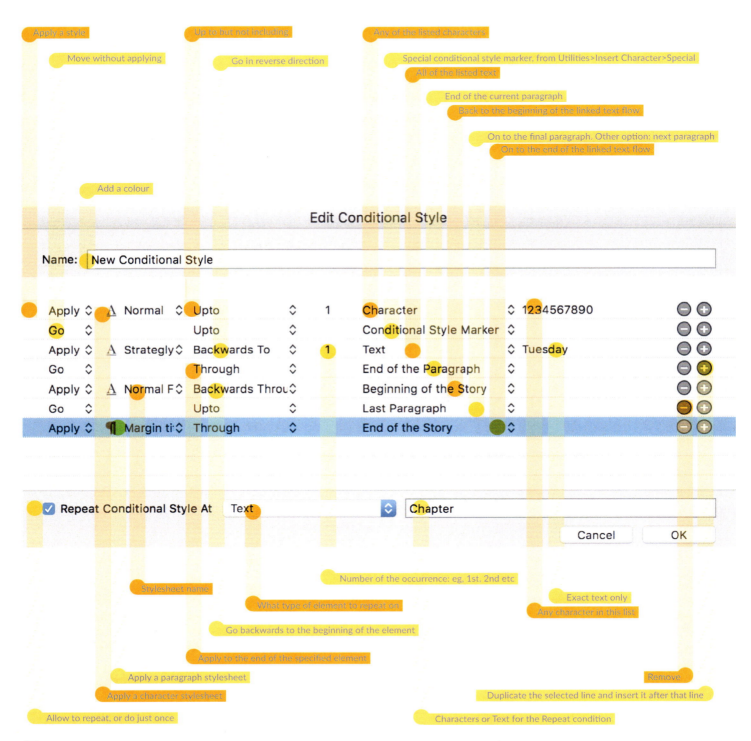

Action—*Apply* or *Go*. This either applies a style sheet, or merely moves the point of activity somewhere else.

Style—Any character or paragraph style already defined.

Motion—*Up to* takes you up to but not including the Position Marker. *Through* acts up to and including the Position Marker. *Backwards to* and *Backwards through* do the same, but in reverse.

#—the occurrence. This section has been formatted with a Body bold until em-dash Conditional Style. If the number were set to 2, it would look for the second em-dash to apply the style. Where the Position has no marker but a number, this number defines it.

Position—There are a number of options. A *Conditional Style Marker* only appears when View>Invisibles are turned on. Apply it with Opt-ctrl-| (Mac only) or Utilities>Insert Character>Special>Conditional Style Marker.

Marker—what marker is looked for. *Character* means any single character from the list you provide, *Number* means any string of digits, *Text* means an exact text string that you specify.

Deep Automation

If you're coming to QuarkXPress from InDesign, you may be looking for GREP or something similar. Conditional Styles do some of the things that GREP can do, but many others are built into the structure of QuarkXPress itself. Rather than constructing a script or GREP style to correct bad kerning in a font, you can manage it with Edit>Kerning Pairs. You can specify that tracking automatically changes with font size in Edit>Font Tracking Tables, and you can automate many other features using Paragraph, Character and Item Styles. Open Type also introduces its own character automation. Other aspects of automation are better managed through Content Variables, Shared Content and Composition Zones.

However, if that is not enough, from QX2018 you can now write your own JavaScripts, in addition to the Mac-only Apple Scripts that QuarkXPress has supported since its early days. There is also a simpler level of script-type automation, which is Find and Change, which can do surprisingly sophisticated manipulations.

If choosing between Scripting, Find/Change and deeper automation, it is almost always better to use in-built 'object oriented' features like styles, rather than linear 'execute once and leave as permanent change' scripting like Java and AppleScript.

8 Content

The Content palette lets you share content between boxes, which could be images or text. It is also where Job Jacket content appears.

The icons across the top are unusual.

✚ adds the selected box as shared content. 📺 imports content into the container. 🆔 inserts the item selected in the palette into the layout. You can edit the name and some characteristics with ✏, and 🖼 unsynchronises all instances of a shared content item.

Begin by creating a box, typing something into it, and pressing ✚.

The Shared Item Properties opens. You can name your item, and then choose whether the box attributes are synchronised, whether the content is synchronised, and, if so, whether this includes content attributes, such as text formatting, or only the content.

Pressing OK saves this, and your named item now appears in the palette. If you click on the arrow, it shows you what it contains.

You can now use the icons to work on this. Clicking on the contents—ie, underneath the main item—you can import content into the box. If you now create another box, you can press the 🆔 icon to insert your content into it. Alternatively, just drag the contents from the palette onto the box, or drag the container onto the layout, which will create a box containing the content.

Any changes you now make will be reflected in every instance, with attributes according to what you chose. If you try to edit with the pencil tool, you will see that you can change the name, but the attribute choices you made on creation are now fixed.

Unsynchronise All makes the content independent. Changes will no longer be reflected in the boxes you already created, but you can still use the shared item to create new, synchronised boxes. Deleting, by contrast, removes the object from the sharing palette, leaving all text in place, unsynchronised.

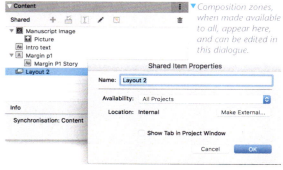

Composition zones, when made available to all, appear here, and can be edited in this dialogue.

Palettes 99

9 Content Variables

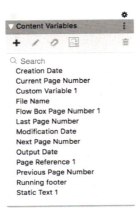

Content Variables are automatically generated short sections of text (though they will line-wrap, from QuarkXPress 2016). The palette is self-explanatory, ✛ to add, pencil ✎ to edit, double-circle-arrow ⟳ to duplicate, an option to convert to text in the document 🗎, and trash 🗑 to delete.

All of them update automatically. If you delete one, it converts everything to static text.

In use, drag the content variable into the text, or use Utilities>Content Variable and choose the one you want. There are various presets, and any that you have defined yourself. The content variables take any format you give them when used. Unlike Content, which has to be in its own box, Content Variables can be inserted into any text.

Clicking ✛ or edit ✎ opens the Edit Content Variable dialogue, and this is where the fun begins. You can also use Utilities>Content Variable>New.

Don't name your variable yet—it will offer a consistent name based on the type. Instead, click on Type, which brings up thirteen options.

▲ *QX2018 offers thirteen kinds of content variables, all of which can wrap onto two or more lines.*

▲ *Watch out when copying content variables from one document to another. If a content variable references something, such as a cross-reference, that does not exist in the new document, it may cause problems saving, opening or exporting.*

Creation Date
Creation date allows you to specify the format and the order the document was first created. This is mainly useful as an internal audit tool: very few readers will be interested in when you pressed 'New' in QuarkXPress, and it will not take account of when the first draft was written on someone's iPad on the train from Tangiers to Casablanca.

Current Page Number
This gives the page number of whatever page it appears on. The result is the same as cmd/ctrl-3 or Utilities>Insert Character>Special> Current Box Page #. In a Book, the page numbers will be ordered throughout unless you have specified otherwise by using Sections.

Custom Variable
A custom variable lets you combine several other variables with any text you define, for example, a Page reference followed by the Modification Date in brackets, for managing complex revisions.

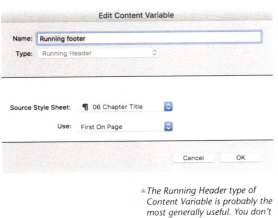

▲ *The Running Header type of Content Variable is probably the most generally useful. You don't need to use it to just produce a running header or footer. You can use it to copy text from any style-sheet to anywhere else.*

File Name
The name of the File. You can choose whether or not to include the extension. If the file name is the title of the document, you can use File Name with the extension turned off to self-refer in the text, for example, the file name of this book is Desk Top Publishing with QuarkXPress 2018.

Flow Box Page Number
If you have boxes which flow across several pages, the Flow Box Page Number allows you to define the previous page, as in 'Continued from Page *x*' or the following page, as in 'Continued on Page *y*'.

Last Page Number
The final page number of the project or section. Note that this is the page number as it would appear on that page, not the page count—if you have front matter numbered i, ii, iii etc, this will not

add in those additional pages, though choosing 'section' rather than 'document' would mean that the last page number shown while in that section would be xvii, etc, rather than the end of the document. If you want to do a word processor style 'Page 17 of 49', which is handy when things are being passed around for meetings, make sure that you only have one kind of page numbering. In a Book, the number is the last page number of the current project, not the entire book.

Modification Date
The date the file was modified. You can specify the format.

Next Page Number
This gives the number of the next page in the layout, or in the section. If you choose 'section', and the current page is the end of the section, it will show <#> instead of a number—ugly, but potentially highly useful in finding out what has gone wrong with some monstrously complicated numbering system.

Output Date
The date on which the file was printed or exported.

Page Reference
This allows you to reference an anchor ⚓ which you have created with Style>Anchor>New. The anchor can be in another document in the same project—especially useful in books, or when referencing sister publications. You can specify text that goes in front of or after it, such as 'See page <number> in Reference Sheet IV'. It will also allow you to create a hyperlink, which will be embedded into a PDF on export.

Previous Page Number
This is the number of the previous page. It works the same as Next Page Number.

Running Header
Running Header is not just for running headers. It looks at the first or last use of a particular style sheet on a page or spread—you choose which—or the most recent previous one if there is no example on the current page/spread, and inserts that as unformatted text.

Used judiciously, this can do many more things than merely putting a header or footer, like the one at the bottom of this page. You can use it for character or paragraph styles.

A word of warning—if the text is very long, QuarkXPress may take a long time to find and place it. You will probably decide it has crashed, and quit and restart it. It will get there eventually, but it probably isn't worth the wait.

Static Text
Static Text is anything you want to type in. It isn't actually static, as every use in the document will change if you change it. Very useful for things such as the name of a venue, the date of an event, and so on.

Index?
List?
Content variable?
Cross-reference?
Which should I use?

QuarkXPress offers several different ways of making your content intelligent. Knowing which to use can save a few headaches.

Lists and Content variables can both address information based on the *Style Sheet* associated with it—Content variables to find the most recent usage, Lists to find all usages.

The Index relies on you *tagging* each occurrence you want to index, and it intelligently organises entries with the same tag as being the same thing (a list will list everything it finds separately).

Content variables can also find individual *anchors*.

Cross references allow you to refer to text by its *structure*, either Outlining or Foot/endnoting, and can quote text and context, or give a page or structural reference.

10 Footnote Styles

Footnotes were introduced in QuarkXPress 2015, and the styles have been upgraded to satisfy user requests.

To insert a footnote, use Style>Footnotes/Endnotes>Insert Footnote (or endnote). There is a ridiculously complicated keyboard shortcut for this. On a Mac, if you are using a lot of footnotes, go to Preferences>Key Shortcuts and create a more sensible one, such as Cmd-`, or anything you find convenient.

To apply a style, just select the marker—ie, the *, or [1], and click on the style you want from the palette.

The styles palette operates as you would expect[*]. It's when you press ✚ to add or pencil ✎ to edit that it gets interesting. Read on:

In **Edit Footnote Style**, first give your new style a name. Each style is for either footnotes or endnotes.[1]

You can use any **numbering style** you have defined. QuarkXPress has additional typographic numbering styles, set in Edit>Bullet, Numbering and Outline Styles, to reflect academic practice, such as using *, **, †, ††.

The **Marker Style** defaults to Superscript, but you can also have Subscript, or inherit from the Numbering Style.

You can set the **start number**, and you can also set numbering to **restart** never, each page, or each section, though this is only for footnotes.[2,3]

Set the **Paragraph Style**[4] with any style you've defined. This specifies the body of the note itself, including any character style and spacing.

The **Character Format** sets the text of the note number before the note itself. It defaults to Inherit from Marker Style, but you can set it to any character style you like.

You can prefix the number, but trailing spaces are not supported here. The same goes for the suffix—leading or trailing spaces are ignored. However, you can set various kinds of space separator, and you can even have more than one—but non-spaces are ignored, and if you try to include them the space resets to \s, which is a regular space. Click the Space Separator drop down for a list of options.

Finally, you can force the Endnotes to begin on a new page.[5]

---

*Except for the * icon, which is for a custom footnote. Sorry, couldn't resist doing this as a footnote.*

Note |1 See side bar. If working with multiple types of footnotes, for example for a journal, make sure the fonts are distinctive.

Note |2 A couple of further thoughts on footnotes and endnotes. People who love endnotes and footnotes are by nature pedantic. Academics love them, as do journal editors. Designers may not love them—though, to my mind, footnotes, if well designed, lend magnificent typographic charm, and go well with a historic typesetting aesthetic. The novel Jonathan Strange and Mister Norrell by Susanna Clarke makes extensive use of footnotes for its fictional history.

Note |3 Footnotes and endnotes are placed within the text box, rather than underneath it. This is correct typographic practice, but it will mean that the useable length of the page is shortened. Footnotes work equally well for single column or multi-column text, where the note is placed underneath the column.

Note |4 When pasting text that began as body text and was later relegated to the footnotes, use Edit>Paste Without Formatting, otherwise it will retain its original formatting, which is unhelpful.

Note |5 And, while we're commenting, you will see that once the footnotes reach a particular length,

---

▶ *The footnote styles palette allows you to edit footnote and endnote styles, but it does not allow you to edit the separator styles, for which you need Edit>Footnote styles. See below.*

▶ *Edit>Footnote Styles opens this dialogue, which is where, in addition to footnote styles, you can also create and edit Footnote Separator Styles.*

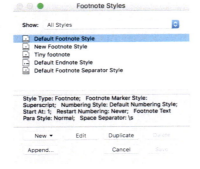

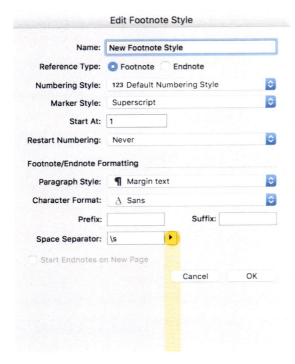

▲ *Footnote styles are fairly straightforward, but it is worth working on them until they are perfect because they play a powerful role shaping the bottom of the layout, which is crucial for taking the reader to the next page. You can specify both a paragraph style and a separate character format.*

▶ *All types of QuarkXPress spaces are available as the separator, and it is worth investing some time in getting this looking right.*

Endnotes, by default, appear at the end of text they relate to.

Now, at this point you are probably thinking: 'this is all very well, but where do I define the separator style?'

Separator Style

For the separator style, go to Edit>Footnote Styles and either edit the Default Footnote Separator Style, or choose New and use the dropdown menu to pick New Footnote Separator Style.

Here, you can define the spacing of the ruling line, and separately define the line style, width, colour, shade opacity and indents for the initial footnotes and footnotes that are continued on subsequent pages.

The **Endnote Separator style** is set by the Default Footnote Separator Style, and is not separately editable.

Introduced in QX2016, you can create cross-references to footnotes with Style>Cross Reference>Insert. From QX2018, footnotes can span columns. This is set in the Footnote Separator Style.

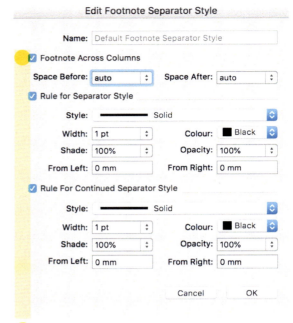

▲ *From QX2018, footnotes can now span columns. This is set in the Footnote Separator Style, in Edit>Footnote Styles.*

11 Glyphs

The Glyphs palette offers you the entire font to select characters from. It would be incredibly tedious to set text this way, but you could try a line or so of dragging (or double-clicking) from the Glyphs palette into the layout, and imagine that you are Peter Quentell in Cologne, 1525, with William Tyndale looking over your shoulder as you set the first printed Bible in English. If you have to set a few letters of text in a script unfamiliar to you, dragging them from the glyphs palette may be the best option.

Essentially, you choose your working font in the top drop-down menu, and then select either the Entire Font, Alternates for your current selection (if there are any), Special Characters, or a variety of other things depending on what features the font supports.

This includes Open Type sets not supported by QuarkXPress—which could be almost anything, as the Open Type specification allows non-standard sets to be created, even if no software can display them.

As you look at the glyphs, you will see a small triangle at the bottom right of some glyphs. This shows that alternates are available for that glyph. If you select a character in your text, choosing Alternates for Selection will show the other versions of that glyph within the selected font.

If you double-click a glyph, it will be inserted at the text cursor.

You can drag a favourite glyph, such as something your keyboard does not support, onto the Favourite Glyphs section at the bottom.

The magnifying glass  increases the size of the glyph and its grid. Below it, the slider changes the proportions of the glyph within the grid, to help examining tiny features.

▶ *Overleaf: typographic characters should always be used rather than their non-typographic equivalents. 'x' the letter is not the same as the multiply symbol ×, and three full stops '...' is not the same as '…', the ellipsis symbol. ° degrees is a different symbol from the ordinal º, used in Nº5, as opposed to °F. For most of these there are key combinations for both Mac and Windows, and these are worth memorising. It is also worth preparing a JavaScript or AppleScript to automate exchanging them in imported text.*

▼ *Below are the symbols created for this book. You can drag any character onto the Favourite Glyphs, and it will persist even when a different font is selected. You can bring a glyph into a document either by dragging or by double clicking.*

---

they move onto continuation footnotes, using the footnotes separator style of the first footnote, not that of subsequent footnotes.

Typographic characters

Name	Usage	Mac	Windows
— em dash	punctuation	opt-shift-hyphen	alt-0151
– en dash	range, 5–7 etc	opt-hyphen	alt-0150
- hyphen	joins/splits	hyphen key	hyphen key
− minus	mathematics	use glyphs palette	
× times	mathematics	use glyphs	alt-0215
÷ divide	mathematics	opt-/	alt-0247
± plus minus	approximation	opt-shift-=	alt-0177
· mid point	punctuation	opt-shift-9	alt-0183
• bullet	punctuation	opt-shift-8	alt-0149
° degree	angles, °F	alt-shift-8	alt-0176
æ (various)	vowel sound	opt-'	alt-0230
" Ordinal	N"	opt-0	alt-8470
' Quote	Open single	opt-]	alt-0145
' Quote	Close single	opt-shift-]	alt-0146
" Quote	Open double	opt-[	alt-0147
" Quote	Close double	opt-shift-[	alt-0148
… Ellipsis	punctuation	opt-:	alt-0133

On Windows, use the alt key and the numeric keypad

▲ *Typographic characters should always be used instead of their typewriter equivalents. Most are accessible directly with hot-keys, rather than requiring the Glyphs palette (previous page)*

▼ *The Gradient palette is too narrow to construct chrome gradients like the one below, but you can easily drag it out to allow you to create the narrow bands of colour which characterise chrome.*

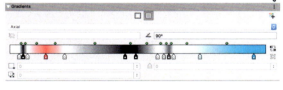

▲ *All four gradient types are involved in creating this chromed look. As text cannot directly take a gradient (though it is possible with some careful work), the letters are first converted to curves using Item>Convert Text to Boxes. The main area is applied using the Axial gradient above. The borders are applied as a rectangular gradient, and the flares are produced blending diamond and circular gradients.*

12 Gradients

Colour Blends, as they were called in previous versions, are now called Gradients, and QX2017 enhanced them to include diamond and rectangular blends, and to allow them to be saved as colours. Furthermore, gradients can now be applied to lines and frames as well as background fills.

Gradients can be either Frame ▢ or Fill ▢.

Type is None, Axial, Radial, Rectangular or Diamond.

The next box, proportions ⬚ only appears for radial gradients. It sets as a percentage the flattening of the circle into an ellipse. Full Radial changes how this is calculated.

Angle ∡ is the angle of the blend. It is often worth setting this to 45° if the blend is subtle and not intended to be too obvious.

The button ⬚ next to it reverses the gradient.

The wide bar is where you define the gradient, clicking once underneath to establish a point, which appears as a marker ⌂ below.

Once you have set the points, you can move them, and also adjust their midpoints with the diamonds ◇ above the line.

Underneath you have the colour ▪ and shade of the selected point, and its opacity ⬚, as elsewhere in QuarkXpress.

On the right you have ⌂ for the exact position of the marker as a percentage. This will show where you have put the marker, and you can edit it numerically if you require an exact percentage.

Gradients across text is sadly all too reminiscent of the Word Art of a famous word processing application. If you are desperate to do this, convert text to box with Item>Convert Text to Boxes and then apply the gradient.

Layering a mixed opacity graphic box over text, however, can produce much more refined effects.

13 Grid Styles

You normally set the text grid for the entire document—if you are locking the text to a grid—when in the Master Pages mode in Page Layout, and using Page>Master Guides and Grids. However, if your design has two or more font sizes that are consistently used in different places, for example the body text and the margin text in this book, you might want to have two separate lock-down grids.

You achieve this with Grid Styles, applied to individual text boxes. The functionality is the same as Page>Master Guides & Grids, but you can save as many styles as you want.

Note that updating 'Normal' in this palette does not change what you have set on Page>Master Guides & Grids.

From the palette, click + or ✎ to open the Edit Grid Styles dialogue.

The main tab is Text Settings; Display Settings just specifies how the grid is displayed.

In the Text Settings tab, specify your font size, its vertical scaling (which should be 100% for normal work) and the line spacing. It will then calculate the total leading. QuarkXPress's default is 20% additional leading, but you can change that in Preferences>Print Layout>Paragraph. You would normally set alternate leading as part of the Paragraph styles.

The Baseline Position section is how the baseline is calculated. This defaults to 25% above the Bottomline (ie, the lowest descender), but if you have settled on your font, you can choose *Read From Font*, which will calculate more accurately.

This only affects where QuarkXPress thinks the baseline is, not the actual spacing of the grid, which is set by the leading, above.

You can specify a baseline offset.

Finally, you can opt to lock your custom grid to the Paragraph Style Sheet Normal. This is helpful if you are going to create several grids and want to duplicate from one grid which matches your Normal.

It's possible to create a grid on which no text can appear. This can be useful for forcing chapter headings onto the right-hand page.

▼ *Grid Styles are for a traditional lock-down text grid, where every line of text falls into exactly the same place. You can also achieve this by specifying text sizes exactly.*

For a highly formalised document, or when emulating traditional processes, Grid Styles can enable you to achieve the standard easily. However, modern grids are usually generated geometrically. For this, use Window>Guides.

▼ *The Grid Styles dialogues give you a high degree of typographic control, and also enable you to specify how it appears on the screen.*

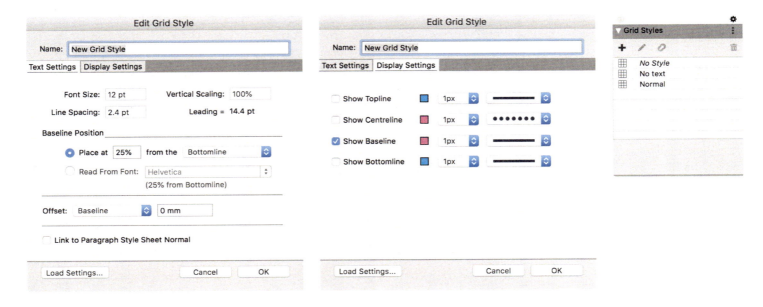

14 Guides

You can drag ad-hoc guides from the rulers at the top and left of the screen at any time, and QuarkXPress's dynamic guides, which appear when you drag or resize boxes, will take away much of the strain of getting things consistent. However, the Guides palette offers a great deal for guide management that is worth knowing about.

There are two things to remember about the Guides palette:

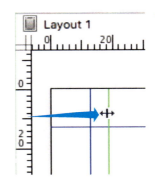

◂ *Dragging an ad-hoc guide out from the rulers. You can do this on any page. If you do it on a Master page, it will appear on every page controlled by that master. Dragged guides also appear in the Guides palette.*

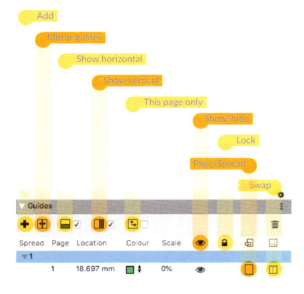

First, it works on individual guides, per page, unlike the various Style palettes. Normally you would expect to set guides on Master Pages. However, if you want to make adjustments on particular pages or spreads, the Guides palette can do that as well.

Second, the palette menu ⋮ in the top right hand corner is much more important than in other palettes, giving access to five separate dialogue panels.

1   The palette

The ✚ button adds a guide, as you would expect. The other icons across the top mirror the guides ⊞ (for a spread), show horizontal ⊟, show vertical ⊞, and show the current page guides only ⤴. There is also trash 🗑, for delete.

The next row is a click-to-sort set of columns.

Spread—sorts by spread.

Page—sorts by page. Double-click to open the edit panel.

Location—the vertical or horizontal position. Double-click to edit directly.

Colour—the display colour. Click and hold to select or create a new colour, using the System's colour setting tool. Note that these colours are not linked with your colour palette. The default is green, but you can change this in QuarkXPress>Preferences>Print Layout>Tools>Guides & Grid. New colours will have their RGB numbers, not names, and are not subsequently editable.

Scale—the minimum view scale at which the guide is visible. Double-click to edit.

Eye—👁 turn visibility on or of.

Lock—🔒 lock guide, unlock.

Page/Spread—⎄ click to confine to page, or take across spread (horizontal guides only).

Horizontal/Vertical—⎄ click to swap (careful here).

Generally speaking, create your guides as much as possible on Master Pages and lock them.

▼ *The drop-down from the palette menu ⋮ opens a range of key features, including plain grids, row and column grids, and bleed and safety guides.*

2   Guide Attributes

By selecting New Guide in the menu ⋮, or double-clicking in the palette, you get to the Guide Attributes dialogue. We will look at the basic attributes here and refer back to them for the other dialogues.

Location—the location, in your default units, from wherever you currently have the origin point. This is by default the top-left hand corner of the page, but if you grab the corner of the main screen where the rulers meet, you can drag it anywhere. Ctrl-click/right-clicking on that corner opens up a contextual menu to set units and ruler direction, and opt/alt-click resets it to the default.

Direction—Horizontal or Vertical.

▼ *Guide attributes. Clicking preview allows you to see the guides appear on your page while you work with them.*

106

Type—Page or Spread.

Colour—from the list, as in the palette (see above).

View Scale—sets the minimum magnification at which the guide will be displayed.

Locked—like it says.

Preview—allows you to see it before you agree it.

Add, Cancel, OK—you can add a guide and remain in this dialogue by choosing Add. Otherwise cancel or OK.

You can create an image of the page including the guides from File>Export As>Image.

3   Create Grid

Create Grid opens an alternate dialogue which has the following extra features:

Horizontal and Vertical check boxes—switches on the controls for each.

Start—the position of the first guide.

End—the position of the last guide.

Number or Step—number of guides or gap between the guides, QuarkXPress then calculates where they go and they are created up to the end point.

Range—you can specify on which pages they will appear.

Create Grid creates an evenly spaced graph-paper-like grid. If you want to create a page-design grid, unless you are a phenomenally hardcore member of the Swiss school of design, the Create Rows and Columns dialogue is likely to be better.

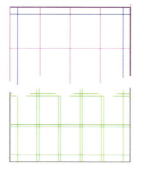

◂ Create Grid creates a table-like grid. This is useful in some kinds of design, but for a Grid-layout, it's generally more useful to create Rows and Columns, using the next option.

◂ Create Rows and Columns creates the kinds of grids that we usually talk about when we consider a grid-based layout. Make sure that these are set to Centre within Margins rather than Page Boundary.

4   Create Rows and Columns

This is similar to Create Grid, but more useful for page design tasks.

Rows, Columns—sets the number of rows and columns.

Gutter—sets the gutters. You can, as in other dialogues, enter a simple mathematical expression, such as 6/85*210.

Centre within—Page Boundary or Margins. Margins would be the usual choice.

Other controls are the same as in Create Grid or Guide Attributes.

This would be the normal place to start if you wanted to create an underlying page grid.

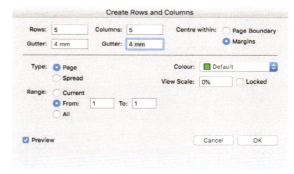

5   Create Guides From Box

To create guides from a box, select the box and open the Create Guides From Box dialogue from the palette menu ⋮. The measurements will be calculated automatically. You can turn the top, left, bottom or right lines off, but the simplest thing to do is to click OK, and your guidelines have been created. This also correctly finds the rectangular outline of an irregular box. This is highly useful for constructing a master page around an optically placed set of boxes and using them for an unusual grid.

▴ Create Guides from Box also correctly finds the rectangular outline of irregular boxes.

Palettes

▲ If coming from InDesign, note that you create Bleed and Safety Guides from the Guides palette, not at document creation.

6 Create Bleed and Safety Guides

The final type of Guides dialogue creates guidelines outside and inside the margins, and colours them appropriately. I have to say that I had been doing this for years by dragging the guidelines from the rulers, and only heard about this feature recently. A massive time saver.

Bleed—outside the page. This defaults to points, but 3mm is fairly standard.

Safety—inside the page. Again, 3mm is standard for trimmed paper, but for a book, which will be trimmed all at once, 6.35mm may be minimal.

15 HTML5

HTML5 was introduced in QX2016, and continues to be enhanced. From QX2018 it is possible to apply animations, buttons, video and audio to groups of objects. You can apply HTML5 features in print layouts, but they will only be active when used in digital layouts.

This palette controls interactions for Fixed Layout ePub and Kindle (readers do not support all features), HTML5 publications, and apps.

The palette is relatively straightforward. Name the object at the top, where you can also specify that it is initially hidden.

Even if you have no intention of using HTML5, you can still use this to **name** boxes, which will then appear in the Interactive Objects list at the bottom of the palette. In a complex document, this can help you quickly track down where crucial boxes are.

To preview, use the diagonal up arrow at the bottom left of the QuarkXPress screen. Note that previewing some of them from a print layout may cause unexpected results.

If you are familiar with web design, or even with creating animations in PowerPoint, most of the options will be self-explanatory.

360° image

If you have a correctly formatted set of images, this will allow you to load them, so that they automatically play a set number of times, and can then be navigated in a 360° fashion with the mouse or a finger. You can either create a set of images, or you can create a set of layouts in QuarkXPress.

Essentially what you have here is a mouse/pointer controlled section of graphics. If you have created a 360° sequence in external software, this will perform interactively or by autoplay exactly as you have seen these things on many websites. If you simply load a collection of images, you will have an apparently random set of images flashing up as you move the mouse: this can create its own unique effects.

QX does not overlay a 360° icon on the image: if you want that, then embed it in the image or create it as a separate item over the object. My personal view is that you are better off encouraging the user to play by some other means than such an icon, which (to me) ruins the effect.

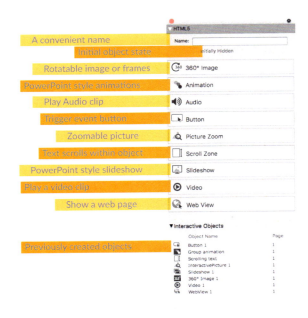

▶ To create a true 360° image, you need external software which will produce a series of blends: QuarkXPress's interactivity essentially allows the movements of the mouse to select an image. This is standard for this type of images, so most software should work correctly.

▶ When you select '+', you can add either prepared images, as above, or a series of QuarkXPress layouts, which mouse movements will then select.

Animation

The animation features should be familiar from PowerPoint animations, with options such as Fly in, Appear, Grow, Shrink and so on. You can set the animation to Auto Play, Allow Interaction, which means that the animation repeats when clicked, and to Hide at Start and End. Duration defaults at 5 seconds with 0 delay and play once. Be careful when setting Loop!

The Timelines offer various gradations, but if you want to control the animation exactly, choose Cubic Bézier which will allow you to set it the start, finish and intermediate speeds mathematically

Audio

Audio plays an audio file, either automatically or on-click, with or without a controller. It can play on loop or once through. Some devices do not necessarily grant access to the audio player, so check that this feature works on the target device if you need it.

Button

A Button initiates one or more actions. Actions possible include navigation, playing or pausing an object, playing or pausing a sound file or animation, resting the page, taking a snapshot, opening a file, displaying or hiding a pop-up, and showing or hiding an object.

It's important to realise that a button does not have to look like a button to be an effective part of a layout. Putting a cube on screen, for example, encourages someone to click different sides of it. Unlike other features, you can apply as many instances of a button as you need to the same object, allowing you to, for example, pause an object and go to a slide show at the same time, thus interrupting a running loop. If you use a button to show a pop-up, it creates a new layout. You will need to create a button on that layout to close it as well.

Picture Zoom

Picture Zoom allows the user to pan or zoom an image, or to do so automatically using the 'Ken Burns' effect.

Scroll Zone

This turns your object into a scrolling container for another layout. You can either select an existing layout or create one. The scrolling layout appears on the current page as if inside the scrolled box.

Slideshow

This presents a standard slideshow with several options. This is essentially a simplified PowerPoint style presentation, with fewer animation options than 'Animation'. However, it is convenient for scrolling through a series of pictures or QuarkXPress layouts.

Video

This makes the object a video controller, either with embedded content, or URL content, or YouTube/Vimeo.

Web View

This offers a browser view of a file, web-page, or embedded image. Web view means that you can effectively embed anything which is supported by web-browsers, including scripts and server-side functionality. You can embed the page, in which case you must ensure that ancillary files are present, or link to an external page. You can also include a static image for when the page is off-line.

Some assembly required

You can copy any print layout to digital layout using Layout>Duplicate, and you will get a functional HTML5, ePub and app layout, especially if you use Adaptive Scaling while duplicating.

However, if you want to create HTML5 publications and iOS or Android apps that feel like real apps, you will need to invest a significant amount of time testing and adjusting to get things which are 'just right'. When it comes to interactivity, anything but 'just right' is 'just wrong'. See File>Export>HTML5, iOS and Android for details of application-level interactivity. Note that your document is already interactive because of the Quark browser interface. That may be enough on its own.

◤There are eighteen different animation effects, but the most useful are appear, disappear, fade in and fade out. All the others have an affected look which jars with most designs.

◂Timelines can be complex, and you can enter mathematical formulae by clicking on the curve tool. The path can be set to match another animation object.
Animate To specifies the angle, scale and opacity of the final object, not the initial object.

◂Buttons offer the richest interactivity. As well as navigation, in the top two panels, buttons can also play objects and show and hide pop-ups. A pop-up can be a QuarkXPress layout, in which case you must create a Hide Pop-Up button on the new layout, or an image, for which QX creates its own scroll and hide controls.

Beware auto-hyperlinking
Some PDF readers try to make things that look like hyperlinks live. These are often wrong. You can use the Hyperlinks JavaScript to create true hyperlinks throughout a story.

16 Hyperlinks

The Hyperlinks palette organises URLs and anchors.

URLs, of course, come from the web. QuarkXPress supports http:, https:, ftp: and mailto:. Naturally, you can use any additional parameters supported by the software that executes the URL. For example, mailto: can include instructions for the subject line.

The icons across the top are new URL, new anchor, edit, and, delete. On the next row, you can opt to display or hide URLs, Anchors or Pages.

Pressing opens the *new hyperlink* dialogue. This allows you to create hyperlinks, link to existing Anchors or to Page links. Pressing allows you to create an Anchor where the text cursor currently is. This is the same as Style>Anchor>New. You can also create hyperlinks with Style>Hyperlink>New, but you can only create a page reference from in this palette.

Unlike Lists and Indexes, Anchors do not work across different projects in a Book.

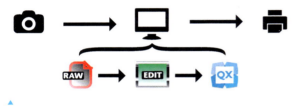

17 Image Editing

Production level image enhancement should be done as close to the output stage as possible. In the ideal workflow, images are captured at the highest possible quality in camera, and Raw Development is done in a specialist processor such as Capture One or DxO. Image Editing, which selectively changes the content of the image, if it is done at all (and this is generally not permitted in documentary photography) is done in an Editor, such as Photoshop or Affinity Photo, so that the image as commissioned and conceived is completed in its full resolution form. Production level enhancement, such as colour balancing to match other images, output sharpening and resampling, should be done after the layout is completed. Previously this required repeated round trips to Photoshop, but this is no longer necessary, because QuarkXPress, since QX2017, can handle these final stage edits non-destructively, meaning that extensive repurposing is relatively simple, and designers are no longer faced with managing multiple versions of the same file.

The effects are non-destructive, and they apply from the top of the palette to the bottom. You can move them up and down in relation to each other with the arrows ▲▼.

They are in two groups, Filters and Adjustments. You can also set the Transparency Blend Mode in this palette. Export opens up a new dialogue enabling you to export and reimport images with all their effects and resampling. The palette menu allows you to copy effects from one image to another.

Filters apply convolutions to the image. This means that, although you apply them across the entire image, the result depends on the context of the individual pixels. Adjustments change the colour values of the pixels without reference to the pixels surrounding them. By their nature, Filters are much more processor-intensive than Adjustments, and, for filters which have a Radius feature, such as Gaussian Blur and Unsharp Masking, the demands on the processor go up exponentially the wider the radius. For this reason, you can save the image, downsized if you like, with all of its effects applied and have it swapped for the image in use. This is not usually necessary, but if you are applying wide radius filters to several images, you may find your computer grinds to a halt. An alternative is to put your images in Composition Zones.

Note that the pixel values relate to the pixels in the image, not to the pixels at the final output resolution.

Filters

Despeckle

Despeckle is a relatively gentle noise reduction filter which removes some noise altogether and lowers the contrast of other noise. The easiest way to see what it does is to use Threshold on an image and then put Despeckle on afterwards. If you zoom into the place where the black Thresholded elements break up unto lots of dots, and then unapply and reapply Despeckle, you will see how some noise disappears entirely, and other noise is greyed so that it's less noticeable.

Despeckle works at the resolution of your image, not of your eyes. In other words, you might have quite a lot of what your eye sees as noise, but despeckle doesn't touch it because it is too large.

When to use despeckle? You will often want to add it as the penultimate filter in a chain, right before output sharpening. Aggressive use of curves, levels or other adjustments is liable to bring out previously invisible image noise.

Despeckling used to be applied to scanned images to deal with inevitable 'salt and pepper' noise. Although today's digital cameras are susceptible to noise at high ISO or in low light, the noise, once noticeable, is generally beyond the reach of Despeckle.

Despeckling has a very slight blurring effect. This should not normally be a problem for good resolution images.

Gaussian Blur

Gaussian Blur is a 'soft focus' blur, like looking at something through a matte screen, as opposed to the 'out-of-focus' blur which you get from lens bokeh. Gaussian blur looks more deliberate than out-of-focus blur, which only really works when there are in-focus elements juxtaposed with it.

In action, it's very simple: increasing the radius increases the blur. You can apply it to the picture, or, often more usefully, to the mask. Masks in supplied files are often not quite right. Blurring the mask has the effect of feathering it, giving a smoother transition, which is especially useful in compositing. Note that Quark only works on TIFF files for this—not on PSD files. You have to turn Alpha channel clipping off if you want to use this successfully.

Gaussian Blur is often an essential component in an effect chain.

Consider an image which has been supplied to you as a harsh black-and-white scan. In the example overleaf, taken from Wikimedia Commons, although the format supplied was PDF, the image was very clearly a bit-map. This produces exaggerated 'stepping' on the curves, as well as random lumps of noise. It is obvious that you can-

▲Image enlarged to 32 ppi in order to demonstrate noise effects.

▲Despeckle applied at the end of an image chain. This is a subtle effect, operating at 1 pixel and 2 pixel noise. Note how it smooths out some noise but retains some of the characteristics. Despeckle has relatively little effect on chromatic (colour) noise.

▼Gaussian blur on a 382 ppi image. Clockwise from top left: 0 pixels, 4 pixels, 8 pixels, 16 pixels.

▲Improving apparent image quality with Gaussian blur.

Unsharp unpacked
At Resolution/200 pixels, Unsharp masking is output sharpening. At Resolution/20 pixels, it improves the appearance of structure. At Resolution/5 pixels, it is a local contrast enhancer, similar to Tonemapping.

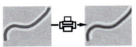

▲How Unsharp Masking works: a regular line is softened when reproduced as a halftone. Unsharp masking sandwiches a blurred version of the same line, which the eye interprets as sharpness.

▲Unsharp masking on a 382 ppi image. Clockwise from top left:
0 pixels, 4 pixels,
16 pixels, 64 pixels.

0	2
64	16

not gain a higher resolution from this image, but it is possible to give an appearance of a higher resolution by first softening the image with Gaussian Blur at 1 pixel radius, and then sharpening it with Unsharp Masking at 4 pixels. As a refinement, you can put a Gamma Correction (or Levels, or Curves) in between the two and this will enable you to make the strokes thicker or thinner. In many cases it may then be advantageous to reduce the overall opacity thereby restoring the idea of a drawing.

Unsharp Masking

Unsharp Masking is a darkroom-derived technique where an image which is not quite sharp can be made to appear sharper by sandwiching the negative against a copy of the negative which is very slightly blurry. This creates haloes around the elements—stronger haloes for stronger elements—which the eye reads as definition.

Unless you are very old, or very, very dedicated, chances are that you've never actually done this in a darkroom. However, the technique is employed in almost every properly processed image you will ever see.

By comparison with the 'sharpen' tool that you will have seen in image editing applications, which simply increases the contrast between adjacent pixels, unsharp masking produces sharpness without jaggedness, and without dramatic increase in noise. Unsharp masking does not refocus a blurry image—for that you need a true deconvolution filter such as FocusMagic.

In practice, photographers dedicated to getting the maximum out of their images have evolved a three stage sharpening process. Capture Sharpening, performed when the image is first developed from RAW, is typically 0.5 pixels and is used to overcome the inherent softness of a digital camera CCD which (except for some rare exceptions such as the Nikon D800-A) have anti-aliasing filters over the sensors which tend to soften everything. Even better than Capture Sharpening is applying a true deconvolution filter, such as Focus-Magic, Topaz Infocus, or DxO's proprietary filter.

Creative Sharpening is applied inside a photo editor, typically with a brush tool and quite possibly a Wacom or other pen.

Output Sharpening must be applied at the very end of the process, just before final export, at the final image size, and is usually 1/200 the image resolution at normal viewing distances, rounded down for regular images on glossy paper, or rounded up for very large images or images on matt or uncoated papers.

It's for Output Sharpening that we want QX's Unsharp Masking.

In terms of upgrades to the world of DTP, having Output Sharpening inside the DTP package is huge. In the past, images were either left as they were, which meant that they were always soft, or else they had to be resized in Photoshop to their final output size at 300 dpi, then Output Sharpened, then reimported into the DTP application. If you subsequently changed the size of the image, you had to resize again in Photoshop, re-Output Sharpen and reimport. Hard disks filled up with hundreds of versions of the same image, and junior designers invariably picked the wrong version.

For output sharpening, always put Unsharp Masking at the end of the chain, and base the calculations on the image resolution as reported by QuarkXPress. Output sharpening will do more to improve the apparent quality of your documents than almost any other process you can apply.

Important: check that there is not an additional output sharpening step being imposed by someone else later in the process. RIPs do not normally include output sharpening, but a helpful print shop operator may be sharpening everything that goes through pre-press as a 'value added service'.

Controls:

Amount—Leave this at 100% most of the time, though you can increase it for very low quality papers, and increase to about 130% if instead of CMYK halftone output you are outputting via stochastic rather than halftone rendering, such as with an inkjet roll printer.

Radius—For most output sharpening, use 1 or 2. If you dramatically increase the radius to, say, 60, you get a local contrast enhancement instead of sharpening. This is also very useful.

Threshold—The minimum contrast in pixels to trigger sharpening. Setting it to around 10 will reduce load on the computer, and also prevent unwarranted noise being added.

Find Edges

Find Edges is an effect which finds the high contrast borders between pixels and colours them. The result is a bit like an unflattering pencil drawing. However, if you make a copy of an image, and set the copy to Find Edges, Overlay at 20%, and place it exactly over the original image, you get a very clean, high-definition sharpening effect, which can be used in conjunction with unsharp masking. Increase the opacity of the overlay, and it will become progressively more cartoonish. At 60% you get a stylised photo-cartoon hybrid.

If you composite an image with Find Edges using Soft Light over the same image with Gaussian Blur, you get a better than usual imitation of a pen-and-ink illustration. This works best with a well-defined image.

If you then apply diffuse to the top image, you get a pointillistic image that is more defined than merely applying the diffuse filter on its own.

Solarize

Another effect from chemical photography, Solarize inverts all the pixels which are above the threshold value. The effect is also known as the Sabattier effect. It's named after what happens to film when it is drastically overexposed, for example when you pointed your Kodak Instamatic at the sun.

Solarisation can produce some dramatic and beautiful effects when used on landscape photography. However, this is, strictly speaking, not what Desk Top Publishing is about. If you want to edit photographs, go and do it in Photoshop. If you have an image which isn't quite good enough for your publication, then adding solarisation may temporarily persuade you to keep it, but it will not age well.

Where solarisation comes into its own in DTP is in constructing harmonious layouts. Imagine you have a beautiful landscape image

Capture sharpening and output sharpening. Note that extensive processing can soften an image even if it was sharp from the camera.

◀ Eyes slightly blurred (perhaps caused by overprocessing).

◀ Image as it came out of the camera.

◀ Slight deconvolution filter applied (FocusMagic).

◀ Best image with output sharpening applied.

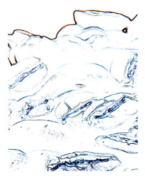

▲ Find edges is rarely a useful effect when used on its own.

▲ Find edges overlaid onto the base image at 50% transparency creates an alternative sense of sharpness, definition and brightness which is superior to unsharp masking for many types of image.

▼ Solarise

▼ Solarise, Colour Dodged onto the base image, has the effect of retaining the dark areas, but increasing saturation of colours in the light areas.

Palettes

▼ *Page spread harmony with solarise and Gaussian blur.*

filling one page, and you want a contrasting background for text on the facing page. If you place the same image on the facing page, solarise it with a threshold of 118, and then Gaussian blur it with a radius of 58, you will get a harmoniously contrasting graphic background which provides good secondary interest to your main image, but doesn't get in the way of the text. This is done in a few seconds. You would spend many hours getting to a similarly organic result attempting to create such a background image by other means.

If you run Solarize after Find Edges over a Gaussian blurred instance of the same image, with Soft Light, you get a craquelure or old oil-painting type result, although the shadows may disappoint.

Diffuse

Diffuse is an alternative to Gaussian blur which replaces the picture with similarly coloured grains, for a pointillistic effect which may remind you of Seurat. The general effect may be overwhelming, but if you set it to darken only or lighten only, you can add a strong sense of movement to an image.

The Radius range is 1–10.

At Radius 1, Normal, you get the Seurat effect.

At Radius 10, Normal, the result is a bit like a sandstorm.

At Radius 1, Lighten only, the picture will look like it has been printed on sugar paper

At Radius 10, Lighten only, particles of light seem to drip off a sunkissed image.

At Radius 1, Darken only, there is a slight sense of peering in the dark

At Radius 10, Darken only, a picture of ears of corn appears to be infested with mites.

The actual result is subject to the image resolution, and, of course, the image itself. As with Gaussian blur, you can apply to this to the image or to the mask.

Emboss

Embossing produces the familiar, and annoying, embossing effect, which is like watching a 3D film without 3D glasses. However, as with other effects, it is much more useful as a step in a wider process.

For example, if you pair it with a Gaussian Blur filter set to 2x the radius of Emboss, and have Overlay it onto another instance of the same image, it becomes a subtle (but highly welcome) local contrast enhancement filter.

You can pair it with Unsharp Masking to perform fairly radical surgery on an image which is too soft to be rescued by Unsharp Masking alone.

Embossing Effects

Embossing Effects does essentially the same thing as Embossing, but with fewer, more visual controls. Like embossing, it is most useful in combination with other effects and overlays over another instance of the same image.

▲ *Diffuse on a 382 ppi image. Clockwise from top left:*
0 pixels, 9 pixels Normal
9 pixels Lighten, 9 pixels Darken.

▼ *Using emboss to create local contrast.*
Left: original image
Right: Emboss settings as left, with Gaussian blur at 18 pixels, overlaid over the base image.

Note how the gloss on the lower bean comes through in the overlay version.

▼ *Emboss radius 18, angle 130, amount 400%.*

Edge Detection

Edge detection is similar to Find Edges, except that as well as providing a maximum contrast edge, it leaves the original coloured areas in black.

Use it as a screen at 30% of the original image to lighten it without loss of contrast, and to add edge definition. Overlay it for a powerful, contrasty, cartoon look.

There are two variations. Sobel puts halos above and below the image elements, whereas Prewitt tends to put them below. Sobel typically produces more, stronger lines.

You can use Edge Detection as a local contrast enhancement by compositing it with Difference over an image. The effect is subtly different from unsharp masking, and particularly suited for recovering contrast in over-smoothed areas.

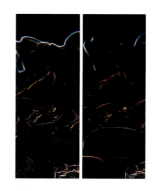

▲ Edge detection: Sobel ▲ Edge detection: Prewitt ▲ Original ▲ Sobel by Difference over original ▲ Prewitt by Difference over original

Trace Contour

Trace Contour traces around the dark elements of an image, filling them in black, based on the Levels control. It is similar to the Threshold adjustment, and, like it, it can be inverted. As with other filters in this group, use it as a basis for more sophisticated surgery on images. Multiplying it over a second copy of the same image produces a powerful cartoon-like effect.

With strong Gaussian blur, you can use it to introduce a shape into the layout which resembles the form of an image. As previously, this would work as a background on a facing page.

If you want to make things glow, Trace Contour can do it for you fairly easily. Composite a copy of your image using Screen mode, apply Trace Contour, Gaussian Blur and turn up the Gamma. To avoid the effect being ridiculous (effects are best applied subtly), turn the transparency down to about 30%.

▼ Original image. Note that the text on the yellow chair is not visible. 478 dpi ▼ Trace contour.

▼ Trace contour composited onto the original image with Multiply produces a powerful cartoon effect.

Add Noise

Add noise introduces any amount of noise from almost none to completely obscuring your image. In addition to the Amount control, you can choose Uniform or Gaussian, and select Monochromatic.

If you choose Monochromatic, then you can set different amounts to gently emulate photographic noise. Not using Monochromatic always looks to me like an analogue television which has gone wrong. I have never found a use for it.

Uniform or Gaussian produce different kinds of noise. Try either—it depends on your image which will be better.

Noise is so important that we could spend the rest of the book discussing it. Put Desaturate on after Add Noise and you get a classic black and white film look. Turn Monochromatic off and reduce to 1 pixels, and you get a very smooth, very tight look, like a magazine image from the 1960s. Overlay an image using Difference with noise on the top layer and 50% transparency and you get a cloth effect.

If an image is irredeemably unsharp, so that no amount of sharpening techniques can save it, you can often overcome the problem with a good quantity of noise, or possibly heavy unsharp masking followed by noise.

▼ Add noise: Uniform, 5 pixels ▼ Add noise: Uniform, 5 pixels monochromatic

▼ Add noise: Gaussian, 2 pixels ▼ Add noise: Gaussian, 2 pixels monochromatic

Palettes

▲ The chair image with added noise   ▲ Median 2 px   ▲ Median 10px

▶ Pantone 293 swatch for reference:

▼ Levels:
▬ straight from the camera
▬ highlights 'tucked in'
▬ highlights and lowlights tucked in.

Pantone 293

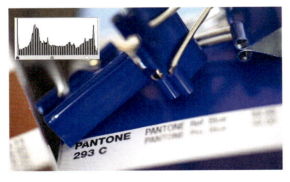

Median

Median is a softening routine like Gaussian blur. However, unlike Gaussian blur, it blurs things within themselves rather than spreading them, and it does so by averaging out the colour and luminosity values. Turning up the Gaussian blur eventually results in a uniform wash of colour across the entire image. Turning up Median results in something which is both blurry and distinct.

At lower values, Median is very good at cleaning up noise. You can pair it with unsharp masking to produce a 'smooth-sharpen' effect, which flatters many images.

Adjustments

Levels

The Levels control sets the black point, white point and midpoint for the image, and, optionally, restricts the output to a range.

If you are working with monochrome images, this is by far the most useful image control.

Channel—RGB/CMYK or Red/Green/Blue or Cyan/Magenta/Yellow/Black. Here you can choose whether to work on the entire image or just one channel. Normally you would work on all channels, which will be RGB or CMYK depending on your image (or greyscale, in which case there are no other channels). You would only choose to work on a particular channel either for a special effect, or because there is something fundamentally wrong with your image. However, in that case, you would generally be better off going to Curves, which offers more control.

Input Levels—This is the important setting. You'll see a curve, with a black marker, a grey marker and a white marker underneath it. The curve represents where in the range of values 0–256 the luminosity of your image lies. This curve will be different for every image, but if there is a gap at the left end or the right end, then the image isn't making full use of the tone available on the printed page.

For CMYK and web work, you will generally want to move the black and white markers so they touch the left and right ends of the curve. However, if you're working in mono for print, especially if the quality of the print is not particularly good, then you will get better results by 'tucking in' the markers (see example top of next page). This means you are losing some of the (largely invisible) difference between totally black and almost black, and totally white and almost white, but giving more space for the image critical mid-values. For mono print, it also helps to move the centre marker leftwards.

To help you see what you're doing, if you are working with a colour image for mono reproduction, use the 'desaturate' Adjustment to see what the result is.

Now, if your values are stacked up at the extreme left or the extreme right, this usually means the image is under- or over-exposed. You can fix this to some extent by moving the levels around, but if you have access to the original RAW file (assuming it's from a digital camera), then you should go back to this and re-develop the image in Capture One, DxO or whatever RAW developer you use.

116

Output Levels—You can restrict the range of values output by the file. This basically makes your image duller and less interesting. Personally speaking, I've almost never used this in print, but it can be important when preparing an HTML5 file which is going to be shown on a projection screen, where the intrinsic contrast is too high, and the whites tend to blow out.

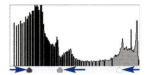

◀ Mono images benefit from more aggressive 'tucking in' of the highlights and the lowlights, but it's also worth moving the mid-point marker leftwards, which overcomes the inevitable darkening that comes from dot gain on most technologies.

Curves

Curves are like Levels, except that instead of just specifying the black point, white point and mid-point, you can set any number of specifications. Curves is set out as a graph of input and output values. The best way to understand this is to try it out. Load up an image, and then click on the curve. This creates a point. If you drag the point down, that part of the image becomes darker, if you drag it up, that part becomes lighter. The dark parts of the image are on the left, the light parts on the right.

Therefore, to increase the overall contrast of an image, lift the top right and drop the bottom left. To decrease the contrast, do the opposite.

▼ Curves:
- straight from the camera
- 'push process' curve
- gamma curve, darken

In the examples, a push-process curve brightens the highlights and darkens the shadows, equivalent to a more refined brightness/contrast, while a gamma curve can intensify the entire image.

You can work on all the channels of RGB/CMYK, or you can work on just one. This can help you remove a green, blue or red colour cast, or warm up the mid-tones by moving the centre of the red channel upwards, without compromising the highlights. Don't try to use Curves to fix a colour cast caused by bad lighting—use Hue/Saturation and Colour Balance for this.

As with other controls, curves enable you to manage the transfer characteristics when compositing two images. You can achieve a dramatic transfer with a highly pronounced push-pull curve on the upper image. This relies on the natural luminosity gradation of the image.

A different, and equally dramatic effect, can be achieved by colour dodgin with a strong darkening curve applied. Without this curve adjustment, the colour dodge composite would be so blown-out as to be unusable.

Entirely reversing the curve is the same as inverting the image using the Invert effect.

Brightness/Contrast

The oldest and most obvious image adjustment, from the days of CRT televisions, is brightness and contrast. The control is self-explanatory and easy to use, but if colour is critical, use levels, curves and the other controls.

In most cases, the Gamma adjustment will do everything you might want to do with brightness and contrast, but does so safely so you don't risk ruining the image. Brightness/Contrast can be a handy tool for managing other effects, including threshold and posterize.

Palettes

▲ *Cleaning up an image shot under mixed lighting. This image was shot in the Plantin-Moretus Museum, Antwerp, under a combination of fluorescent and incandescent light—not uncommon in public venues. Colour balance is ideal for this kind of work, because the different types of lighting will tend to act separately on the highlights and shadows. Afterwards, we applied a push-processing curve and output sharpening.*

▲ *Preserve Luminosity off. In most cases you will need to apply curves afterwards with this setting, but it gives more control.*

Colour Balance

Colour balance enables you to re-emphasise the colour channels based on highlights, midtones or shadows. They are in pairs of complementary colours, which, as it happens, correspond to print cyan versus screen red, print magenta versus screen green, and print yellow versus screen blue. There's an option to preserve luminosity so that the overall brightness of the picture is adjusted to compensate.

If you move the Cyan/Red slider to the right, the luminosity of the red channel goes up by about 25 levels out of 256. If you move it to the left, it goes down by about 25 levels. You'll notice that the Colour Levels indicator actually says '100' and '-100'. This represents 100% of the range of the control. If you want to go further than this, you'll need to use the Curves control. However, in most cases, the controls as given here are the most useful.

A word of warning. Unless both your monitor and your output process are very well calibrated against each other, you may well be creating rather than solving problems with this control. If colour output is critical, but you can't get the calibration right (my Colour LaserJet, for example, no matter how long I spend with the ColorMunki, never seems to get some things quite right), then the best thing to do is a series of test prints for your particular image, where you put it up next to the screen and then make small adjustments until the image is perfect. Any commercial output, such as a digital press, roll-printer or CMYK press, ought to be properly calibrated. If there are problems, check that your monitor isn't the cause of it. As always, calibrate regularly, and calibrate for the lighting conditions in your room.

▶ *The Hue/Saturation/Lightness model from the colour palette. In this model, Hue is the angle from the centre, starting at vertical which is green. Saturation is the distance from the centre, with 100% being the maximum, and Brightness or Lightness, set from the control on the right, is the percentage illumination, from 0 (black) to 100% (full illumination).*

▼ *Rotating the hue*

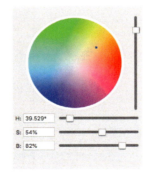

Hue/Saturation

Hue/Saturation and Lightness allow you to make adjustments as if you were using the HSB colour model. If you've never experimented with the HSB model, it's worth playing with it now in order to understand this control. To do so, go to the colours palette, click '+' for New, and select the HSB colour model. The wheel will be familiar. However, HSB assigns a percentage for each of Saturation and Brightness, and a value in degrees ° for the hue, which is the rotation round the circle. Play with it for a bit.

Now, back to this control. Saturation and Lightness do what you would expect them to do—in fact, within QuarkXPress, this is the best way of increasing or decreasing saturation, though, for maximum results, use the LAB colour method instead in an external editor.

The Hue control shifts the entire image around the circle by a number of degrees. Obviously you can use this to create weird and wonderful effects, but it is generally most useful when applied at, say -3° to remove the colour cast caused by photographs taken under fluorescent lighting when the camera white balance has not been correctly set. You would normally want to do this when RAW developing the image, but there are plenty of times when someone sends you an image with a greenish cast.

Selective Colour

Selective Colour works like colour balance, except that instead of operating on a range of tones based on their overall luminosity, you are operating on a range of tones based on their colour channel.

As with Selective Colour, you have sliders for Cyan, Magenta and Yellow, which also correspond to Red, Green and Blue (though, confusingly, this information is not included). You also have a slider for Black, which corresponds to the overall luminosity.

The colour groups you can work on correspond to the colour groups of RGB and CMY, with white, neutrals and black added.

Why is this tool here, when it seems to overlap the others? Essentially, this and Colour Balance are the surgical tools you need when you have an image which has been shot in mixed lighting, where you will have differing levels of colour contamination in various ranges. Mixed lighting is a mistake which ought to have been fixed before the photograph was taken. It is very hard to fix afterwards—of the main Raw developers, only DxO really makes a good fist of it, although a similar, more advanced, set of controls in Capture One mean that you can largely overcome it. Others, such as Lightroom, offer controls for selectively adjusting highlights and shadows.

Gamma

Gamma Correction moves the entire curve of luminosity in a particular way that is pleasing to the eye and produces generally good, consistent results. When you have an image which is just a bit too bright or a bit too dark, moving the Gamma with this control is generally the fastest and most reliable way of fixing it. Whenever you are tempted to use Brightness/Contrast, go to Gamma instead.

Gamma provides a powerful tool for managing image compositing.

To give a little background, gamma correction was a method of encoding a signal in the days of Cathode Ray Tube television so that the maximum amount of information was available at luminances where the eye discerns the greatest differences, recognising that a CRT was not a linear device. If the decoding gamma is the reciprocal of the encoding gamma—for example, 2.2 after encoding at 0.4545—then the result is that the final output is the same as the original input. Gamma encoding and decoding is still used by computer monitors and by colour spaces such as sRGB to enable the most efficient communication of relevant image information. RAW files, which include all the data captured by the camera, are not gamma encoded, which is why it is possible to recover vastly more data from them if the exposure is not correct.

Mathematically, gamma correction is a power law correction, where $V_{out}=V_{in}^{gamma}$. It closely resembles the way the eye perceives light.

For all these reasons, moving the gamma correction adjusts the entire image in a way which seems natural to us. It should be one of your first choices for making an image tonally balance better with the layout. You can achieve any gamma setting in Curves, above, including more extreme versions than possible with Gamma alone. Of course, you can also stack two instances of Gamma on top of each other in the same image.

▲ Cleaning up the image using selective colour. For this image, Colour Balance would be better, because the main issue is mixed lighting. However, if there were issues with the original image itself, for example fading over time, Selective Colour offers more precise control.

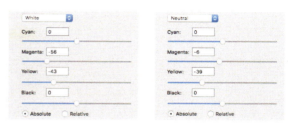

Colour temp	Source	Cast/tint/hue shift
1700 K	Sodium Vapour	3.4°
1850 K	Candle, sunrise	
2400 K	Incandescent	-
2700–3200 K	Fluorescent	4.3° – -11.9°
5000 K	Horizon daylight	
5500 K	Vertical daylight, flash	-0.3°
6500 K	Overcast	
15000 K +	Blue sky	

▲ Colour temperature and tint for common natural and artificial lighting. Note that Sodium Vapour and Fluorescent both have a significant tint, which comes out as a rotation of Hue. However, in mixed lighting you cannot simply correct this with an overall Hue-Saturation-Lightness control, because parts of the image will be affected differently because of their distance from light sources. Strong reflectors, such as blue, green or yellow tinted walls, will also have an effect.

▼ Gamma curves:
All of these curves look good, even though our examples cover the extremes of the Gamma range. If you did the same thing with brightness and contrast, most settings would be unuseable.

-100   -50   0   50   100

Palettes

▲▲*Original image*
▲*Colour balance followed by desaturate.*

▲▲*Desaturate only*
▲*Left image 'finalised' with levels and output sharpening.*

▼*In this version, Threshold is followed by Invert, and then Selective Colour, which allows us to colour what is now the white area any colour we like, while removing all the black from the black area. We composited this with Difference over an orange background.*

▼*Threshold can be used effectively on images with strong contrast, such as this which was originally shot to be used as a silhouette.*

▶*'Out of the box', Posterize produces fairly unappealing effects. Here, Gamma is used to control the image going into Posterize, set at 3 Levels, and the opposite Gamma is applied afterwards. This gives the overall feel of the image, but the result is noisy, so we apply Median at 7 pixels (1031 ppi image). Going up to 10 pixels would create an almost abstract, pop art image.*

Desaturate

Desaturate removes all of the colour values from your image, leaving only the monochrome image. If you put it after Selective Colour in the chain, it will respond to Colour Balance or Selective Colour's treatment of the colour image's values. In combination, this gives you good options in controlling the conversion from colour to mono. This is essentially reproducing the yellow, green or orange filters which black-and-white photographers used to put on their lenses to enhance particular kinds of contrast.

Desaturate has no options. If you are producing a document in mono, you don't need to desaturate every image individually, just turn on View>Proof Output>Greyscale and you will see how all the images are reproducing.

You would normally, therefore, use this to create a mono image in a colour document, or else to create a mono overlay on another image.

Invert

Invert creates a colour negative of your image. It has no options.

While the most obvious use of this is to create 'X-ray' type images (though, in fact, this isn't how X-ray images actually work), it can be very powerful when used in conjunction with Threshold, and also when preparing overlays.

Threshold

The threshold control assigns every pixel with a luminosity below the threshold to black, and every picture above to white. The result is a black-and-white (not merely monochrome) version of the image. For many images this will produce an unsightly scribble, but images that have intrinsically high contrast and clean lines will come out looking like drawings.

Threshold, along with Invert, is a crucial tool in Image Logic. You can combine the two to create masks to selectively adjust one part of an image while leaving the rest untouched.

Posterize

Posterization replaces shades of a colour with flat colour. It's called Posterization because, until CMYK print, colour posters had to be produced with bands of flat colour, and the number of colours had to be restricted to cut cost and production time.

The Levels control goes from 2–255, but '2' does not mean that there are just two flat colours in total.

In my experience, the most successful settings are between 3 and 5. At 2, everything looks like a cheap 1960s comic. After 12, it becomes hard to see the posterization effect—rather, everything just looks poorly done.

I usually put Selective Colour ahead of Posterize in the chain, so that I can control what colours are being affected in what way. 'Out of the box', posterize rarely produces a result that you will like—you need to help it with tonal controls going in, or going out, or both.

Using Posterize ahead of Threshold can help to control what Threshold does.

Export

The export icon ⤴ opens up a dialogue which lists all of the adjustments, filters and transformations used on the image. These can be previewed so that you can see the effects of turning on and off the various adjustments and filters and crop.

In terms of resolution, although the dialogue only offers 'downsample', you can also use it to upsample. This is fairly rudimentary, so upsampling is really only for quick fixes.

With a cropped image, you can export bleed. Turning off the crop greys out the Bleed setting. You can change Colour Mode and Format. However, in practice, only PDF-output supports other colour modes than RGB, so if you want to save as bitmap, greyscale or CMYK you have to change format to PDF. From PDF you can save RGB to any of the others.

You can overwrite the original (careful!), which automatically sets 'Link to New Picture'. Rather more safely, you can automatically Link to New Picture without overwriting.

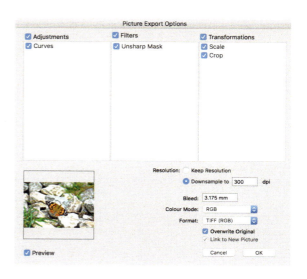

18 Index

The Index is a powerful tool that replaces a job which might—in a long document—previously have taken someone weeks or months. Even so, the Index is not automatic: it does not produce a concordance of everything in the file. Each word to be indexed must be selected once, and it may need to be cross-connected to linked words.

Further, although the Index can be built across an entire book, each chapter must have the index words selected in it.

Hands on with indexes

To begin, select a word in the text. It automatically appears in the Text box in the Index palette.

Before you can do anything with it, you need to add it to the index, so, from the row of icons just above the word Entries, you can choose either ▤ which adds that occurrence only, or ▤ which adds all occurrences in the current project (though not in the rest of a book). ▸ goes to the next occurrence. Adding all occurrences is usually the most convenient.

You can now mark the level at which the item occurs, and, optionally, specify that it should be sorted with a different term. You might do this if you wanted to sort typeface and fonts together. Let's assume we pick the word 'font' to index, and add 'typeface'. For level, we choose First Level for 'font', and Second Level for 'typeface'. Additionally, we enter 'font' in the Sort As box for 'typeface'.

It's now time to go to the menu in the top right hand corner, underneath the cog, and choose 'Build Index'.

For now, we will choose Nested, the default, Replace Existing Index, and also select Add Letter Headings, for which we will give the *Paragraph title* style sheet, which is one we have been using in this book.

▼ *Build index is accessed from the palette menu ⋮ of the Index palette or Utilities>Build Index. A Nested index can work on four levels, which appear as separate paragraphs. Run-in indexes put the second level on the same line as the first. Only Master pages which have automatic text boxes can be used for indexes.*

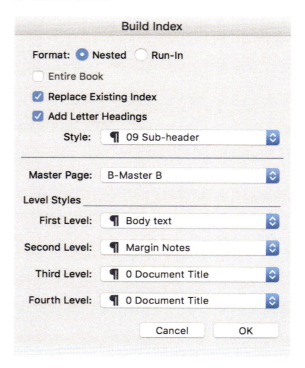

We will assign B-Master B as the Master Page—often we would construct a special index page Master Page—and choose level styles of *Body text*, which is the text you are reading, and *Margin text*, which is the style we have used for the margins. Choose OK.

The following appears (if we only have those two index entries defined), on a new page after the final document page.

F
font 153, 154, 170, 180, 183, 184, 194, 195, 199
typeface 192

The 'F' is the Letter Heading we added.

The 'font' entry has page numbers from this project only (we have not yet defined it in the other projects that make up this book). It is in the *Body text* style; 'typeface' has been sorted in with 'font', in the second level *Margin text*. On its own, this is sufficient to build a complete index, if you go through and identify all your key words. Every indexed entry is marked in the text with red markers ⌊-entry-⌋. You can set the marker colour in QuarkXPress>Preferences>Color Theme.

Going deeper
An **entry** can be one word or several. Each entry also has one or more **references**. It's important to keep this in mind, because otherwise the editing options make little sense.

The part of the palette marked 'Entry' refers to the overall keyword—or text, as it can be more than one word. To edit this text, click on the pencil icon ✎. Click it again to save the change.

The part of the palette marked 'Reference' refers to a specific occurrence of that Entry.

If you go to your entry in the list, and click on the triangle so that it points down, a list of all the actual page references will come up.

Click on one of these, and click edit ✎. You can now change the Reference's style, and also the Scope.

The default scope is the page number, but you can suppress the page number for that Reference, or you can extend it to any number of paragraphs, for example because you know that the index item introduces a twelve paragraph topic. You can also set the range to the end of the story or the layout. When you have finished, click pencil ✎ to apply it. The page number should change (or disappear). Click the pencil ✎ a couple more times if it doesn't.

Additionally, for a reference, you can point it to a different key word, using Cross-Reference.

Indexes can be nested or run-in. Nested indexes can go four levels deep, run-in just two levels, in the same paragraph. With nested, the paragraphs are separate. ↪ determines what levels ar available.

If you Opt/alt-click on the ⊞ or ⊞, it creates a reversed entry with a comma, so that William Caxton becomes Caxton, William. Set the punctuation used in Preferences>Index.

19 Item Styles

Item styles take some or all of the attributes of the selected box and create a style from them. Like paragraph and character styles, you can change all of the boxes of a particular style in one go subsequently, though if you have adjusted them, for example by reshaping, your changes are persistent.

Unlike paragraph styles, when you create a style from a box, only certain parameters will be copied—but you can copy all of them by Cmd/ctrl-clicking on the style or pressing pencil ✎ for edit. This opens up a tabbed dialogue.

Essentially, each of those tabs mirrors the parameters set in the equivalent Measurements panel tab. You can turn any of them on or off—they begin by being mostly off except where you have specifically set an attribute, for example in the Measurements panel. If you turn one on, it will take whatever parameter it can deduce from the box you are making it from.

If this sounds complicated, it's actually very simple in use. Make your box, set it up the way you want, click ✚ in the palette, and name your new box. If you prefer, you can base it on another box (which will override what you've specified for this box) and the box

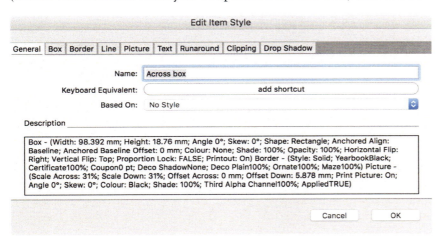

will update with its inherited settings when you change the other box. In this way, you can have a structured set of boxes which self-update as required.

This is a good way of managing a lot of common settings, such as standard insets for text boxes, a standard corner radius, setting images to be at 100%, or setting a particular offset for the image. You can even set the position of the box, for example with Item Styles for column 1, column 2 or column 3 which automatically places boxes correctly.

Cmd/ctrl-clicking brings up the Item Styles Edit list, where Item Styles can additionally be exported and imported.

Note that some settings override each other. For example, you cannot specify corner shape and corner radius.

You should also be aware that Item Styles do not cover Image Editing or Transparency settings. You can copy those separately in the Image Editing palette.

Why a computer-generated index is only the beginning

Computers are by their nature exhaustive. QuarkXPress can (and will) automatically search for every instance of a word. However, this produces data, not information. If you look at the index of a well-produced academic book from the 1940-70s, for example, FM Stenton's Anglo-Saxon England, you will see that the selection of indexed words is relatively streamlined, being almost entirely proper nouns. An example is:

> *Durham, 602; see of, 659, 660 n., 665, 666 n.; foundation of cathedral 435; monks introduced into, 678 […] bps of: see Æthelwine; Ealdhun; Walcher; William.*

However, this does not list every occurrence of the word 'Durham'. For minor figures, on the other hand, who are only mentioned in footnotes, all occurrences are given. The scope of the index changes with its content. While QuarkXPress will find all the occurrences and list them, it is for the editor to turn this into a true index.

▶ *Some of the item styles used in this book.*
Item styles operate the same set of parameters as Edit>Item Find/Change and the Eye-dropper tool ✐.

◀ *Item styles cover 90% of all the formatting not managed by Paragraph and Character styles.*

▼ *How the three key style palettes, Item, Paragraph and Character relate to the other styles.*

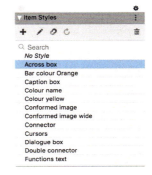

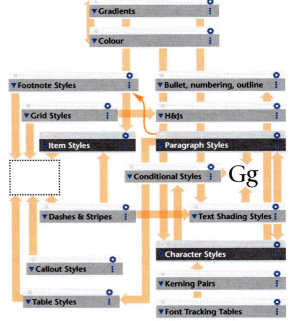

📄 *21: Text boxes in depth*

▶ My thanks to Matthias Guenther for contributing the JavaScript sections.

20 JavaScript

One of the key new features of QuarkXPress 2018, is scriptability using JavaScript. Though QuarkXPress had AppleScript support on Mac since v3, JavaScript has several advantages. First, it is cross platform. And second, as it is the programming language of the web, there are many people already knowing how to program JavaScript.

QuarkXPress 2018 is using ECMAScript 6+ (ES6+), which is a modern version of JavaScript. Advantages of using a modern version allow you to use modern constructs (lice classeS), built-in regular expressions (GREP) and the ability to use 3rd party frameworks and libraries.

Quark included the V8 JavaScript in QuarkXPress to handle JavaScript.

To manipulate QuarkXPress objects and layouts, JavaScript uses a Document Object Model (DOM). You can image a DOM like a tree structure of the document, containing all boxes and items and all content, including type properties. You can read about their attributes and modify them (write).

As the DOM of QuarkXPress (which is called QXML) is similar to the HTML DOM, which is how browsers construct documents, JavaScript programmers should have a low learning curve to learn the DOM of QuarkXPress.

Quark included many sample scripts with QX2018, for example to create a caption based on IPTC information of the image. Or to do a regular expression find/change (GREP). Or to sort paragraphs. And more. You can find more samples here: github.com/qxpjs/

All you need is a text editor, though using a code editor with syntax highlighting is probably easier. Quark recommends Visual Studio Code, which is free-of-charge and available for Mac and Windows:

code.visualstudio.com/

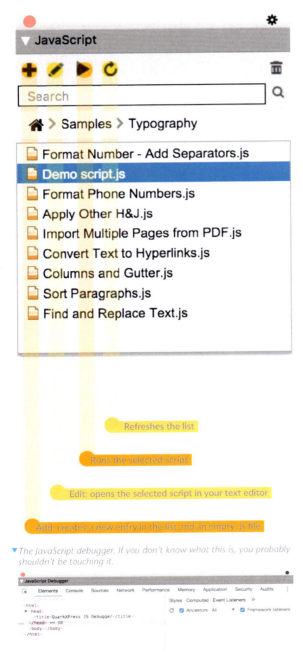

Refreshes the list

Runs the selected script

Edit: opens the selected script in your text editor

Add: creates a new entry in the list and an empty .js file

▼ The JavaScript debugger. If you don't know what this is, you probably shouldn't be touching it.

21 JavaScript Debugger

Troubleshooting a script can be difficult. For that Quark built-in Chromium, which gives you a familiar debugger. You might have seen the same in Google's Chrome browser.

If you are curious to see what the DOM of QuarkXPress looks like, open a document, open the JavaScript Debugger palette, go to console and enter *app.activeLayoutDOM()* (without quotation marks. You now see the object model of the current layout. Double-click the lines with arrows and you can drill down in the object model of the layout.

22 Layers

By default, objects in QuarkXPress stack over each other like pieces of paper and photographs pasted onto each other on a sheet of paper. Just as you would with a paste-up, you can move things to the front or back, or shuffle them up and down, but moving a lot of stuck together pictures and scraps of text is tedious and confusing.

Layers goes beyond that idea by allowing you to put things on different layers. You can make layers visible or invisible, printing or non-printing, locked or unlocked, and you can move things between layers.

As usual, the ✚ icon creates a new layer.

The diagonal down arrow icon moves the selected object to a different layer—once you press it, you then specify which layer it is.

The two-box icon merges layers.

Double-click on a layer to edit it. As well as locking, visibility and output, you can control whether text on a lower layer runs around an object on a higher layer, and set the colour and name of the layer. Visible layers are shown in the dialogue with the eye 👁 and locked layers with the padlock 🔒.

▲ Layer palette with palette menu. Double-clicking a layer opens a dialogue box.

23 Lists

Lists are automatically generated tables of contents and other similar lists, based on what style sheets are in use. They can be formatted to provide just a plain list, or a list with page numbers before or after. The lists are also structured, so you can have different levels, and different formatting for each level, or even for items based on a different style sheet within a level.

Lists can apply to the current layout, or to an entire book.

To create a list, choose the ✚ icon. The Edit List dialogue then appears. On the left of this dialogue you have a list of all your defined styles. On the right is a pane which is initially empty. Double click on a style to move it across, or use the arrow icons between the two panes.

Once inside the right hand pane, the style sheets will be listed in alphabetical order. However, this is not the order they will appear in the list. To set that, used the Level column, using the up/down arrow to increase or decrease the level, with 1 being the top level.

You can then number them text…Page#, Page#…text, or just text.

In the final column, you specify the style they are going to appear as. It's worth making a special Table of Contents (or ToC) style. When using page numbering, QuarkXPress inserts a single tab, which you can format using a paragraph style. Without formatting, the result will be haphazard.

Normally the items will appear in the order they are in the document, with whatever level styling you have set. Alternatively, you can have them appear in alphabetical order, for example for a glossary or gazetteer.

How layers work
A normal Quark document is like a collection of cut out pieces of paper laid on top of each other, which is the way that paste-up layout use to take place. Layers is like putting in glass sheets with artwork on each sheet.

▼ Artwork seen from the side, as if loosely laid on top.   ▲ Artwork as if cut out, placed and pasted, like manual layout.

▼ Using Layers is like placing artwork on glass plates, with collections of work on separate plates.

◀ The lists palette is not only where you create and manage lists, but also enables you to navigate around a complex document. Use 'Find' to locate an element in a heading. Double-click any line to be taken straight to that place in the document. You can have as many lists as you want, though you can only assign one of them at a time to be the Table of Contents for Kindle or ePub. Find this in the File>Export>ePub or Kindle options.

Palettes   125

▲ The Edit List dialogue box. Double-click a style in the left pane to add it to the list, or use the arrows. Double-click in the list to remove it. You can use both paragraph and character styles. Making an item second level indents it in the list display. If you want to indent it in the built list, create an indented paragraph style and assign it under 'Format As'.

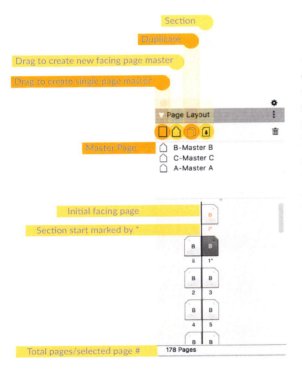

▼ If you want a page preview, use the ▲ arrow at the bottom of the screen, next to the magnification and page number. This will show a live preview horizontally of all the pages, which you can use to navigate the document.

Press OK.

Back in the lists palette, Update synchronises the list with the document. Build inserts the list into whichever text frame is currently selected. If none is selected, Build will be dimmed.

Lists are highly useful for a number of tasks.

As well as a table of contents, you can use a list of all headings to create the skeleton of a document summary.

You can also use lists to navigate round a document. Clicking on a list item in the palette will take you there.

If exporting for ePubs and Kindle, it is possible to set a list as the Table of Contents, rather than using the article names. This is useful if you have a book with chapters rather than separate articles.

You can list all the figures or illustrations as a separate list.

When working collaboratively on a document, you can set a style to mark sections for discussion, for example setting a highlight background. It is then a simple matter to provide a list of them.

Finally, lists can be layout-wide or book-wide, enabling you to keep a running list which encompasses separate chapters.

24 Page Layout

One of the oldest features in QuarkXPress—and among the most useful—is the Page Layout palette. Every page in the document is shown, and you can move the pages around, delete them or create new ones. Additionally, you access the Master Pages from here, and from them a number of options otherwise not available.

Clicking on the four icons at the top does nothing at all: you have to drag them. Normally you would drag them into the Master Pages area, but you can drag them onto the main, numbered page area if you prefer.

The flat sheet icon ▢ creates a blank non-facing page. The folded corner icon ⌂ creates a facing page—it will automatically change its margins in the layout if put on the left or the right to match the page margins.

The double sheet icon ▢ duplicates—but only in Master Pages. The down arrow icon ▢ creates a new section.

1 Master Pages

The power of Page Layout is in the Master Pages.

In a new document, A-Master A is created automatically. You can add other masters by dragging the single sheet ▢ or facing pages ⌂ icons into the Master Page area.

Double-click A-Master A to go to that page. If you have created a single side document, you are faced with just one page. If you have created a facing pages document, you will be looking at a double page spread. The margins will be whatever you set them to when creating the document.

After creating the document, it is only in Master Pages that you can change the document margins (with Page>Master Guides & Grid).

If Guides are not currently visible, press F7 to turn them on. You should now see your page margins.

Anything you put onto the Master Page will appear on every page you create using that Master Page. If you then edit that thing (box, guideline, etc), it becomes static and will not be updated, but if you leave it unedited, it will change with the Master Page. You can change this behaviour in Preferences>Print Layout>General.

You can use **Layers** on the Master Page, which is highly useful if you have a set of guidelines and boxes which you never want changed—for this, lock the layer—and others which are optional. If you are working on a shared project, you can also have an instructions layer, with output turned off, which the other users can switch on and off in the Layers palette as they work on the page.

Auto page insertion
On the Master Page, there is either a broken chain link or an unbroken one in the top left hand corner. This is on both pages of a spread. If the link is unbroken, it means that text that overflows from your main text box will automatically create a new page. If it is broken, this Auto page insertion is off. In a new document, this reflects the decision you made in the New Document Layout dialogue. Preferences>Print Layout>General is where you set the auto page behaviour.

You can use the **Link** tool to link a broken chain to any empty text box on the page, and this will then cause reflowing text to create new pages. You can use the **Unlink** tool to break this.

You can have any links on the page you want. For example, you can have the automatic text chain flow through as many boxes as you like. Equally, you can link another set of boxes together, though you can't have these auto-create new pages.

Content variables
Content variables are especially suited for use on a master page. These include page numbers, running headers, last page numbers (for the '37 of 82' page numbering format), modification date for document control purposes, output date and file name. Typographically speaking, the less extraneous matter there is in the headers and footers, the better. However, for many corporate and technical documents, version control is more critical than aesthetics.

Shared content
Shared content can also appear on master pages. A company logo may need to be consistent throughout a document. You can also use Shared Content for the document title or a version number in a header or footer. This may be a better solution than a Content Variable because you can then change it from any page, and they will all update together.

Master Guides & Grid
At other times greyed out, Page>Master Guides & Grid is active when you are working in a Master Page. It combines two things: the margin and column guides, using the same method which you used in the New Layout or New Project command, and the grid con-

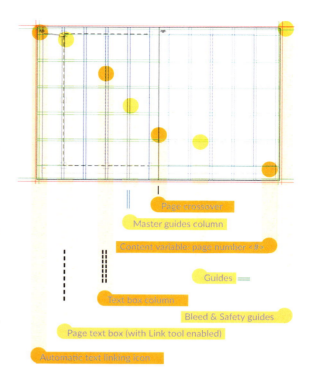

Ways to access Master pages
You can access Master Pages in three ways:
From the Page Layout palette.
From Page>Display.
From the bottom left of the screen, using the icon.

Turning on View>Highlight Content Variables enables you to spot the Content Variables when they appear in text.

Watch out with Content Variables: if you copy them from one document to another and they have nothing to refer to, Quark may become unstable and exporting may fail.

Grid tricks

If you have set up a page grid for boxes, you might be relaxed enough to let running type fall where it may, but want to avoid major titles falling just off a major grid position. You can set just the Section headings to conform to the grid, and a wide grid which conforms to your underlying layout grid, set in the Guides palette.

Equally, you can create a left page grid which prevents a chapter heading from ever appearing on it, forcing the chapter headings to always appear on the right page.

▶ *The Section dialogue, from the palette menu ⋮ or the ⊞ icon.*

Name only applies when exporting from a digital layout with a Designer Table of Contents.

Prefix can be up to four letters. Of course, you can have a much longer prefix on the page itself. You can set the starting number, and also the format as 1,2,3,4, I,II,III,IV, i, ii, iii, iv, a,b,c,d or A,B,C,D.

trols, which are similar to Window>Grid Styles. There are a couple of refinement here: for Margin Guides, you can lock the top and bottom and the left and right (or inside and outside). For Grids, there is an additional button for Adjust, and a button for Load Settings.

Adjust takes you to a new dialogue where you can nudge the settings and QuarkXPress will calculate the lines between the top and bottom margins that this produces, based on your Master Page size and margins, as set in the previous dialogue. If Preview is on (from the main dialogue), you can see these adjustments change as you nudge.

Load Settings allows you to load the settings from any other Master Page, any Paragraph Style, and any Grid Style.

2 Sections

A document can have several sections. To see the section, Ctrl/right-click on any page in the Page Layout view and choose Section, or go to the mini-menu ⋮ and choose Section.

Section Start allows you to specify this page as the start of a new section. This means that it begins a new numbering sequence, with, if you choose, its own prefix (eg, 'Page') and its own numbering system, such as '1,2,3' or 'A,B,C'.

From QX2017 onwards, you can now give a section its own name. This only affects digital output, and you use it in the export Options, Table of Contents. This allows you to specify a named section as a 'Designer' table of contents, where you create your own digital navigation. Otherwise, you can use it to remind yourself what the section is for.

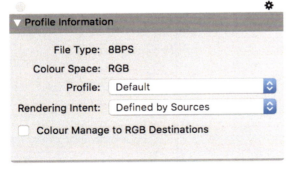

▲ *Profile Information gives you details of the file type, colour space, profile and rendering intent. Normally these are greyed out, as settings should be defined in the source image and interfering with them will cause unwanted colour shifts.*

▼ *You can turn on access to these profiles in Preferences>Print Layout>Colour Manager. You should normally only do this if you i) know what you're doing and ii) for some reason are unable to set the profile in the source application.*

25 Profile Information

The Profile Information palette offers some simple information about an image: bit depth and colour space. If you turn on colour management in the Preferences, then you can also set Profile and Rendering Intent here. Be careful: this should normally be set in the originating application, and you would only change it here if you know there is a problem in the origination.

For most images that have come from a camera, you will not want to change the settings unless somehow they have got lost or been incorrectly changed elsewhere. If the image was generated by software, for example 3D rendering or a natural media paint application, perhaps on a smart device, it may have no profile attached to it at all. In that case, the final RIP will let the values pass through—which, chances are, will not represent what was on the screen when the image was created. For normal work, if there is no profile, assign sRGB, unless you have the calibration for the monitor in which it was created.

Rendering intent is usually best left on Perceptual, unless there is a good reason to change it.

26 Redline

Redline offers a simple set of controls for tracking and highlighting changes, as you might find in a Tracked Changes Microsoft Word document.

To use it, you must turn Tracking on. This is in Utilities>Redline, or in this palette by with the Track Changes button, the left-most icon. Once on, you can turn Highlighting on (second icon) to see what changes there are. The next two icons move you backwards or forwards to the next change. You can then accept or reject changes, with a choice of all or current. The options button, at the end, allows you to specify what is highlighted based on the individual reviewer.

27 Reflow Tagging: See Articles

In QX2015–QX2017, Reflow Tagging sets the way that ePub and Kindle articles flow. From QX2018 this is now the Articles Palette, which also sets behaviour for Tagged PDF files.

28 Scale

The Scale palette, which replicates the Item>Scale dialogue, appears to be a simple tool to set scale, either as a percentage of the existing scale, or by typing absolute measurements. Underneath are calculations showing the original and scaled size, and a button which enables you to scale an entire layout (careful with this) rather than just a box. The measurements are normally connected by the chain icon, but if you click on this, you can rescale disproportionately.

It's only when you click on the palette menu, that you see the scale settings. This has been entirely revamped from QX2017 to reflect the settings in Adaptive Layout.

In addition to the settings, you also now have an 'increase size' and 'decrease size' feature in this menu, which acts as a nudge increase/decrease.

The scale (and adaptive layout) options are organised as General, for miscellaneous layout options such as margins and grids, then into Text/Picture/None, which deals with boxes with different kinds of content and is where you set synchronization, Table, which allows scaling of table size and grid, and Interactivity, which applies only to digital features. Generally the 'out of the box' settings are good, but when using this in Duplicate Layout, it is often better to turn on Synchronization if you will be editing content.

The only way to change the size of a Composition Zone, once one has been created, is to use this palette.

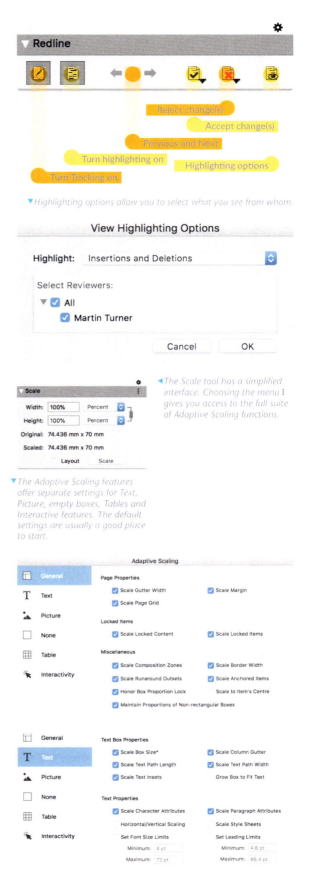

▼ Highlighting options allow you to select what you see from whom.

◀ The Scale tool has a simplified interface. Choosing the menu gives you access to the full suite of Adaptive Scaling functions.

▼ The Adaptive Scaling features offer separate settings for Text, Picture, empty boxes, Tables and Interactive features. The default settings are usually a good place to start.

29 Style Sheets

Paragraph and Character style sheets are critical to consistent typography. The actual controls in them are explained under the Measurements panel, Character and Paragraph tabs. This section will look at how the style sheets work, aside from the formatting aspects.

The palette itself is straightforward: ¶+ or A+ creates, respectively, new paragraph and character styles, the pencil ✎ edits, the ⊕ icon duplicates, ↻ updates the style to match the selected text (can have unwelcome effects), and the trash 🗑 deletes.

Option-clicking on a style marked with +, to indicate that the current text deviates from its style, restores the selection or paragraph to its styled state. Ctrl-click/right-click or using the corner menu offers a much broader range of choices for updating styles or text.

Cmd/ctrl-clicking opens up the Styles dialogue, which, in addition to the options here, allows styles to be imported with Append.

How styles work
When you create a paragraph style, a panel appears which contains:

Add shortcut allows you to create a shortcut key, such as F9 for Body text. This is useful when quickly formatting long text, and overrides defaults.

Based on is the style sheet that the new style sheet is going to follow. If based on 'Normal', then when you edit the Normal style, your new style will change as well, except for the things that you have altered from the normal style. If coming from digital, you will recognise this as the same concept as Cascading Style Sheets. This allows you to control all the typography of a document consistently.

Next Style specifies the style sheet that will automatically be applied when you press the return key while in that paragraph. For a title, for example, you might well want to have the next style Body Text rather than itself. Body Text, on the other hand, would want to be followed by more Body Text.

Character Style allows you to apply a previously defined character style sheet, make a new one, or, with 'default', just make some ad hoc changes that go with this paragraph style sheet. If you change your mind later and want a character style with that format, you can come back here and choose 'new'.

If you create a new Character Style, either here or directly from the menu, a panel opens up, and the first three lines are similar to what

Tagged PDF
New in QX2018, you can export Tagged PDF. You access this from File>Export>PDF>Options>Tagged PDF, but before you do this, you have to prepare the document. See the Articles Palette for tagging objects. You also need to set the Heading Style in the Paragraph styles.

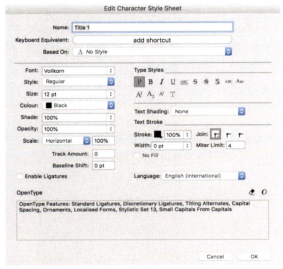

▲ The character styles replicate the same functions that are in the Measurements palette, Character tab. See that section for details.

▲ Text Shading is applied from the styles created in the Text Shading palette, rather than directly.

▼ OpenType Styles are accessed from the O icon. To reset them, use ⟲.

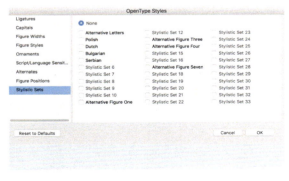

we just looked at: Keyboard Equivalent allows you to assign a key, and Based on allows you to follow another character style. Note that if you choose 'based on', any changes you had made to this dialogue will be replaced by what you are basing it on.

New in QX2018, you need to set a Heading Style for each paragraph style if you intend to output as Tagged PDF. The options are fairly simple: you have six levels of Headings and one Paragraph level.

The rest of this dialogue offers you controls which are in the Measurements>Character panel. Note that the language is set here, rather than on a document-wide or paragraph-wide basis. You can set the entire document language, or change one language into another (for example, US to International English while keeping French the same) with Utilities>Convert Project Language.

Changing the format

Reformatting is relatively straightforward. In Character Style, all of the controls appear in a single dialogue.

In Paragraph Styles, you have five panes. The first one, where you establish the paragraph style, we have already looked at in part. As well as the controls about what it is based on, what the next style is and what the character sheet is, it will show you a summary of what the paragraph style contains. In an unstructured paragraph style, where it is based only on defaults or an example paragraph, there will be a long list. For a structured paragraph, based on another style, it will show something like "Normal+Left Indent: 3mm".

If you want to streamline your document and maximise consistency, it is best to use structured paragraph styles as much as possible.

The next four tabbed panels are Formats, Tabs, Rules and Column Flow. See the Measurements Palette for information on these.

It is often better to use the Measurements: Paragraph, Tabs, Column flow and Rules to set those attributes, as you can see the effect as you work. Afterwards, update the style with ↻, or by ctrl/right-clicking on the style in the list to invoke the contextual menu.

Space Before/Space After versus Lock to Grid

Setting before and after spacing is a fundamentally different design aesthetic from working to a text grid.

Traditionally, narrative text was set with indented first lines and no extra space between lines. This is not consistently Renaissance practice, but it was well established in 20th century printing. Typewriters, though, often used a space between lines, being an extra carriage return. Word Processors followed this practice, with the default style usually expecting two hard returns instead of providing a first line indent. Web-based design—and the user interfaces of most software—use an improved version of the typewriter style, with a spacing between paragraphs which is more than the inter-line, but less than an extra hard-return.

Aesthetically, provided you don't use both at once, you will not be incorrect (there are Renaissance and medieval examples of using both, though).

▲The Formats panel replicates the settings in the Measurements palette Paragraph tab.
Note that from QX2017 onwards you can enter a percentage in the Leading.

▲Drop Caps increases the size of the first letter(s) and drops its baseline to match its line count, but it does not change the font. To create 'true' dropped caps, combine this with a Conditional Style.

▼The Tabs panel replicates the settings in the Measurements palette Tabs tab. It's generally easier to set these interactively from Measurements, especially if setting tabs at the right of the column.

▲Note that H&J options are substantially upgraded in QX2018. Use Edit>H&Js to specify the quality of hyphenation.

▲Text shading applies a style from the Text Shading palette.

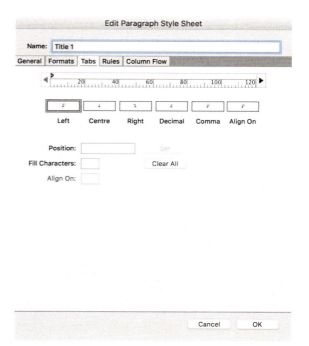

Palettes

131

Locking to Grid is the extreme version of the Swiss school of typography, which insists on identical frames on every page, and the text falling at exactly the same place on every page. This means that all baselines must fall in exact multiples, so there can be no smaller gaps between paragraphs. In other words, locking to Grid will override your *space before* and *space after* settings. This can cause the text to suddenly 'hop' if you have specified anything other than full grid lines in before or after, or have any text with different leading. On the other hand, if you are working with a number of different sizes of text, setting 'tight' with no additional leading and then relying on the grid to space the text correctly may be the most efficient solution.

What should you do? There is no doubting the beauty of a truly consistent grid layout. However, in the real world, you may be doing violence to your photographs (which are also the work of an artist) by forcing them into bad crops, and making nonsense of your charts and technical diagrams. Also, to web-accustomed eyes, the inter-paragraph spacing looks more natural.

The bottom line is that you should let the work dictate the form. Just be aware that switching from one to the other mid-job can create inconsistencies that will only come up occasionally, and will be hard to track down.

Widows and Orphans, With Next

A single line at the top of a page looks bad. Called an orphan, this, and widows, which are the less bad single lines at the end of a page, can be controlled with the 'Keep Lines Together' settings. Likewise, titles need to be immediately above the text they refer to, not widowed at the bottom of the previous page. For this, the 'Keep with Next' setting is perfect. If you combine the two, though, especially if you set all text in paragraph to be kept together, you can get into situations where all text suddenly disappears, because there are no conditions in which it can reflow correctly.

You may be confident that you will never allow this to happen. However, if you are working on a draft document in which you insert all the titles with the intention of returning later to put in the text, then this is exactly what is likely to happen. The moral is, if your text disappears, first check your *Keep Together* and *Keep with Next* settings. If that fails, you may have pasted in a table or box which is too big for its container, and will thus never reflow.

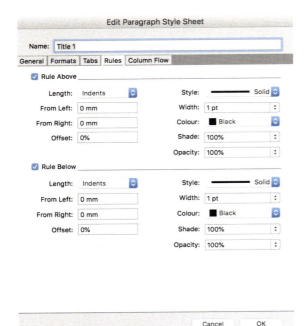

▲ The Rules panel replicates the controls in Measurements>Rules.

▲ Normally, Offset defaults to %, which is a percentage of the inter-paragraph spacing. Because space-above and space-below only apply when there is a paragraph above or below, this means that a rule will not apply at the start or end of the page. If you set an absolute value, eg 5mm, the rule does appear. You can also use this with a transparent rule to push the first paragraph down the page.

▼ Span/Split columns replicates the settings of Measurements>Column Flow.

30 Table Styles

For Inline Tables only—being tables which are edited in the source application, such as Excel, and then formatted by style in QuarkXPress—table styles offer a highly consistent and convenient solution to a vexing problem.

Tables have been in word processors and DTP applications for years, but they are never as convenient as working in a spreadsheet, where you can have an infinite number of new cells without having to think about making a new row and fitting the text in. Tables are most often supplied as Excel these days. Even if they are not, they can be rapidly imported into Excel.

When creating the table, you can set it to be linked with a style, as we saw in Tools: Table Tool. This is where you create and manage those styles.

The style palette itself is very simple: ⊞+ creates a new style, pencil ✎ edits it, ⊕ duplicates and trash 🗑 deletes.

It's when we create or edit a style that the complexity emerges.

Let's take a simple calendar example. This is a fairly common problem. There are lots of free templates for calendars in Excel available on the web. In principle we could just export one of them as a PDF file and convert to native objects, but the design on these files is usually terrible, and importing in this way breaks the link with the Excel file, which means that the data is no longer live.

In this example, we use the Table tool and choose Link to External Data. We need to specify A1:G11 as the range, and then choose 'Inline Table'. Pick 'Default style' for now.

The Excel file should import as plain text. We could otherwise import it with plain text, which would bring in the gaudy formatting.

We're going to create a very simple table style. New table style will open the Edit Table Style dialogue, which will have just one line: Default. Here we set the Text Style Sheet, and then go on to create an All Odd row with +. Here we add some above and below padding and a Bottom Grid Line. Finally, we add in All Even and put in some further padding. The result is as given at the top.

The Conditions stack from the bottom, with the higher Conditions overwriting the lower. All Even and All Odd are the simplest. You can also set 'Every' which allows you to format, skip a number of rows (or columns) and then format again, as well as Row#—Column#, which allows you to specify down to the level of single cells. You can also set Header Rows, as long as you specified these in the original import. If you realise that you should have done that, just delete the table and re-import, this time applying the style at the point of import.

Once you've created a table style, you can apply it to any number of Excel tables. You can update the table in Utilities>Usage>Tables whenever its data changes.

▲ This simple calendar is an Inline Table taken from Excel.

▼ The clean formatting is based on a very simple Table Style.

▼ The Excel file on which the table is based. This is characteristically overcomplex in its formatting.

7: Creating a calendar with tables and table styles

▶ Text shading styles can be applied as paragraph or text styles. This makes using them slightly easier than working from the Measurement palette, though it's often easier to develop the style using the Measurements interactively and then click + to add it.

▶ ¶ applies the style as a paragraph style, and A applies it as a text style. However, if you simply select text and click the style it will apply as character, and otherwise as paragraph.

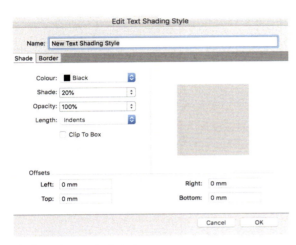

▲ Shading styles cover both shading and borders, but the styles themselves are not separated by Paragraph or Text type. You get a simple visual preview.

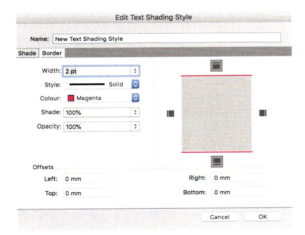

▶ The Welcome Screen is opened by default the first time you open QuarkXPress 2018. Arguably the most useful resource is the QuarkXPress Facebook group, which has a strong community of experienced users and QuarkXPress staff. It is usually the fastest way to get help on difficult issues.

31 Text Shading Styles

In QX2017, the Text Shading Styles palette enables you to create the styles which can then be selected from the Character Styles and Paragraph Styles dialogues, or applied directly.

The functionality is very nearly identical to the Measurements panel ✏ Text Shading tab, with one difference. In the Measurements panel, you specify whether the shading is to be applied to the paragraph or the selected text. This is not necessary in the styles panel. If you apply the style directly, it will apply Text mode if you have selected some text, or Paragraph mode if the cursor is on some text but you have not selected anything. When you attach text shading to a Character Style, it is always text mode, and when you apply it to a Paragraph Style, it is always paragraph mode.

QuarkXPress has for a long time included a custom underline function, but it has never been integrated into style sheets. This function is still there in QX2017, but in most cases you can use text shading instead, which can be integrated into paragraph of character styles. With some careful work in Conditional Styles, you can have underlining which elegantly breaks, or partially breaks, for descenders.

Note that you can set the colour in both shading and framing to 'none'. This is useful if you have a lot of highlighting in a document that you are using in the drafting process. You can simply switch the highlighting colour to 'none' at the point you want to export a public version, and then return to the highlighted document afterwards.

32 Welcome Screen

The Welcome Screen, Mac only, is a visual display that gives you an easy route to App Studio, Designpad (for iPad), the public Facebook page, Twitter feed, and also takes you straight to where the documentation is hidden on your drive.

27: Text stroking and framing

Menus

This section describes and comments on the Menus briefly. Where possible, it references explanations elsewhere.

1 QuarkXPress (Mac)

With the exception of Preferences (below), items in the Mac QuarkXPress menu are in the Help menu on Windows. Preferences on Windows are in the Edit menu.

About QuarkXPress—opens the About Screen which gives Licence Code, version number and build number. Tech support may want to know this.

Edit Licence Code—allows you to change your licence code.

Quark Cache Cleaner—if Quark has recently crashed, or you are having difficulties, the Cache Cleaner utility can delete the image cache and optionally delete the preferences. This was previously available only as a separate utility, but from QX2017 is integrated as a menu item. It closes QuarkXPress before acting.

Check for Updates—forces checking for updates now.

Quark Update Settings—goes to the settings for Quark Update, an external application.

▲ *Preferences dialogue*
▼ *The Preferences List*

1 Preferences (for Windows: Edit>Preferences)

The Preferences are extensive. Some refer to the project currently open, some to the application as a whole. If you want to make project-specific settings the default, close all documents and then make the changes. This also applies to all other menu items that are not greyed out when no document is open.

Display—sets the Pasteboard width, allows you to add the Pasteboard colour in Trim view to the colour theme (below), allows you to make Text boxes opaque during editing, and sets the computer monitor colour profile. Note that the pasteboard width can be decreased from 100%, but not increased.

Colour Theme—allows you to create new colour themes (Mac), redefining most of the interface. This does not affect your palette of print colours. In Windows you can select pre-defined colour themes. QX2017 introduced a new 'flat' colour theme for Mac, similar to the Windows theme. You can go back to the old theme, which has the old icons, if you prefer.

Key Shortcuts (Mac)—allows you to define any menu command, measurements palette command, text formatting command and some others with a particular shortcut key. It's helpful to have a couple of keys that you keep reassigning based on the task at hand. For example, on a Mac, Cmd-~ is an easy control to assign for combining boxes in a table, assigning a particular size when formatting boxes, and so on.

You can save your choices as sets.

Input Settings—selects the type of smart quotes and turns them on or off, sets the Page Range separators for specifying sequential and non-sequential pages (by default, '-' and ','), sets keyboard controlled drag-to-zoom, allows or disallows drag-and-drop text, and turns maintaining picture attributes on and off while importing. QX2017 introduced types of smart quotes, and smart dashes, converting -- to an em dash—.

Font Fallback—sets whether or not to fallback to other fonts if characters are not present, how far to search for an active font in that case, and which fonts to use per language if no active font with that character found. This only works for scripts that QuarkXPress knows about. If you enter the Runic character ᛝ (for Gandalf, or grand) and the current font does not support it, even specifying a fallback font that does support it will not work, as Runes are marked in Unicode as language: none. Also sets the slug line (text outside the registration marks giving file name, output date).

Open and Save—sets the all-important auto-save and auto-backup, and its location.

```
▼ Application
   Display
   Colour Theme
   Key Shortcuts
   Input Settings
   Font Fallback
   Open and Save
   XTension Manager
   Sharing
   Fonts
   East Asian
   Index
   Job Jackets
   Notes
   PDF
   Redline
   Spell Check
   Tables
   Fraction/Price
▼ Project
   General
▼ Print Layout
   General
   Measurements
   Paragraph
   Character
   ▼ Tools
      Item Tool
      Zoom Tool
      Content Tool
      Table Tool
   Guides & Grid
   Colour Manager
   Layers
```

5 and 6: Setting the Preferences

135

If you have deleted preferences because you are having trouble, make sure you go back to turn this on immediately—these are things that get you out of trouble. Also sets the auto-library save and whether to maintain its position, and (somewhat oddly) the script language for non-unicode support. QX2017 introduced an option to set the number of instances that Find/Change remembers. If you find these annoying and want to go back to classic QuarkXPress behaviour, set this to zero.

Xtension Manager—sets the behaviour of the Xtension manager, either always opening when QuarkXPress starts, when something changes, or when there's a problem. You can open the Xtension manager at any time in Utilities: Xtension Manager. Unlike Photoshop Plugins, which only activate when invoked—and may cause an instant hang—Xtensions are checked when QuarkXPress opens. The default behaviour is that the Xtension manager will then open if there has been an error. Typical errors would come from Xtensions which have not been updated to match a change in the Operating System, Xtensions that only work with older versions of QuarkXPress, Xtensions which have been damaged—for example when a component has accidentally been deleted or moved elsewhere—or Xtensions which are in conflict with each other. Where there is a problem, Quark will switch off the Xtension.

Sharing—this sets the defaults for Content sharing. If you share content via the Content palette, you will get access to these whenever you create new shared content. If you use the Content Sharing Tool (in the flyout menu from the graphic rectangle) then these defaults will be applied directly.

Fonts—this pane allows you to turn off font previews, as well as setting the behaviour when fonts are missing, along with the default replacement font. Although QuarkXPress is quite intelligent with its font replacement, you may want to consider FontExplorer Pro, Suitcase Fusion or some other font management utility.

QX2017 brought in a couple of important font enhancements—first, the font menu now remembers your most recently used fonts and puts them at the top. If you have a long list, option/alt-click it and the cursor will go right to the top. In this preference, you can set how many it remembers. Also, you no longer (necessarily) need a separate Xtension to install fonts 'on the fly'. This relies on the OS, so check that it works on your system. However, if you were thinking of paying to upgrade your font manager to include the latest Xtension to do this, you may not need to.

East Asian—this turns on the East Asian functionality. You will need to restart QuarkXPress for the changes to take effect.

Job Jackets—sets when Job Jackets are evaluated, and where they are stored by default. See Utilities>Job Jackets.

Notes—sets the attributes including colour and font for the sticky notes. The default is yellow, Arial. Use Item>Note>Insert to create a note.

PDF— sets the PDF workflow. If PDF creation is causing problems, you can increase the Virtual Memory. If that doesn't work, you can switch to exporting to a .PS file and distil later, either via Preview (Mac), Acrobat Professional or Callas PDF Tools. You can also set the default project naming and the error logging.

Redline—sets the colour and style of redlining. Unusually, this will be set from the print colour palette.

Spell Check—sets preferences for the spell checker, especially German, and for ignoring URLs and numbers.

Tables—allows anchored tables to break automatically. I would strongly recommend leaving this on. Turning it off could leave you with serious reflow problems.

Fractions/Price—sets how QuarkXPress constructs faux-fractions and prices. This does not affect the behaviour of true font-based fractions in Open Type.

Project
General—turns auto-picture import on or off, allows single layout mode to be turned on globally as the default, allows Open Type kerning to be turned off, and allows Multi-coloured Open Type Transformations to be turned on. Auto-picture import reimports modified files when the project is opened. This slows down opening, but speeds up exporting. Open Type kerning should nor-

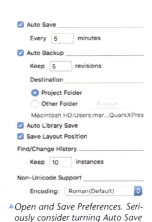

▲ Open and Save Preferences. Seriously consider turning Auto Save and Auto Backup on. This is also where you set the Find/Change behaviour.

▼ The sharing pane: This sets the default for new Shared Content from the Content palette. You can change these when you create the content.

mally be on. When using Chartwell fonts, Open Type Transformations should be on.

Print Layout

General—allows you 'Greek' text below a certain size and/or pictures. This may marginally speed up performance, but will degrade the look of the layouts on screen. It does not affect print or export. You can also recolour hyperlink display, set the behaviour of Master Pages, overriding page changes, set where automatic pages are inserted (or not), specify whether frames are inside or outside a box, turn auto-constrain on or off, and auto-justify for Chinese, Japanese and Korean (CJK) characters. Frames by default are inside a box, so reduce the imaged area of the box or the space available for text. Putting them outside means that boxes grow larger as the frames grow. If you find that new pages are not being automatically created when text overflows, it may be that this preference has been reset at some point.

Auto constrain is a neat little feature which is a real time saver if you need it. When you check Auto Constrain, every item you create and paste in the layout is constrained by the borders of a box stacked behind it, if those borders surround the borders of the new box. Every box you create automatically becomes capable of constraining another item.

If Auto constrain preference is checked and a box is active, items will be pasted in the center of the active box. For example, if a text box is active and you paste a picture box, the picture box will be pasted within the text and constrained to the centre of the text box.

Measurements—sets the units of measurement for the document. Also sets how many points per inch and the size of a cicero, and whether coordinates are page or spread relative. The reason for allowing the size of a point or cicero to be set is because historically, these have had different sizes in different countries.

Paragraph—this sets the auto-leading, normally at 20% but better at 30% for novels, allows maintained leading to be turned off, sets the way in which grid-locking takes place, if in use, and sets the hyphenation algorithm for all supported languages. Usually, the most advanced algorithm is the best one, but in case of problems, you can return to an earlier type.

Character—sets the defaults for superscript, subscript, superior and Small Caps when generated by QuarkXPress instead of true OpenType glyphs, along with options for ligatures, minimum kerning size, flex space width, cap accents and standard em space.

Tools

Item—sets the nudge increment. Opt/alt-nudging (ie, moving with the arrow keys) nudges by 1/10.

Zoom— sets the minimum zoom, maximum, and increment. The increment is especially useful if exact 1:1 representation on your monitor is an odd amount, such as 155%.

Content tool—sets the behaviour of the Content tool to create or select boxes.

Table tool—sets the defaults for the Table tool and allows you to turn off the dialogue on creation. If you intended to create numerous identical tables, you could set the defaults here and turn off the dialogue. You cannot link to external data or create inline tables as part of these default settings.

Guides and Grid—sets the snap distance for guides, their colour, and whether they are in front of or behind content. You can also set the page grid visibility (ie, the size at which it appears and disappears), whether it is in front of or behind content, and, potentially, in front of or behind the Guides. Normally, the Guides are in front of content and the page grid is behind. If you find the snap to guides distance annoying, here is where to reduce or enlarge it.

Colour Manager—defaults for low-level colour management decisions. You would not normally need to change these. The proofing options can be set directly from View>Proof Output. Colour management of EPS and Vector files is now on by default (this is different from previous versions). This is where you can turn on editing in the Profile Information palette.

Layers—sets the defaults for new layers. You can change these in the Layouts palette.

▲ *Measurements is a preference you will want to change early on. Note that there are a number of marginally different specifications for units such as Ciceros and Points. QX uses the most common ones, but you may need to vary this.*

▼ *Auto Page Insertion is in Print Layout>General. If your pages are not automatically being added, look here first.*

▼ *Note that borders can be inside or outside.*

▼ *The character preference pane allows you to set values for Quark-made 'faux' superscript, subscript and small caps. Note that these will never be as good as true OpenType variants.*

▼▼ *Flex Space width allows you to compromise with people who prefer a wider space after a full stop. To do this, change double-spaces to Flexible Spaces from Utilities>Insert Character when you run your clean-up script after importing text.*

2 File

1 New Project

New, or Cmd/ctrl-N, creates a new project, opening the New Project dialogue box. This is visually identical to the Layout>Layout Properties dialogue, but Margin Guides and Column Guides and Facing Pages on/off can be set here, whereas they can only be viewed in Layout Properties.

Layout Name—this will be incorporated in PDF export default naming (subject to Preferences>PDF, see above), and will appear on printer slugs.

Layout Type—print or digital. All previous digital versions are now wrapped up in a single digital layout type.

Single Layout Mode—this removes the layout tabs from the interface. Essentially Single Layout Mode saves around 7mm of screen space. You can still add another layout using Layout—New, which then switches multi-layout back on again.

Page

Size—offers the most common presets, and a New option which allows you to add your own. You can also create layout specifications in Job Jackets, which offer many more refinements.

Width, **Height**—the width and height.

Orientation—swaps between narrower than height (portrait) and wider than height (landscape).

Page Count—how many pages to create initially. Leave as 1 if using Automatic Text Box.

Easier in QX2018
Previously, you could duplicate a print layout to digital, but not the other way round. You can now start with either type of layout and duplicate it with linked content and adaptive scaling in either direction, from Layout>Duplicate.

Looking for Bleed and Safety?
In QuarkXPress, you set bleed at the point of output, in the File>Export>PDF options. If you want bleed and safety guidelines, use the Guides palette in Window>Guides. Choose bleed and safety guides from the palette menu ⋮.

Facing pages, allow odd pages on left—sets the document as a facing or single page document. You can change the 'allow odd pages' setting in Layout Properties.

Margin Guides—Top, Bottom, Left, Right, or Inside, Outside for facing pages. To edit

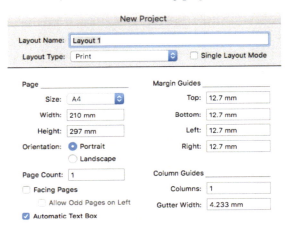

these later, you need to be in Master Pages and go to Page>Master Guides and Grid.

Column guides—sets the number of columns and gutter width. Also only adjustable later from Master Pages, Page>Master Guides and Grid.

2 New Project from Ticket

Project from Ticket opens the list of previously defined JDF Job Jackets tickets, and enables one to be selected to create the new project file. See Utilities>Job Jackets for information on how these are created and managed. A Job Jacket can contain styles, rules for job evaluation, paper sizes and language resources, and many other resources.

▼ *To create a new project from a Job Jacket, use New Project from Ticket. If you are using it simply as a template, turn Share Jacket off. If you are using it to manage a suite of documents which will all share the same brand and typography, then leave it on.*

3 New Project from IDML

IDML is Adobe's InDesign cross-version format. From QX2018, you can import IDML files from with InDesign CS5 or later, including Adobe CC. Not all features are supported, and you are likely to see at least some text reflow. Nonetheless, it means that you can now directly access a wide range of files directly. Consider Markzware's transfer service if exact equivalence is critical, or import a PDF and convert to native objects.

11: Job jackets explained

4 New Library

A library file is a collection of graphics and text which can be used at any time. Libraries are independent of projects, so you can have the same library file for numerous projects. Equally, you can open two or more libraries and drag items between them.

To put an item in the library, drag it there. To use it, drag it from the library onto the layout. To delete it, Cmd-backspace/ctrl-delete. If you double-click a library item, you can give it a label. Any label you give it will join a list of labels that appears when you do this. You can therefore use a label to uniquely name or describe a library item, or to label a whole category of library items.

Libraries store links to files, just as QuarkXPress does, except where the file does not have a separate existence—for example because you pasted it onto the layout—in which case it will be stored in the library in addition to being stored in QuarkXPress. Ordinary graphic files update in the same way that project graphics do.

Libraries save when you close them, unless you have turned Auto-Save on in the Preferences.

▲ *A library file stores Quark objects, which can contain graphics or text, or be vector shapes. All the attributes of the objects, such as fill and image editing, are retained. You can move content variables from one document to another through libraries, but watch out: if the content variable has nothing to refer to in the new document, it will cause problems.*

5 New Book

This creates a new book, which combines a group of projects into a consecutively page-numbered publication which can be indexed, listed, printed and exported as if it were a single document. See the Book palette section for more information.

6 Open, Open Recent

This opens a QuarkXPress project, book or library file. You can open project files from QuarkXPress version 7 or up. There is a free document converter available on the Quark.com website to convert versions 3-6 to current formats. This also does batch conversions.

QuarkXPress has a number of problem-solving routines which are automatically applied on open. It will come up with the dialogue 'This project requires minor repairs'. Normally you should let it go ahead and do them. The project will not open until the repairs are made.

If Quark quit unexpectedly while working on a document, it will offer to restore an auto-backup. This does not overwrite the saved version until you save it.

Open Recent shows a list of recent files, for convenience.

If things go wrong

If QuarkXPress crashes while you are working on a document, it saves a copy of the file in the Quark Rescue folder, usually on your desktop. You can open this with File>Open.

QX also creates a folder, usually in Documents, called Quark_Backup. This will be a different version from the one at the point of the crash, and may be successful where the other fails.

Always ensure that you have an automatic backup system in place. You can turn on Saving of extra versions and auto-save in the Preferences (see above). If you are saving to a Drop-Box or similar managed drive, you may not need to save additional versions, as Dropbox will do that for you.

If QuarkXPress or your entire machine should crash, you may need to Delete Preferences using Quark Cache Cleaner.

The bottom line is that no matter how well managed your system is, unexpected issues will occur. If you don't have a system of backups in place, you will at some point lose data.

7 Close Window

This closes the currently open window, like clicking on the close window button. If the current window is the only window open for the project, QuarkXPress will offer to save it, if unsaved, and close the project.

8 Save, Save As

Saves the project. If you have backups turned on in the Preferences, saving first renames the existing version of the file as a backup, and then saves the current version. I strongly recommend having this turned on: if something goes wrong while saving—power outage, system hang, Quark error—you will still have a properly saved file.

Save As saves with a new file name.

9 Save a copy as/Downsave

Downsaves to QX2017.

10 Revert to Saved

Reverts to the most recent saved version.

Menus

11 Import

Imports text or graphics, depending on the type of box selected. If no box is selected, it will create a new box depending on your imported file.

Graphics:
QuarkXPress will import JPEG, TIFF, PSD, and PNG images, and EPS, AI, PDF, vectors. Xtensions may be available to import other formats.

It will also import a chart from an XLSX Excel file—however, it will come across as an image file. To import Excel charts as vectors (much better), either copy them via the clipboard and Edit>Paste as Native Objects, or save as PDF in Excel and import the PDF, which can be converted to native objects if you want to work on the styling (which you usually would).

For PDF files, you can specify which page to import for a multi-page document. You can't change this later without reimporting. You can also specify whether to import using the bounding box, the media box, etc. For most files this will make no difference—experiment if the result isn't what you were expecting.

For all types of graphics, a summary of information is given underneath the file list. This includes size, resolution, format, colour depth and date. You can choose whether or not to maintain the attributes of the box you are importing into. The default for this is set in the Preferences—Input Settings.

Text:
QuarkXPress imports plain text, Word Docx (but not legacy Doc), HTML, RTF and Xpress Tags XTG, which is a special Quark format highly suitable for constructing with a database such as FileMaker Pro for automating publishing.

All text imports offer smart quote conversion, which, usually, is worth leaving on.

Xpress Tags offers to interpret Xpress Tags, which should usually be on unless you want to display the tags themselves for the purposes of writing a book like this one.

Word import brings in footnotes and formatting, but only graphics which are anchored in the text. To bring in other Word graphics, you can copy them, and Paste as Native Objects, although Word often sends its graphics as images, which is unhelpful, or PDF the Word file, import the relevant pages, and then Style>Convert to Native Objects, which will bring them in as vectors for editing. From QX2017, you can choose whether to bring in Footnotes as Quark footnotes, or as static text.

Word also has an option to import styles. Be very careful before you choose this! A typical Word document may contain dozens or even hundreds of styles, as Word adds styles on the fly when tables are formatted.

If any of the styles you are importing have the same name as styles in your document, you will be shown the Style Conflict box, which allows you to Replace, Use New, Auto-Rename or Use Existing. Styles not in the project already will be added to the styles list. Even if they are the 'correct' styles, they will not be structured, so changing Normal will not then change all the styles that are similar to Normal.

The best workflow—in my opinion—if you know that a Word document has been carefully tagged with the right styles, and you want to follow the original structure, is to create a new document and import it into that. Then rename the styles in that document to match those you have already defined in your main project, File>Save Text as Xpress Tags and reimport. You will be shown the Style Sheet Conflict again, but this time choose 'Use Existing', and select 'Repeat for all conflicts'. In this way, all of the structure of the document will be imported fully formatted, but it will be in clean QuarkXPress typography.

12 Save Text

You can save text in any of the supported formats—Docx, HTML, RTF, Xpress Tags and plain text. Only the text is saved, not the layout. If you want to create a Word version of the entire document—some clients want this—then export as PDF and convert in Acrobat Professional.

XTG format
XPress Tags is a special format which allows QuarkXPress to tag text with paragraph and character styles, and a variety of other formatting options. The easiest way to start working with XTG files is to save text as XTG and use this as a template.

42: Importing from Word and 49: XPress Tags

13 Append

Append lets you add styles, colours etc to your project from another project. It does not allow you to import text or graphics, though you can import a layout, which is highly useful. The dialogue will ask you which you wish to import. This may generate the Style Conflict dialogue if the items have the same names as ones in your current document. You can set default styles for all future documents by doing this when no document is open.

14 Export As

Export allows you to export the project as PDF, an iOS app, Android app, as an HTML5 publication, as an Article, as ePub or as Kindle. It also allows you to export the current page as an EPS or image, or the current box as an image. This is especially useful if you have a lot of pasted images and want to slim down your QuarkXPress project while also making the images available in other documents. From QX2017 you can also export images from the Image Editing palette, which provides more options.

PDF

The PDF engine for QX2018 is entirely different from previous versions, and now uses Callas technology. This means you can now export Tagged PDF.

When you export to PDF, you are offered a list of presets, an options button, and an option to open the job in your default PDF viewer once the export is complete.

The presets have been carefully constructed to industry specifications such as those of the Ghent group. Generally speaking, pick the Press option for sending to a print house. Slightly confusingly, the 'Print' option is for sending to someone to print on an office laser printer. PDF/X options are for verification to particular industry standards.

Although you generally don't need to work with them, we will now look at the Options.

Page—turns on spreads, allows you to send every page as a separate PDF, includes blank pages, and embeds a colour or mono thumbnail. All of these options are off by default and in the presets. Including blank pages is liable to prompt a telephone call from your print house—why are we printing a blank page? I personally detest 'this page intentionally left blank', but there should at least be a page number, otherwise, the chances are that it will go missing at some point and the spreads of your layout will suffer.

Metadata—up to QX2017, this allows you to enter Title, Subject, Author and Keywords. From QX2018, all the metadata is managed in one place, in Layout>Metadata. In earlier versions, the title of the Layout is automatically loaded. The rest you have to specify yourself if you want it included, for example if you are going to upload the document. Up to QX2017, the data is not copied over from Layout>eBook Metadata.

Hyperlinks—irrelevant to output for printers, but highly useful for document sharing, the hyperlinks panel sets which links are included in the PDF, and how they are presented. By default, links and indexes are exported as clickable links, and lists are exported as bookmarks (also becoming clickable links when they appear in a table of contents). If you have several lists, some of which were just to help you navigate round the document in draft, you might want to specify just one list. By default, hyperlinks are invisible, which makes the PDF file represent the printed version best.

This panel also allows you to set the appearance of hyperlinks, offering borders and highlights. Visually, these are useful but unattractive, and it's generally better to create a specific style within the document if you want users to know where the hyperlinks are, though, these days, most users will expect to click things that look like they refer to other things.

Do not be taken in by the fact that Acrobat and some other readers identify hyperlinks in the document and live-link them. This is haphazard at best. If you are importing from Word, you can set hyperlinks to be automatically brought in. Otherwise, run the supplied JavaScript: Convert Text to Hyperlinks. This will create proper QuarkXPress Hyperlinks which will appear in the Hyperlinks palette.

This option pane also sets the default zoom.

▲ The PDF Export options. Normally, you would want to either work with the predefined presets, or else create your own presets to ensure that you are consistently complying with requirements.

▼ The panels list for PDF export options. Tagged PDF is a new feature in QX2018. Metadata is now in Layout>Metadata.

Pages
Hyperlinks
Tagged PDF
Compression
Colour
Fonts
Registration Marks
Bleed
Transparency
JDF
Layers
Notes
Redline
Summary

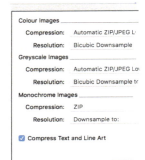

▲Compression Warning! 'Low' compression means high quality, high compression means low quality. If you are used to software that offers 'high' for quality, then you may find yourself making the images steadily worse as you try to increase the quality. Downsampling to 300 dpi is right for most work. Subsampling up to 300 dpi is rarely going to produce a good result if 300 dpi is required. However, many images will reproduce well as low as 200 dpi.

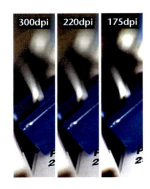

▲Composite workflow leaves decisions about separation as late in the process as possible, so that profile conversions take place only once. Instead of setting the inks in Quark based on a profile, QuarkXPress sends the raw CMYK numbers along with the profile. The RIP sets the final inks based on this and the output device's own profile. If working without a RIP direct to an output device, use Print and select individual plates.

Compression—this sets the compression for colour, greyscale and black and white images, as well as compression for Text and Line art. Important: the compression controls do exactly what they say—compress. Therefore, 'Zip/JPEG low' means that low compression is used, and therefore high quality. This is the opposite of the Quality setting that many applications have for JPEGs, where 'high' means low compression.

This option also allows downsampling of images. Generally speaking, use the defaults for this that come with the presets. If you don't select a default, the images will not be downsampled, which may mean you have a file of several gigabytes: far too big to email, and occupying a large amount of disk real estate. The default for press is 300 dpi with bi-cubic sampling.

Colours—this sets how colours in your document are exported. Note that these are the colours used. Unused colours which are in your palette will not appear. Also, this is not synchronised with your View>Proof Output settings, although the same settings are on offer, including any that you have defined via Edit>Color Setups>Output.

As a general rule, the Composite workflow is now preferred, though a pre-press or print house may specify In-RIP separations. When you send Composite, the RIP settings will determine how the separations are made. The key is to set out clearly in your job specification what process you are expecting, eg, CMYK + 1 spot colour. If the print house can't separate what they need from your file, they will tell you. The Press preset is for CMYK. You will need to change this to CMYK plus spot if you want additional spot plates.

For printing Pantone Extended Gamut (XGC) colours, which allow up to 95%[1] reproduction of Pantone PMS colours using CMYK + two of Orange, Green, Violet plates, consult your printer about how they should be output. 50% of printers in the USA are expected to offer Extended Gamut by 2020.

Fonts—normally you should *select all*. Some fonts have copyright restrictions on them and will not embed in a PDF. QuarkXPress will warn you of that when you try to export, and the rogue fonts will be unchecked in this dialogue. You have a couple of choices here. If the text is example text, such as Lucida Casual earlier in this book, you can use Item>Convert Text to Boxes>Anchored, and then use Find/Change with Ignore Attributes switched off to track down any phantom text, such as spaces.

Alternatively, you can look for another version of the font which has embedding allowed—embedding restrictions are often a mark of a pirated font. Certainly any font you have actually paid for should allow you to make a PDF. You might go back to the font vendor and ask either for your money back, or for an unlocked version. It is somewhat possible that a font is in the public domain, with a Creative Commons free-to-edit licence, but has embedding turned off—possibly due to user error earlier. If the font is genuinely public domain, you can go into FontLab or another font editor and re-export with embedding allowed. However, it is worth doing just a bit of research first. A number of so-called public domain fonts are in fact copyrighted fonts which some poorly advised individual has chosen to make public. Sometimes, people specify 'non-commercial use only' and disallow embedding because they have heard that this gets round copyright. It doesn't. If in doubt, set the text in a different font, or find the 'real' version and pay for it.

Registration Marks—these will be on by default in the Press preset. You can have them set centred or off-centre, if, for some reason, a layout element is going to get in the way. However, you would generally be better advised to not have any element protrude beyond the bleed area (or turn on 'clip at bleed' in the next box. You can additionally include Bleed Marks. This could be important if you have a nervous printer who wants to know if there is supposed to be bleed on something. On the other hand, having the registration marks, which include the crop marks, should tell them that you know what you're doing.

Bleed—bleed can either be symmetric, typically at 3.175mm, which is the press settings default, or asymmetric, for whatever complicated reason you've agreed with your printer, or 'page items' which is the same as 'off'. If you are using press preset but there is no bleed in your publication, it might be worth turning this off, though most imposition software is clever enough to work out what to do either way. Turning on 'clip at bleed edge' is a good idea, again, unless there is some complicated and agreed reason not to.

Transparency—this sets both the transparency and also the rendering of images in vectors, blends and drop shadows, as well as upsampling rotations. Normally, the presets will sort this out for you, but there can be problems.

First, QuarkXPress normally exports transparency natively in imported PDF and AI files. This is fine, unless there is a transparency problem with the file, in which case flattening transparency should preserve the look of the file, using the flattening resolution at the bottom of the screen. However, if that causes QuarkXPress to quit unexpectedly, or produces an error, then the file problem is one that even Quark can't solve. You could go back to the application that created the document, but that isn't always possible. The best bet would be to convert to native objects, but if the file is in a very poor state, that might not work either. The last resort is to turn transparency for imported PDFs off entirely. This will affect all the PDFs in the document, but it might not actually look much different—applications that are cavalier in how they handle transparency may have it on by accident, and without function.

Resolution of Vector Images and Blends should be fine at 300 dpi for the press preset. Because shadows (by definition) contain no sharp lines, 150 dpi is sufficient. However, some pre-flighters will flag up any file at 150dpi as an error, and your printer will tell you that you've prepared the file wrong. There is no point arguing. Change the drop shadow resolution to 300 dpi and resend the file.

Transparency will be off for PDF/X-3 verified documents, as the standard doesn't support them. X-4 allows transparency.

By default, image rotations are upsampled to 300 dpi for images less than 225 dpi. You can only turn this off or change it when flattening transparency.

JDF—this allows you to include a Job Jacket JDF, and, optionally, the name of the contact. This streamlines the process if your print house has a JDF workflow, provided that you are yourself working to a Job Jacket. See Utilities>Job Jackets.

Layers—this allows you to select which layers to print, and tells you what plates are needed for those layers. It reads from your Layers palette. If you make changes here and check 'Apply to layers' it will write those changes back to your layers palette. Otherwise, they will be retained when you export to PDF until changed.

Notes—Includes your Notes from Item>Note in the PDF. Useful for client approval, highly embarrassing if left on during final export for print, or if you've left unflattering internal comments about the client on them.

Redline—allows you to include changes marked up according to your Redline settings. Again, good for client approval, not good for final export.

Summary—this contains no settings, but is a useful sanity check that your file is as intended.

As well as using the presets, you can make your own. This is highly useful for organising your own internal and client-facing workflows, as well as for providing files just the way your print house wants them.

EPS

This exports single pages or spreads as EPS files. The options are essentially the same as for PDF, except that you are given Preview options, as an EPS file usually contains a preview. You can choose Tiff or none, set the data to be ASCII, clean-8 bit or binary, exclude the page background from the output, and output a spread. You can save the options as an Output Style, which you can manage from Edit>Output Styles. Generally speaking, the defaults will work without problems. Note that EPS files cannot contain transparencies, so the default is to flatten everything. There is an option to ignore this: it may well enable you to transmit EPS transparencies to some applications such as Illustrator, but it will not produce true portable EPS files. The Advanced options allow you to choose PostScript Level 3 or 2. Only choose 2 if you know you will be outputting to very old equipment.

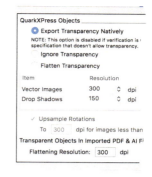

▲ *For preference, export transparency natively for print output. However, be aware that Apple's Preview and some other PDF viewers do not support transparency blends. Therefore, if exporting to share a PDF for electronic viewing, you need to flatten transparency if you are using transparency blend modes. You can either do this directly in QuarkXPress, or through Callas PDF Tools or Acrobat Professional.*

Composition Zones
When you convert Composition Zones to picture, the format it creates is EPS. Since EPS does not support transparency, doing this flattens transparency for a single item. It does so in the CMYK colour space, enabling you to mix RGB and CMYK transparency blends in the same document.

Image blurring
Outputting an image that contains text over a transparency blend will pixellate the text.
Item>Composition Zones>Create followed immediately by Item>Composition Zones>Convert to Picture fixes this, although it will interpret the blends in the CMYK colour space.

Image

This allows you to output to JPEG or PNG, either as pages or the selection, and can include page guides and text grids, which is often useful. Options cannot be managed as Output styles, but they are persistent.

HTML5 Publication

HTML5 output has continued to improve in each version since it was introduced in QX2016. Layouts are now fully responsive, causing the browser to automatically select the correct layout for the device in use. You must still create a separate layout for each target device, exactly as you would if designing a native Android or iOS app, but QuarkXPress will now insert the correct JavaScript for the browser to seamlessly choose the right one.

You can save HTML5 output styles. You can save these from the Options in the output dialogue, and manage them from Edit>Output Styles.

There are new options in QX2018 for reader controls, with transitions: slide, fade and none.

Many options can be set from within QuarkXPress that were originally hard-coded.

Pictures—sets the default resolution and maximum resolution and dimensions.

▲ Creating a section title for a designer Table of Contents

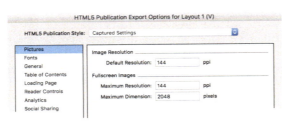

Fonts—a simple confirmation that you wish to collect fonts, and a warning about 'faux' fonts. Note that Open Type special features are supported from QX2018.

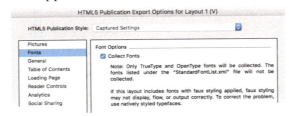

Page Stacks—this (rather nicely) allows you to have the sections as the 'pages', and the pages within the sections as scroll-down windows. As this can be disorientating, you can lock the orientation in desktop and mobile devices respectively.

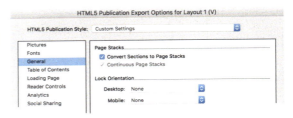

Table of Contents—you can opt to have a 'designer' table of contents page, which is a separate named section (from the Page Layout palette). This is essentially any design you want which links to the various pages. You can optionally give this its own banner name.

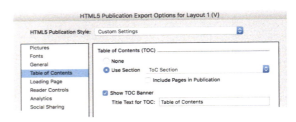

Loading Page options—this allows you to set the background, text colour, and, crucially, the loading page icon, so that it doesn't default to the QuarkXPress icon.

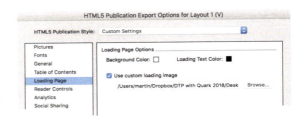

Reader Controls—this allows you to turn off various reader features that may be superfluous based on your design. For an en-

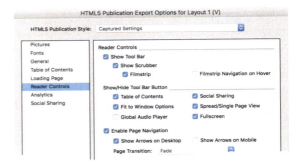

tirely web-like appearance, turn everything off. For a book-like appearance, leave things on. From QX2018 you can set the transitions between slides.

Analytics—lets you turn on Google Analytics using your Tracking ID, and also set Geolocation. You need a Google tracking ID and an API key to do this.

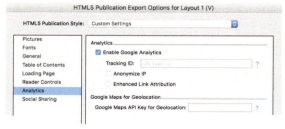

Social Sharing—allows you to specify a Facebook App ID, and turn on or off Twitter, LinkedIn and Email sharing.

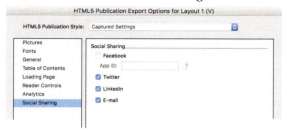

You Export directly from the bottom status line, as well as previewing your HTML5 output locally in your browser. From QX2018 there is a new addition to the 🌐 preview: ▼. This now allows you to select a page preview, layout preview or full project preview.

> **What digital format?**
> Apps have a tremendous allure, but the reality is that the vast majority of apps in Apple and Google's stores are almost never downloaded. If there is not a clear demand for your app, then you are going to a lot of work for little benefit.
> An HTML5 publication is not as smooth as a true app, and subject to the connection speed of the device accessing it, but it is much easier to get someone to visit a website (which is what it is) than to download an app. If you want to sell an App, it may be worth offering the functionality for free as HTML5 in order to create interest.
> Fixed format Kindle and ePUB can technically support some animations and HTML5 features, but the results are sporadic: you need to test every device to which you are deploying. Fixed format is better suited to giving an eBook equivalent of a print layout.
> By far the most distributable format is PDF. If you want to monetise content and distribute it, flow-format Kindle or ePub will not do favours to your design, but they do allow you to reach the maximum audience.

iOS and Android apps

QX2017 introduced ad-hoc publication of iOS Apps, and QX2018 extends this to Android Apps.

There are essentially three steps to creating either kind of App, but most of step three is outside QuarkXPress.

Step one is creating a digital layout, exactly as you would for an HTML5 publication, using the HTML5 palette to add interactions and animations. You need to create a separate layout for each vertical and horizontal orientation of each size of device you are going to support. It's possible to lock to just one orientation, but you must do this explicitly.

Step two is setting the export options. These are a subset of the HTML5 export options. Essentially, this is Picture, Fonts, General and Table of Contents.

Step three, which only appears when you press 'continue' after passing the export options, takes you to the authorisation and other information you need for the app to appear in the Apple App Store or Android stores.

To create an iOS App, you need to register with Apple as an App Developer, which costs around $90 a year, depending on where you are. This allows you to create a number of certificates. QuarkXPress tells you what those certificates are in the output settings, but you must work through Apple's relatively complicated site in order to obtain these and download them. iOS App output will not work at all without these certificates.

The same is true, though slightly less complicated, for Android Apps.

Check the help and documentation provided by Apple and Google.

You also need to provide graphics for splash screens and links to help pages and other information.

Once you have provided this information, press continue and your files are uploaded to Quark to be processed. An internet connection is required. This will take perhaps as much as 20 minutes if nothing has gone wrong. The ℹ️ icon will tell you its progress. If the app is not successful, go back and check your settings.

What next with HTML5 output?

You can preview HTML5 on your computer using the 🌐 icon, but you cannot open up the files Export produces on your local computer and preview the publication. It can only be run on a web server.

To try out the site, upload it via FTP to an FTP server. If this is too technical, contact your Internet Service Provider or Webhost for help.

If your FTP software supports folder synchronisation, you can set it to synchronise with the output folder on your local system. This will substantially reduce load time.

It's worth holding off on uploading your files until you are completely ready, because most web servers involve some kind of caching or mirroring, which means it can take some time for your changes to be live.

Fixed layout or flow layout?

You create fixed layout ePubs and Kindles in a Digital Layout. Reflow type (the original format) can be created from either layout.

Fixed layout is extremely easy: design your document as you would for print, but in the digital layout. Export it. Done. Reflow layout requires you to first tag the document. See the Articles palette for more details.

Reflow layout takes more work to set up, and the results are less attractive. So why not just stick with fixed layout? Classic Kindle readers, which are by far the most popular, can only read Reflow type Kindles. Generally speaking, if your layout can survive Reflow format, it's a better choice.

ePub, Kindle

These two output formats share a similar set of options. To export for Kindle, you must download Amazon's free Kindle Gen application. You set the Metadata for eBooks, Kindles and tagged PDF in Layout> Metadata. Reflow format eBooks and Kindles can be created in either type of layout, print or digital. See the Articles palette for more information on Reflow eBooks and Kindles.

To create fixed layout Kindle or ePub output, you must be in a digital layout. Most often you will be creating such a document as a print layout first. To convert it, go to Layout>Duplicate, choose Digital as the type, and decide whether or not to set Adaptive Scaling, which is similar to the Scale palette, but with additional options for Shared Content, which is helpful if you want to continue to edit the two documents in sync with each other. If you have a long book to duplicate, this will take a long time! Allow at least twenty minutes for a book the size of this one. The more memory you can free up before you start, the better.

Once you have your digital layout, you are ready to export fixed layout straight away.

At the point of export, you choose Reflow or Fixed Layout. This option will not appear from a Print layout, as only Reflow is exportable from there.

The options are:

Pictures—Overrides Default Settings to render images at a higher or lower resolution, in a different format or quality.

Text—Exports Dropped cap as native (default) or ignore. QuarkXpress now supports native dropped caps, but it is possible that some ePub or Kindle readers do not. Experiment to see what works.

Table of Contents—Enables you to use a List as the Table of Contents, to change the name of the cover in the Table of Contents, and to change the name of the Table of Contents. If you are publishing a novel, there may be only one article, which is the main text. By default, Kindles and ePubs would include solely that article as the only item in the Table of Contents. If you have a List of the chapters, this would be much better. You can select any one list as the table of contents. QuarkXPress is dependent on Amazon's KindleGen to create Kindle Mobi files directly.

East Asian—options for setting East Asian text.

Page Layout—sets how footnotes are exported and whether page layout is automatic, portrait or landscape for fixed layout, with spread options.

Miscellaneous—for the ePub option only, allows you to target Windows readers or iBooks, Kindle and universal readers.

Watch out!

When you export for Kindle or ePub using flow layout, QX will ask if you want to export fonts. You need copyright permission to do so, which you will have if your fonts predate separate permissions and allow all uses, or if you paid for the eBook rights. However, even when you do this, there is no guarantee that Amazon's Kindle processing system will honour them. In one book we were working on, dingbat fonts previewed fine when exported for test on a local Kindle device, but when passed through Amazon's system, they had reverted to plain text. Always test on each device you intend to deploy to!

Further thoughts

When preparing an ePub or Kindle publication, look at what is already on the market. Consider whether all the elements in the print edition should be included. For example, if you are using a List for the Table of Contents (good) it would be odd to have a Table of Contents separately in the document. Consider whether some elements would be better linked together. Where there is frequent opportunity for linking, it may overcomplicate matters to do so. Should you include the Index? It can autolink, but, given that you can search in ePub and Kindle, does it make sense? Also check where you have page references. These *will* work in fixed layouts, but make no sense in Reflow Kindles, as the pages are entirely notional.

Article

This publishes the selected story as a Quark Copy Desk QCD article. These files are for use with Quark Copy Desk, an external editor for QuarkXPress article. You can import them into QuarkXPress, which can be helpful in collaboration.

15 Collect for Output

Traditionally, the way to send files to print houses from QuarkXPress was by collecting for output. This meant that all the files arrived at the printer's, and any problems could be fixed there. This is no longer standard practice: print houses now generally expect you to send PDF files, and there are less opportunities for error when you do.

Collect for Output is still an option, but it is more suited to creating off-site backups, for example on DropBox, than communicating with a print house.

Essentially, Collect for Output saves a selection or all of the files necessary to work with your Quark project on a different computer, provided that it has a copy of QuarkXPress 2018. This includes not only the Quark file, but also colour profiles, fonts, pictures, and a report saying what should be included. The report is in Xpress Tags format, and can be imported into a Quark document for reading—this in itself is a useful tool if you want to see what all your style sheets are doing.

In my workflow, if I'm working with a key client on an important document—potentially an official submission with hard deadlines and enormous ramifications if they are not met—I will Collect for Output to Dropbox prior to leaving the house, with or without my MacBook Pro. I then send the client a link to the Dropbox folder, with instructions to download the 3-day trial version of QuarkXPress should I get knocked over by a bus. (I'm not being morbid—this is actually a standard expression in organisational resilience). If my laptop gets stolen, the house goes up in smoke, or I lose my memory and am found wandering in Scotland with no knowledge of my own name, the client can still open the document and finalise it.

However, I haven't sent a client a QuarkXPress collect for output since 2001. Print houses no longer all keep the same versions of the software (QuarkXPress 3.32 was the version people used for years), and they no longer expect to make final changes on behalf of the client.

This reflects the dramatic change in technology. We used to take files to printers on Syquest Drives and Zip Drives, or send them over ISDN. It might take hours or days to get a new version of a file to the print house if an error was detected. PDF was nowhere near ready for print workflows, and most printers would not accept them. During the 1990s, I frequently used to drive from Belgium to Holland with a laptop and a .ps Postscript output file, and drag the document through the imagesetter myself (I worked for a charity and the printer was sympathetic enough to allow me to image and develop the films after hours, at reduced cost). My first use of QuarkXPress was when I found an error on the films and quickly had to open Quark for the first time on their Macs (we were Windows Ventura-based) and output a tiny box of text to the Agfa imagesetter, and subsequently stick it onto the film with blue tape, having first removed the offending original text with a scalpel—those were the days. But I digress.

These days, a composite PDF for an entire book can be emailed and on the RIP within twenty minutes. Corrections made by the design team are likely to be more reliable than those made by the printer's assistant anyway. There is less work at the other end, which cuts down cost, and leaves less chance of error. File sizes can be a few megabytes, because the PDFs are fully optimised for press. Things can still go wrong, but it is less likely, and easier to fix.

Technically, it is a breach of copyright to send the font files, even if the print house deletes them afterwards (and, seriously, did print houses ever do that?) In an increasingly litigious society, it isn't worth the risk. Collect for Output is still important, but not for those reasons.

16 Job Jackets

See Utilities>Job Jackets for a discussion on what they are and why they are important.

Link Project—this links a job ticket to a project. A list appears of available tickets to attach, or you can browse files. When linked, project resources become available, and editable.

Modify Job Ticket—this allows you to make certain modifications to the current job tickets.

▶Evaluate Layout enables you to check the layout against all the specifications in the Job Description, and also optionally add further rules relating to various aspects of Boxes, Text, Lines, Paths, Pictures and Fonts. Rules can be as specific as identifying text boxes with a rotation, or a fractional point size.

▶Running an evaluation either produces a green tick to show that the test is satisfied, or a number showing how many failures there were. You can then go to Show Case to view them.

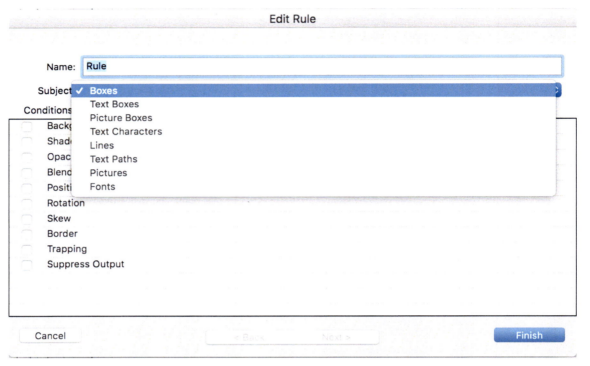

Evaluate Layout—this allows you to set rules and run a pre-flight to check that your publication is compliant. You can set Preferences>Job Jackets to force evaluation of the document at particular times.

You can create rules which impose minimum text sizes, reject indexed colours, GIFs, or pictures enlarged above 100%, unprintable shades or colours, and many other formal issues with files which would not prevent them from printing, but would produce unacceptable results. See Utilities>Job Jackets for more information.

17 Print

The Print dialogue is by far the most complex thing in QuarkXPress. However, it is relatively easy to manage and, with a couple of exceptions we will look at here, the settings are identical to the PDF Export options above.

Main Dialogue

The main print dialogue has four panels. The main panel changes as different panes are selected.

At the top is the physical printing machine which you installed through your Mac or Windows system. You can use this setting to switch between installed printers.

Underneath is the Print Style setting. By default, this is 'Captured Settings', which means any edits you have made. If you press Print, these are stored with the document. If you've made changes but aren't yet ready to print, you capture them with Capture Settings at the bottom.

However, once you have made the basic settings, you would do well to use this box to save as an Output Style. This will also ap-

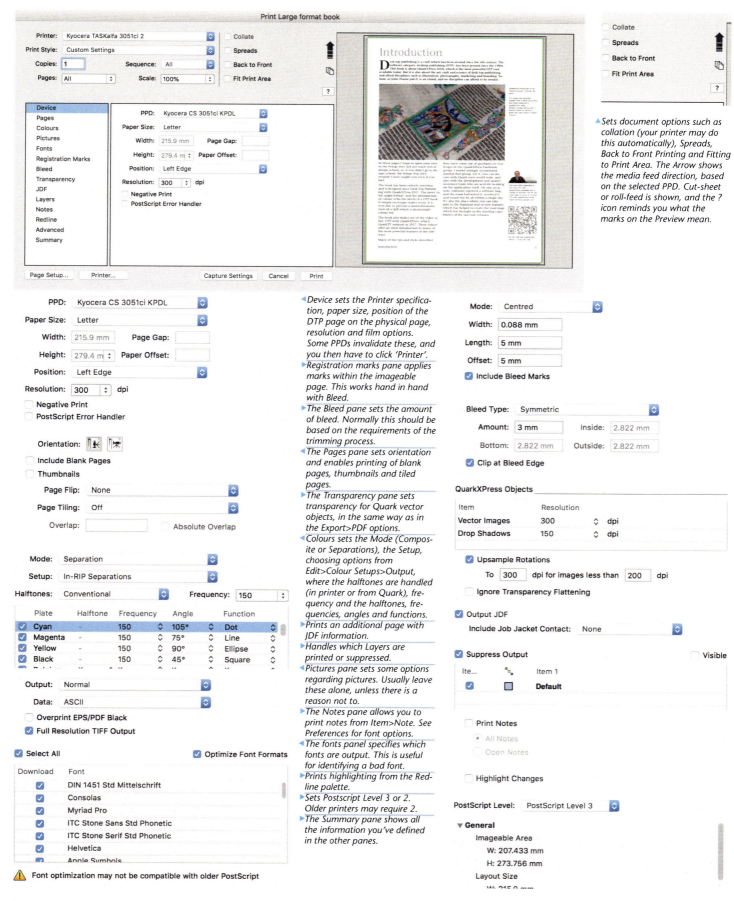

▲ Sets document options such as collation (your printer may do this automatically), Spreads, Back to Front Printing and Fitting to Print Area. The Arrow shows the media feed direction, based on the selected PPD. Cut-sheet or roll-feed is shown, and the ? icon reminds you what the marks on the Preview mean.

◀ Device sets the Printer specification, paper size, position of the DTP page on the physical page, resolution and film options. Some PPDs invalidate these, and you then have to click 'Printer'.
▶ Registration marks pane applies marks within the imageable page. This works hand in hand with Bleed.
▶ The Bleed pane sets the amount of bleed. Normally this should be based on the requirements of the trimming process.
◀ The Pages pane sets orientation and enables printing of blank pages, thumbnails and tiled pages.
▶ The Transparency pane sets transparency for Quark vector objects, in the same way as in the Export>PDF options.
◀ Colours sets the Mode (Composite or Separations), the Setup, choosing options from Edit>Colour Setups>Output, where the halftones are handled (in printer or from Quark), frequency and the halftones, frequencies, angles and functions.
▶ Prints an additional page with JDF information.
▶ Handles which Layers are printed or suppressed.
▶ Pictures pane sets some options regarding pictures. Usually leave these alone, unless there is a reason not to.
▶ The Notes pane allows you to print notes from Item>Note. See Preferences for font options.
◀ The fonts panel specifies which fonts are output. This is useful for identifying a bad font.
▶ Prints highlighting from the Redline palette.
▶ Sets Postscript Level 3 or 2. Older printers may require 2.
▶ The Summary pane shows all the information you've defined in the other panes.

Menus 149

pear (and be editable in) Edit>Output Styles. You can make a separate setting for each printer.

The rest of this area is self-explanatory: number of copies, which pages—you can specify a range using a hyphen and non-sequential pages using commas, and combine these as much as you want. Sequence sets all, evens or odds, scale sets the scale, you can set collation on (if your printer doesn't do this automatically), which will then print as many complete, ordered sets as you have set copies. You can print to spreads, print back to front, meaning last page first, for printers that do not manage this, and fit to print area, which will override scale.

All these changes (and any other visible changes you make later) will appear in the preview on the right, which will also allow you to look at previous and later pages. The ⌘ reveals the colour code used. In our example, dark border is the clipped area that is not part of the final trimmed sheet.

The left hand lower pane has the options for what will appear in the centre pane next to it. By default it is set to Device when you open the dialogue.

Device pane
The first item in this pane is the PPD. This should be installed on your system by the printer's own software. Often the manufacturer will have bundled all of its printers into the same installation, so you will need to scroll down the list until you find your model. If it isn't there, and you have no time to hunt for it, pick Generic Colour, Generic B&W or Generic Imagesetter. For colour and B&W, you will have to go into printer and page settings, bottom left hand corner, to set paper size. With the correct PPD, QuarkXPress will handle those settings itself.

If you have the correct PPD installed, Paper Size will offer you the range of available paper. At the bottom of the list, 'Custom' will allow you to define your own.

By default the position is top left, but you can centre it horizontally, vertically or both. This becomes important when using crop marks, as these will otherwise be off the page.

Resolution nominally changes the printer resolution. With my LaserJet CP5225n, it does nothing of the kind, as the printer's own built-in RIP captures and discards uninformed instructions by computer users of that nature.

You can print negatively—useful for some imagesetter/platemaker combinations. Oddly, the other command of that vintage, Flip Page, is in the next pane, Pages.

The Postscript error handler should normally be off. It prints a page if there is a Postscript error. This is mercifully rare these days, and will not mean much to you unless you understand the Postscript language.

Pages
Orientation—also slightly oddly—is in this pane, along with 'Include Blank Pages'. You can also print page thumbnails—useful for analysing the shape of a document.

Page Flip mirrors the page vertically or horizontally. Page Tiling allows you to print oversize pages. Before the roll-printer era, in-house PR teams across the world used this function as they busily cobbled together displays for projects with aspirations larger than their budgets.

Colours
This pane is the most important for colour proofing. Assuming that you have set up the correct colour profile for your printer in Edit>Color Setups>Output, you choose it here. If you have profiled your printer and your monitor, you should be seeing a reasonably consistent colour workflow from camera to monitor to printer, subject to the capabilities of the devices.

You can also (bravely) try to set the frequency, angle and function of the line screen here. This would mean that you could print with a line, ellipse, diamond or tri-point screen, and also lower the frequency to the point that your laser printer gives good photo rendition. In practice, I haven't found a printer since the 1990s that actually allowed you to do this, as resolution enhancement technology takes over. The result will be better than the straight 600 dpi of our old LaserJet III, but less flexible.

Pictures
This pane allows you to output in low resolution or rough, or to send TIFFs at full resolution. There is very little point in doing either using today's technology. You can also send pictures in different formats.

Again, unless you are trying to solve a technical problem, these settings should not be changed. The same goes for overprinting EPS black.

Fonts
Like the PDF Export dialogue, this allows you to turn fonts on and off, and also to send them in a slightly different format. This is really only for tracking down problems.

Registration Marks
This is identical to the PDF Export panel of the same name.

Bleed
This is identical to the PDF Export panel.

Transparency
This is identical, but with slightly fewer functions, to the Transparency panel in PDF Export.

JDF
As with the PDF Export, this outputs a JDF in addition to the other pages.

Layers
As with the PDF Export, this allows you to choose which layers to print.

Notes
This prints your notes, from Item—Note.

Redline
This prints out redlining, defined in the Redline panel.

Advanced
Subject to your printer's PPD, you can pick which Postscript level to use. You should not normally need to do this.

Summary
This is a summary of your settings.

3 Edit

The Edit menu begins with familiar functions such as Undo and Redo, and becomes progressively less familiar as it resembles increasingly the job of an Editor, as opposed to the metaphor 'Edit' adopted by computers.

◂ *The order of this section is the Edit menu order on a Mac. The same items are present on Windows, with the addition of Preferences (see under QuarkXPress menu, above), but the order is slightly different: Grid Styles, Hyperlinks, Item Styles and Underline Styles are all at the bottom of the menu on Windows. Kerning Table Edit is under Utilities on Windows.*

1 Undo and Redo, Cut, Copy, Paste, Select All

These all function as they do in most other applications.

You can set the number of levels of undo in the Preferences on Windows.

2 Paste without formatting, Paste in Place

Pastes without any attributes. Paste in Place pastes an item in the same position as on the page it was copied from.

Preferences
The Preferences menu item is found under Edit on Windows. On a Mac, it is found under the QuarkXPress menu. See that menu (above) for details.

3 Paste as native objects

Introduced in QuarkXPress 2016 (along with Style>Convert to Native Objects), Paste as Native Objects does something very simply which every other application has so far failed to do: it pastes from pretty much anywhere, and inserts as native, editable Quark Objects.

This applies not only to well-behaved files, such as those from Adobe Illustrator and InDesign, but also to the notoriously badly behaved graphics from Excel.

A few types of graphics will not paste well—the more lurid Excel charts, for example, are sent across as images. For those, export as PDF and then Style>Convert to Native Objects.

For an Excel chart, which is a challenge that, up to now, Illustrator has not been able to manage without turning the text into gobbledegook, simply copy from Excel and then Paste as Native Objects in QuarkXPress. As much as possible, Excel sends across the outlines as vectors, though its gradient backgrounds will come across as images clipped by those vectors.

On paste, a dialogue comes up. You can ignore the settings unless you aren't getting what you want.

▾ *The Preferences menu on Windows is found underneath Select All. See Preferences on p135.*

Menus 151

▲ *The Excel pie-chart as it arrives pasted into QuarkXPress—fussily overstyled, with fonts too small to read, and almost certainly not brand-compliant for colours or typeface.*

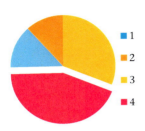

▲ *After 30 seconds reworking in QuarkXPress*

▼ *Special characters for Find/Change and Conditional Styles (*only Find/Change)*

Wildcard	\?
Tab	\t
New paragraph	\p
New line	\n
New column	\c
New box	\b
Backslash	\\
Punctuation space	\.
Flex space	\f
Discretionary hyphen*	\h
Indent here	\i
Discretionary new line	\d
Em space	\m
En space	\e
3-per-Em space	\5
4-per-em space	\$
6-per-em space	\^
Figure space	\8
Hair space	\{
Thin space	\[
Zero width space	\z
Word joiner*	\j
Conditional style marker	\r
Footnote/Endnote*	\o
Content Variable *	\v

What arrives is a grouped file, in colour. If you have View>Proof Output>Greyscale on, these colours may not be visible, so turn off proofing for the moment.

Ungroup the file. For any Excel file, even the Cones, which are sent across as an image, the text should have come across correctly in editable format. This is absolutely essential, because, imported as a straight PDF, the text of an Excel chart is usually in the wrong font and typically illegibly small. If you want to edit a whole host of tiny text boxes that have come across, either use Utilities>Linkster to make them all one story, or, from QX2017 onwards, use Item>Merge Text Boxes. You can then apply character or paragraph styles as a block.

The backgrounds are still in their lurid, Excel state. You can keep them as they are, but they will not usually gel well with a properly designed layout. To remove the backgrounds, click on them with the picture tool and press Delete. You can now recolour them as you like—recolouring them before this will have no effect, as the background will be hidden by the image file. Remember to recolour any keys in the same way. You can explode the pie, or part of it, if you like. Once you've done this a few times, the whole process takes about 30 seconds.

4 Find/Change

Find/Change, and its sister, Item Find/Change offer a uniquely powerful way to typographically rework text and items.

It's also a user experience triumph, working, unlike most advanced search/replace functions in other applications, in human-understandable left-to-right format, rather than vertically.

Essentially it has two modes. On first open, Ignore Attributes is on, giving you the simplified view. Everything you enter on either side is remembered, and you can retrieve it by clicking the double arrows. This is exceedingly helpful when working with a client who insists on adding double spaces after full stops, doing two carriage returns for a new paragraph, or using '…' (with dots) instead of '…' (ellipsis).

There are various special codes you can enter for special features. You can also paste any text, including invisibles such as tabs, returns and special characters, and they will appear with their correct special codes. For example, if you've imported a document from Word with Styles turned off (highly recommended), all of the bullet points will come across as bullet-tab: "• text".

If you copy that and paste it into the Text frame of Find What, it will appear as •\t, because \t is the code for tab. Most glyphs will come across natively, though specialist glyphs may come across with their standard version, and you will need to specify the font as well.

You can combine attributes in any way you like. For example, if you have the mistyped 'fair' consistently in French passages instead of 'faire', you can find *Text: fair, Language: French*, and replace with *faire*, without upsetting correctly spelled English 'fair', meaning 'juste' or 'égale', or possibly 'foire'.

You can now distinguish between breaking and non-breaking characters, and also find and change Open Type features. From QX2018, these open up a new dialogue similar to the dialogue for Open Type in Character Styles.

If you have a very complex set of changes, for example if you were changing a docu-

G 44: Finding and changing power tricks

ment in Dutch old spelling to new spelling, there is a QuarkXPress script (Mac only) that supports replacing long lists of things in batch mode. You can also, from QX2018, use the supplied GREP JavaScript.

In operation, Find Next finds the next item, Change, then Find changes that one and finds the next, Change just changes what you found, and Change All (the dangerous option, though you can unchange it all with a single Edit>Undo) finds and changes everything. Your choices apply on story (the default) or whole layout, whether locked text is affected, and whether footnotes are searched.

Find/Change now allows you to search for the non-breaking attribute, as well as for Open Type features. You can set the number of previous items that Find/Change remembers in the Preferences.

Pressing option/alt changes the buttons to 'Find first' and 'Find last'. You can search for wildcards using cmd/ctrl-shift-?, or just by typing in \?. Finding 'Th\?r' would find all instances of Thor, Thør and Thursday.

What about GREP?

GREP is an old UNIX command-line utility to "Globally search a Regular Expression and Print". If you are coming from InDesign, you may be wondering where GREP is. Find and Change provides some of the functions that you would use GREP for, and Conditional Styles provide others. If you absolutely need full GREP functionality, it's built into JavaScripting and you can GREP all you like.
However, unless you've grown up using GREP, it isn't especially intuitive. Rather than trying to turn QuarkXPress into something else, it's worth first learning QX's own, more intuitive, tools. If these are insufficient, feel free to move onto GREP through JavaScripting.

5 Item Find/Change

Item Find/Change uses the same left—find, right—change format. However, as there are so many more attributes, it is tabbed into Box, Box Colour, Frame, Line, Picture, Text and Drop Shadow, with a highly useful Summary at the end, so you can check what you are really finding and changing.

This works exactly like—and looks exactly like—the Item Styles.

Underneath, across all the tabs, you can specify what kind of items you are searching for—Text Boxes, Picture Boxes, None Boxes (ie boxes defined to have Content: None), Lines and/or Text Paths.

The level of changes goes down to every settable attribute of a box or line. If it's too complicated, you can use the corner menu (top right) to acquire all the attributes from a selected item, or just those that relate to the currently open panel.

If you want to use this to check, for example, for accidentally rotated boxes, you can't: it will only find an angle of rotation, not a >0°. However, you can accomplish that with File>Job Jackets>Evaluate Layout, where you can set a rule to forbid, or to flag, rotated boxes, and, indeed, many other potential problems.

6 Colours

This brings up the Colours edit list. See the Colours Palette section for a discussion.

7 Style Sheets

This brings up the Style Sheets edit list. Please see the Style Sheets Palette section.

8 Item Styles

This calls up the Item Styles Edit list. See the Item Styles Palette for more information.

9 Callout Styles

This calls up the Callout Styles Edit list. See the Callout Styles palette.

10 Conditional Styles

This calls up the Conditional Styles Edit list. See the Conditional Styles palette.

◂All of the Styles lists in the Edit menu have approximately the same format. As well as the functions from the relevant palettes, such as Style Sheet functions from the Style Sheets palette, colour functions from the Colours palette, and so on, they all include ways to import or append styles from other files.

Import, as here, linked with Export, uses a separate external file to transmit the list. Append, as in Colours, Styles and most others, appends a list from another Quark file, similar to File>Append.

If you want to have certain colours and styles as defaults in all new documents, then close all documents and go to the Edit menu for what you want. If you import or append, these elements will then be available to all new documents up to the point that you delete preferences. You can also edit those elements from within these lists.

Menus   153

11 Bullet, Numbering and Outline Styles

Edit>Bullet, Numbering and Outline Styles calls up the Bullet edit list, which allows the creation and management of three kinds of styles.

Edit Bullet Style

Here you can set a bullet's character style. It defaults to Inherit from Paragraph, but can be any defined character style. You can then set the actual character, and control alignment and outset.

Essentially, this allows you to put a character of your own choice and styling in the margin.

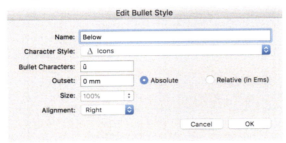

▶ *The arrow pointers in this book, such as the one in this caption, are created as bullet styles and managed as outline styles.*

You can create side-stripes, of the kind seen in many popular manuals of a particular type.

Achieve this by creating a character stylesheet that stretches a dingbat vertically 400% and adjusts its offset.

You need a new paragraph every couple of lines, but the effect is fairly convincing and easy to achieve. This could also be achieved using text shading.

The outline styles used to manage the arrows.

Edit Numbering Style

Edit Numbering Style works in the same way as bullets, except that sequential series are generated. These are Arabic, Roman, alphabetic, East Asian, and typographic symbol sets. Typographic sets, *, **, †,††,‡,‡‡, etc enhance footnote typography. For automatic numbering, prefixes and suffixes can be added.

Edit Outline Style

An outline style organises previously defined bullet and numbering styles, with the ability to include lower (or higher) levels and a separator, as required. Indents are set per level. Combining Numbering Styles with prefixes and bullet styles, we could have:

§1 Preamble

　§1·¶1 Introduction

　　§1·¶1·1 Wherein that the people…

　　　❋ upon the first of the month

　　　　∗ and subsequently each Thursday

　　　　　i) shall first make good…

Lists continue from where they left off, unless you restart them. If you want to include numbered points in the text, but also have section numbers, simply create two separate Outline Styles. These will then not interfere with each other.

You can create cross-references for numbered sections with Style>Cross Reference.

12 Footnote Styles

This opens the Footnote Styles Edit List. For an explanation, see the Footnote Styles Palette, page 102.

13 Hyperlinks

This opens the Hyperlinks Edit List. See the Hyperlinks Palette, page 110.

14 Underline Styles

This allows you to create new Underline Settings. You can apply these using Style>Type Style>Underline Styles. You can't currently integrate these into character or paragraph styles, but you can create a set of consistent underlining options which will generally be superior to the default Underline. This includes setting the colour, shade, width and offset. Underline is not a 'proper' typographic feature—it is a hangover from the days of manual typewriters where typists went back and created underlining with the _ character. This was used to denote italics in typeset text. However, with the rise of underlined URLs, you may (on rare occasions) wish to choose to underline one. My opinion is that people now know what URLs are, and it is sufficient just to write out www.etc. Word processors insist on underlining URLs, whether you want them to or not, which makes the text look amateurish.

From QX2017 onwards, consider using Text Shading to create custom underlines. These can be integrated into stylesheets.

▲ *Underline settings in Underline Styles.*
This feature is still available in QX2017 and QX2018 for compatibility reasons, but in most cases you will be better off creating underlines using Text Shading. Unlike custom underline, Text Shading styles can be integrated with character and paragraph stylesheets, making them much easier to manage and use consistently.

15 Hanging Characters

Hanging Characters allow significant typographical refinement, provided that you are willing to invest a little time in specifying which characters should hang and by what amount. They can be applied in the Measurements: Paragraph tab, or as a paragraph style.

The Edit list contains two types of items: Classes and Sets. The classes have narrow icons, the sets have wide icons.

Classes

Use New>Class to create a class. You are offered the choice of Leading (pronounced 'lee-ding', not 'led-ding', as in the inter-line spacing), Trailing, or Dropped Cap. You can set the hang to any percentage between -50% and 200%, but the default list of options offers useful increments, which you can refine afterwards.

What we are doing here is moving characters into or away from the margin so that they line up to the eye. While Open Type kerning should enforce good spacing between the letters, it does not currently take account of the beginning and end of lines, although this could be programmed in as a contextual alternate. This means that, especially in fully justified or right justified text, punctuation appears overly indented at the end of a line, and leading punctuation, mainly as inverted commas, appears to push the text inwards.

Dropped caps create their own problems (see example). Leading inverted commas create an enormous gap, without adding anything to the visual interest of the page. One solution is to set them at ordinary size, followed by the dropped capital, using a conditional style sheet. This can be further improved by creating a dropped cap class.

Defaults are in place for Hanging and Leading Punctuation, which can be switched on for all text. If you want to refine the way the page appears, you can also set a 5% or less leading hang (which pushes them into the margin by 5%) for W, Y, and possibly V. Examine your extended text carefully to see if these create a problem: this is not only font dependent, but also related to the leading, column width, and other page interactions.

A V X W Y

▲ *Gap between standard and optical margin alignment.*

As well as hanging punctuation, you can use Hanging Characters for Optical Margin Alignment. As the name suggests, this is done optically, which is to say, with the eye. Some software offers 'automatic optical alignment', which is something of a contradiction in terms. Doing it properly produces better results, though the effort may not be worth it in terms of overall document improvement. For Stone Serif Medium, we have realigned the A, V, W, X and Y, with a minimal adjustment to M, S, T and U, and a virtually invisible adjustment to D, K, R and Z. The results are given above. Although the offsets look quite different, measuring the letters suggests that 7.5% will do for all of them, W being a wider letter and 7.5% therefore having more effect. The more invisible adjustment to T could be 2%, and to

"My Name," said the girl at once, "is Aravis Tarkheena and I am the only daughter of Kidrash Tarkaan, the son of Rishti Tarkaan, the son of Kidrash Tarkaan, the son of Ilsombreh Tisroc, the son of Ardeeb Tisroc, who was descended in a right line from the god Tash."

—*The Horse and His Boy,*
C.S. Lewis

▲ *Although an alternative solution is to begin with an ordinary sized pair of inverted commas, QuarkXPress allows you to create a Dropped Cap hanging character class which will automatically push leading punctuation (or any character you wish) into the margin. Either solution is significantly better than a three line punctuation mark followed by an ordinary sized letter. We also superscripted the inverted commas, with a Conditional Style. Note also the trailing punctuation for the comma in the attribution, allowing the words to line up.*

It is also worth noting, here, the way the text creates its own visual rhythm, which is further developed by the incantatory quality of the names, which Lewis made up entirely for their sound and effect. It is important in children's literature to let the typography carry some of the magic of the text being read aloud.

▼ *Optical margin alignment in action. You need to do this optically, which is to say, with the human eye. Pseudo-optical margin alignment, done automatically, produces an inferior result.*

▼ With ▼ Without

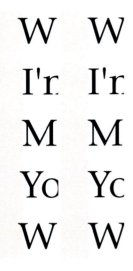

Typographer's ragged
Out of love for the truth and from desire to elucidate it, the Reverend Father Martin Luther, Master of Arts and Sacred Theology, and ordinary lecturer therein at Wittenberg, intends to defend the following statements and to dispute on them in that place.

Left justified
Out of love for the truth and from desire to elucidate it, the Reverend Father Martin Luther, Master of Arts and Sacred Theology, and ordinary lecturer therein at Wittenberg, intends to defend the following statements and to dispute on them in that place.

▲▲ *Typographer's ragged text.*

▲ *Left justified text. Typographer's ragged uses a hanging margin of 200% for the whole alphabet, in conjunction with Very Narrow Measure H&Js. Because of the way the two interact, hyphenation is relatively infrequent, but the justification function creates a gently ragged right margin.*

(Text—Ninety-five theses, Martin Luther, 31 October 1517.)

Margin alignment in action:
   Where are you going, my pretty maid?
   I'm going a milking, sir, she said.
   May I go with you, my pretty maid?
   You're kindly welcome, sir, she said.
   What is your fortune, my pretty maid?
   My face is my fortune, sir, she said.

And not in action:
   Where are you going, my pretty maid?
   I'm going a milking, sir, she said.
   May I go with you, my pretty maid?
   You're kindly welcome, sir, she said.
   What is your fortune, my pretty maid?
                              English nursery rhyme

the others 1%. It is certainly worth improving the quality of the margins for A, V, W, X and Y. There will be an inevitable slowing down for long text if you do the others as well, and the results will probably not be visible even in extended copy.

Once you have set up your classes, you can assemble them into sets. This is a relatively simple matter: create a new set, and select the classes that you want included. QuarkXPress will not allow you to include contradictory classes. For example, you can have the letter W in three different classes for leading, trailing and dropped cap, but you cannot have W set to, say, 7.5% and 5% in two different classes that are included in the same set.

16 Lists

Opens the Lists Edit List. See the Lists Palette for details about how to use lists.

17 H&Js

Edit H&Js brings up the Hyphenation & Justification styles list. Create New or double-click to open the Edit dialogue.

From the point of view of typography, Hyphenation quality in QuarkXPress 2018 is arguably the biggest upgrade to the look of text for twenty years. Currently only QuarkXPress offers this.

As a personal note, I have had more disagreements with clients about hyphenation than any other single issue. Hyphenation is

If you just want to try all this out, do it on a short document. The more text you have, the longer it will take for document-wide changes to be applied. Once in place, you shouldn't notice much difference in speed. However, if you are just experimenting, waiting while a 400 page novel reformats is perhaps not the best use of time.

Typographer's ragged text
If your client objects to hyphenation (see below) then you will find that your Flush left, Ragged right text, which gently curving right margin like a torn piece of paper, resembles a hedgehog, with lines sticking out all over the place.

Rather than going through and reworking every line, you can set the entire alphabet to a Trailing class at 200%. If you now turn on justification and set the hyphenation to Very Narrow Measure, you will be treated to the much desired gently torn right margin. Justification controls are working for you to keep the lines a more or less constant length, but the 200% trailing adjustment allows some but not all into the margin. You will find that your text now overflows the margins, ruining your beautiful design grid, so introduce a couple of millimetres of paragraph right indent to compensate. Despite the availability of hyphenation (which you can turn off in a custom H&J if the client really objects to it), almost all of the management is done by justification, so hyphenation does not occur.

generally invisible to us unless we're looking for it, which means we are fine with it in other people's documents, but become paranoid when scrutinising our own. Until now, professional-grade DTP software has offered the ability to set where hyphenation takes place, and to limit the number of hyphens in a row, but never which words are hyphenated, except by going to manual hyphenation only. Some designers always do this. From QX2018, we can now specify how aggressively the words hyphenate.

Auto Hyphenation

Auto Hyphenation turns automatic hyphenation on and off. You can still put in manual hyphenation with cmd/ctrl-hyphen, and you can ask for suggested hyphenation with Utilities>Suggested Hyphenation. When auto hyphenation is on, you can prevent a particular word from hyphenating by putting a cmd/ctrl-hyphen at the beginning of the word, and you can insert a manual hyphen at any point in the word, which overrides automatic hyphenation, but is itself overridden by prevent hyphenation.

Auto Hyphenation has the following options:

Smallest Word—the smallest word that will hyphenate.

Minimum Before—the number of letters that must be before hyphenation to allow it to hyphenate.

Minimum After—the same, but for the end of the word.

Strictness Level—the new setting in QuarkXPress 2018, this offers:

❏ Compounds only
❏ Nominal
❏ Aesthetic
❏ Prevalent
❏ Everywhere
❏ As QuarkXPress 2017 and Earlier.

See the side-bar for examples: the difference is a subtle one. In our example, with showing the right edges of some standard length lines from the start of A Tale of Two Cities, there are only three different results for five different settings, and the difference in length between Compounds Only and Everywhere is just the length of one word. Nonetheless, over the course of extended text, the difference is palpable.

Hyphenation is always a balance. In justified text with narrow columns, anything less than 'Everywhere' will produce unsightly rivers of text.

Break Capitalized Words—allows or prevents words starting with capitals to break. This affects both the start of sentences and proper nouns.

Hyphens in a Row—you can specify the maximum number of hyphens in a row. Automatically hyphenated text requires inspection to ensure that the paragraph has not become 'spikey'. Ideally, you should never have more than two hyphens in the same paragraph, so it is probably safest to set this to one and then hyphenate by exception.

Hyphenation Zone—the distance from the right hand margin where hyphenation is allowed. A word that does not fall into this space will not hyphenate.

Justification Method
This only applies to Justified text.

Space—sets minimum, optimal and maximum width of a standard space.

Char—sets the minimum, optimal and maximum tracking of a character.

Flush Zone—the zone in which the last word on the line must fall for it to justify if it is the last line of a paragraph. A very large setting for this is equivalent to Forced Justify.

Single Word Justify—allows a single word to justify, preserving the column appearance at the expense of the word.

East Asian functions can be turned on in the Preferences. This gives you access to additional specifications, for example preventing a line breaking before an em-dash. If you subsequently turn off East Asian functions, the choices you made remain persistent.

18 Grid Styles

Opens the Grid Styles List. See the Grid Styles palette, above, for more information.

> **Strange boxes**
> In QuarkXPress 2018, you can apply multiple borders to rectangular boxes. If you want rounded corners for these, edit Dashes and Stripes. Only saved gradients can be applied—you can't use the gradients panel.

▶ *Edit Dashes. You can create rounded and flat dashes, in unusual patterns, and then set the colour of the dashes and the gaps differently from the Measurements panel or the Item Styles. If you set no dash, but rounded corners, you get automatically round-cornered boxes which still allow vertical justification and multiple borders, unlike boxes using the round-corner function.*
Edit Stripes works like Edit Dashes.

▲ *Different Arrows? We used Text on a Path with a Zapf Dingbat at each end separated by opt/alt-Tab to create alternative arrows. Play with Hanging Characters to get the ends perfect.*

> **Round Cornered box**
> Many boxes benefit from a slight softening of the corners. If you do this by creating a round-cornered dash or stripe style, all the Text Box attributes are available.

▶ *The house font of the UK's National Health Service (NHS) is Frutiger. In 2012, the NHS introduced a new acronym: CCG, for Clinical Commissioning Group. However, in Frutiger the spacing for CC and CG is too wide. Editing the Kerning table in QX is th best way to fix this, without breaching font copyright.*

▼ Corrected   ▼ Original
CCG   **CCG**

19 Dashes & Stripes

Opens the Dashes and Stripes editor. Clicking New offers you a choice of a dash style or a stripe style.

Dashes

To specify dashes, click on the ruler and drag a little way. Arrow markers will appear pointing to the beginning and end of a dash, and the dash will appear in high, short preview, and the long, low preview.

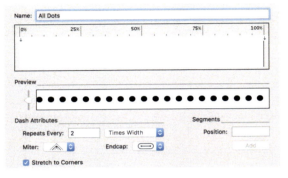

You can then move the arrows, or drag them off the ruler to delete. Up to five dash components are allowed. You can change the proportions of the preview using the slider to see a longer, thinner line, or a shorter, fatter one.

Dash Attributes—you can specify how often the dash repeats in points or as a multiple of width. You can set the Mitre to angular, rounded or bevelled, which determines the shape of corners. By default the dash maintains its shape at corners, but you can set it to stretch. You can also set the endcaps to flush square, rounded, projecting square or projecting rounded.

Segments—you can type in a position as a percentage if you prefer that to clicking with the mouse.

If you are returning to QuarkXPress after a long absence—perhaps lured by the glitz

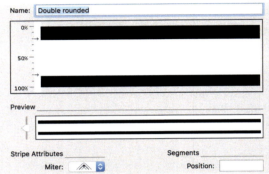

and glamour and early price breaks of other applications—you may be wondering where the old exciting borders are. These were bitmaps, and don't really stand up to today's publishing needs. You can achieve the same—and many more—results with Utilities>Shapemaker and Item>Super Step and Repeat, or by pasting vector art from elsewhere.

Stripes

Stripes work in the same way as dashes, but without the Endcap or Stretch options.

20 Kerning Pairs

With the Kerning Pairs dialogue, you can individually edit troublesome kerning pairs which are either not kerned in the font definition, or where the kerning does not meet your needs. There are 516 common kerning pairs, and these must be applied to each weight of a font. If you want to comprehensively re-kern a font, QuarkXPress is not the tool to do it with[2]. However, if you have an abbreviation, such as CCG, which does not fit well in, say, Frutiger, you may find that there is no previous kerning, 'CG' not being a common component in English. To

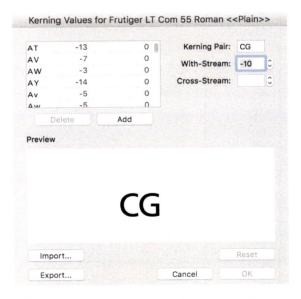

158   🖥 *19: Line drawing and editing | 4: Fonts and kerning*

change it, go to the font you want (typing a couple of letters will take you there more quickly) and double-click to edit. The dialogue will come up, with pre-kerned pairs in the top left, along with their adjustment.

Kerning Pair—type in the pair you are interested in. If already defined, the list will move to show you, and the values will be loaded into the boxes.

With-Stream—horizontal kerning. Changing it is immediately updated in the preview.

Cross-Stream—vertical kerning.

You can export and import kerning for entire typeface weights. Any kerning you apply will affect every use of the font in the document.

21 Font Tracking Tables

As fonts get larger, their tracking should usually decrease. Equally, at small sizes the tracking should be slightly wider to improve legibility. You can create a tracking curve graphically for particular fonts. This is not directly exportable, but you can copy your QuarkXPress preferences round the office to share the values. As with kerning, this has to be done on a weight-by-weight basis.

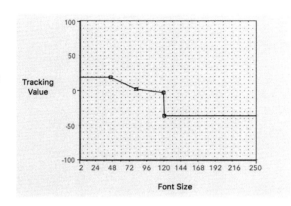

22 Set Tool Preferences From Selected, Restore Tool Preferences

For tools with settable preferences, such as the Starburst tool, you can set the current preferences for the tool for this document, or for new print layouts, and restore them to the defaults.

23 Colour Setups

Colour Setups allows you to control how QuarkXPress treats incoming colours and how it controls them for output. Normally speaking, you will need to create a profile for output devices you control, such as printers. Your monitor's profile should be set automatically, or you can change this in Preferences>Display. For incoming colour, and for standard devices such as Standard Web Offset Printing, you should not need to change any settings, though you can if there is a particular problem. Use an X-Rite or Spyder tool to calibrate your monitor and local printing device. You should then be able to see the calibration in Utilities>Profile Manager. You can also browse an auxiliary folder if, for some reason, your profile is not in the default location.

If you need to edit the Source Setup, duplicate the Quark 7 defaults and work from there.

Output
If you have a proofing device, it will be necessary to enter its profile. This is relatively painless. From Edit>Colour Setups>Output, click New and the dialogue appears. Give it a reasonable name, and then choose your profile from the drop-down list. Leave the defaults as they are, unless you know they should be something different. Save the profile, and then apply it in Output Styles.

24 Output Styles

You can save the options for Print and Export as Output Styles. This can also be done from the relevant menus, but you can manage them all together here. Print, PDF, ePub, Kindle, HTML5, EPS and Apps can all have output styles, but PNG and JPEG cannot.

▼ *The 516 most common kerning pairs.*

A' ac Ac AC ad Ad ae Ae af ag Ag AG Ao AO ap ap Ap Aq AQ at At AT au Au AU av Av AV aw Aw AW ay Ay AY b, B, b. B. BA Bb BE Bi Bk bl Bl BL BP br Br BR bu Bu BU BV BW by By BY C, C. ca Ca CA ch ck CO Cr CR d, D, d. D. da Da DA dc DD de DE dg Dl DL DM DN do DO DP DR dt du DU dv DV dw DW dy DY e, e. ea EC ei el em en EO ep er et eu Eu ev Ev ew ey f, F, F, F; F: f. F. F. fa Fa FA FC fe Fe ff FG fi Fi fl fo Fo FO Fr Ft Fu Fy g, g. ga ge GE gg gh gl go GO GR Gu GU hc hd he He hg ho Ho HO hp ht hu Hu hv hw hy Hy ic Ic IC id Id ie ig IG io Io IO ip Iq it It iu iv j, J, j. J. ja Ja JA je Je jo Jo JO ju Ju ka kc kd ke Ke kg ko Ko KO Ku L' la lc LC ld le lf lg LG lo LO lp lq LT lu Lu LU lv LV lw LW ly Ly LY M ma Ma mc Mc md Md me Me mg MG mn mo Mo MO mp mt mu mv my N, N. Na nc NC nd ne Ne ng NG Ni no No NO np nt nu Nu Nu nv nw ny o, O, o. O. Oa OA ob Ob OB OD OE of OF oh Oh OH Ol oj ok Ok OK ol Ol OL om OM on ON op OP or OR OT ou OU ov OV ow OW ox OX oy OY p, P, P; P: p. P. pa Pa PA Pe PE ph pi pl PL Po PO pp PP pu PU PY qu QU r, r. ra RC rd Rd re Re rg RG rk rl rm rn ro Ro rq rr rt Rt RT Ru RU rv RV RW ry RY RY s, S, s. S. sh Si Sl SM Sp st ST su Su SU t, T, T; T: t. t. T. ta Ta TA Tc TC td te Te Ti to To TO Tr Ts Tu Tw Ty U, U. ua Ua UA uc UC ud ue ug Ug UG Um Un uo UO up Up uq Us US ut uv uw uy v, V, V; V: v. V. va VA vb vc VC vd ve Ve vg VG Vi vo VO Vr VS Vu vv vy w, W, W; W: w. W. wa WA WC wd Wd we wg WG wh Wi Wm wo WO Wr Wt Wu wx Wy xa Xa xe Xe xo Xo Xu Xy y, Y, Y; Y: y. Y. ya YA yc YC yd Yd ye Ye Yi yo YO Yp YS Yu Yv ZO

4 Style

1 Font

Up to QX2017, sets the font. If the font menu takes too long to come up, you can turn off previewing in Preferences>Fonts. However, this is probably a sign that you have too many fonts loaded. Shift-clicking temporarily invokes the non-preview font list.

Fonts in QX2018
From QuarkXPress 2018, fonts are accessed from the Measurements palette on both Windows and Mac. Instead of showing all the variations of a font in the main font drop-down, the lettertype is shown to the left, and the variants to the right.

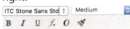

2 Size

Up to QX2017, sets the size from harmonic presets. It is more flexible to use the Measurements panel or Character styles.

3 Type Style

This generally replicates the functions of Measurements>Character, but with three exceptions.

Make Fraction
This combines 2/3, 1/16, etc, on selection, into ⅔, ¹⁄₁₆. Although highly convenient, these are 'faux' fractions, inferior to true Open Type fractions. The method is controlled from Preferences>Application>Fractions/Price.

Make Price
This turns £5.00 into £5^{00}, €2.50 into €2^{50} and $3.20 into $3^{20}. The method is controlled from Preferences>Application>Fractions/Price. Both this and Make Fraction are done by offsetting and changing sizes. If you change the Preferences later, the prices and fractions will not update automatically.

Underline Styles
This is the only place you can apply styles created in Edit>Underline Styles. You can also create ad-hoc styles. Consider using Text Shading instead, as it can be applied via style sheets.

4 Colour, Shade, Opacity

Sets colour, shade and opacity. This is context dependent.

5 Alignment (text)

Sets alignment to left, right, justify or forced. See Measurements>Paragraph.

6 Centre Picture, Stretch Picture, Scale Picture to Box, Fit Box to Picture

These controls only appear when a picture is selected, and are self-explanatory.

7 Convert to Native Objects

See Edit>Paste as Native Objects, page 151, for a discussion of this. If pasting does not work, consider importing as PDF and using this method. It is slightly slower, but converts from more different sources, especially on Windows.

8 Character Alignment

Sets the alignment to Top, Centreline, Baseline or Bottom. See page 78.

9 Paragraph Style Sheet

Chooses any paragraph style sheet. See the Styles Sheets palette, page 130.

10 Character Style Sheet

Chooses any character style sheet. See the Styles palette.

11 Footnotes/Endnotes

Inserts a footnote or an endnote, or moves to the relevant footnotes, or back to the text. See the Footnotes Styles palette, page 102.

12 Footnote Separator Style

Applies or creates a footnote separator style.

13 Update Style Sheet

Updates the current paragraph character stylesheet to match the selected text, if different. See the Styles palette, page 130.

14 Item Styles

Applies an item style. See the Item Styles palette, page 123.

15 Change Case

Changes the case of the text to UPPER CASE, lower case or Title Case. This permanently changes the case. If you want to apply upper case as a style, use the Type Style ALL CAPS, available in the Measurements panel, Character, or Style>Type Style. Note that Title Case sets the first letter of every word in upper case, including 'of', 'and', 'the' and so on. This is therefore not true title case, and will need manual adjusting.

16 Non-breaking attribute

Applied to a word, this prevents breaking across lines. You can search for it and replace it in Find/Change. In View you can turn on highlighting of non-breaking attributes.

17 Flip Horizontal, Vertical

Flips the content of a picture or text box. To flip a shape or group, use Item>Flip Shape, page 164.

18 Cross Reference

The cross-reference pane is persistent, so you can have it open like a palette while you add in references.

You can reference Numbered items, Footnotes or Endnotes, and show the Page number, the Full text, the number either With or Without context (paragraphs) or formatting (notes), along with automatic 'above/below'. You can synchronise cross-references either from the dialogue or the menu. Use View>Highlight Cross References to see them in grey.

19 Hyperlink

Creates, edits, removes hyperlinks. See Hyperlink palette, page 110.

20 Anchor

Creates, edits, and removes anchors. See Hyperlink palette.

21 Remove Manual Kerning

Removes manual Word Space Tracking, as opposed to regular tracking which is available in the Measurements Panel. You can only apply Word Space Tracking from the keyboard.

Mac:
Increase space by 05 em   Command+Control+Shift+]
Increase space by .005 em   Command+Control+Option+Shift+]
Decrease space by .05 em   Command+Control+Shift+[
Decrease space by .005 em   Command+Control+Option+Shift+[

Windows:
Increase space by .05 em   Control+Shift+@
Increase space by .005 em   Control+Alt+Shift+@
Decrease space by .05 em   Control+Shift+!
Decrease space by .005 em   Control+Alt+Shift+!

Is lower case more legible?

Most books about typography will tell you that lower case text is more legible than upper case. Sofie Beier reviewed the evidence in her more-or-less definitive book Reading Letters.[1] The reality—as with the old debate about serif and sans-serif—is that familiarity is what makes things legible. In running text (body text) we are used to Sentence case. Sentences without capital letters at the start or for proper nouns seem just as hard to read, or harder, than all caps. In titles, we are quite used to Upper Case, and it should not create problems.

[1] Bis Publishers, 2012

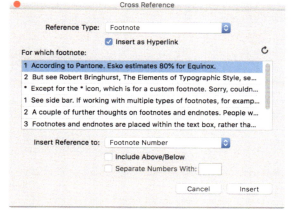

▲Since QX2017 Cross References, can reference Text Anchors, in addition to Footnotes, Endnotes and Numbered items.

As previously, you can insert a reference to the Item Name, Paragraph Number with or without context, or the page number, and the Reference can be set to act as a hyperlink when exported. Unless the anchored item is a numbered item, paragraph numbers will not return a result.

In the Preferences, there are two options in Project>General. They are:

Synchronise All Cross References During Output—which runs the synchronisation process when printing or exporting.

Retain Local Modifications to Cross References—as stated, if you modify the cross references, these can be retained.

Cross Reference to Footnote
Example:
See Page 142 above According to Pantone. Esko estimates 80% for Equinox.

Cross Reference to Numbered Item
Example:
See Page 151 above 3 Edit .

The order followed here is for Mac. The Windows order is slightly different. Most importantly, Super Step and Repeat is near the bottom, with a regular Step and Repeat at the top. On Windows, you can also access Runaround and Clipping modal dialogue boxes, which reproduce the functions discussed under Measurements (above), and further down, Drop Shadow.

5 Item

1 Duplicate

Makes a copy of the selected item, with the same offsets as the last time an item was dragged or drag-copied.

2 Super Step and Repeat

Super Step and Repeat allows you to repeat an object while changing its position, angle, size, frame width, shade, skew and contents size. It can act relative to an object's centre, corners, or a selected point. The best thing to do is to open it up and play with it.

Repeat Count—how many times to repeat.

Horizontal, vertical offset—how far to move it. This defaults to the most recent values when you dragged something with the mouse.

Angle—how much to turn it by.

Scale contents—scales text and pictures.

Rotate & Scale Relative to—pick the reference point.

End frame/line width, box shade, item scale, skew—sets parameters for the final item. Everything in between will be a gradation of that with the original.

Nb: on **Windows**, Super Step and Repeat is near the bottom of the menu, with regular Step and Repeat at the top of the menu.

3 Delete

Deletes an object.

4 Lock

Locks either the position of an item, or the text of a story, or the picture in a box.

5 Fit Box to Text

From QuarkXPress 2016, this fits the box to the height of the text it contains. This is very useful if you want to align boxes of text. Likewise, when you convert imported vector graphics to native objects, or paste as native objects, the boxes will be their original size, but if the text is not in the same font, it will overflow. Fit box to text will sort this out.

6 Merge Text Boxes

From QX2017, you can select a set of text boxes and merge them. The options are to do this in the order of selection, or else from top to bottom. This is especially useful when you have converted a PDF to native objects and the text comes across in numerous small boxes, which some applications use to manage kerning.

7 Send & Bring

Moves objects to the back, to the front, or shuffles them up and down. See the Layers palette for an explanation of how QuarkXPress stacks things.

▲ Super Step and Repeat can be
▼ severely practical, but can also produce dramatic effects.

8 Group/Ungroup All

Usually shortcutted to cmd/ctrl-G and cmd/ctrl-U, Group and Ungroup clump the selected boxes or unclump them, so that they become (for many operations, but not all) equivalent to a single item. You can still access the content from the Text and Picture content tools. As well as being more convenient, Grouped items respond more quickly, which is important when dragging a set of reflowing items across long text, causing it to reflow. From QX2018, you can flip groups using Item>Flip Shape.

9 Export Options

This adds Tagged-text to an object for use when exporting Tagged PDF. See the Articles palette for more information.

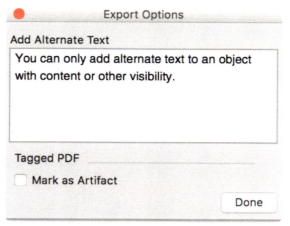

◀ Export options dialogue. Mark as Artifact is for specifying decorative items that should not be read by an accessible PDF reader.

10 Insert inline table

Inserts an inline table to fit the existing text box. See Measurements>Tables tab and the Table styles palette for more information.

11 Space/Align

Spaces or aligns boxes. See Measurements>Space/Align tab for details. Additionally, you can access Apply Last, which repeats the most recent Space/Align action on the selected objects. It also provides a convenient reminder of the shortcut keys.

12 Constrain/Unconstrain

If Constrain is turned on in Preferences, removes it, if it's off, turns it on. See Preferences>Print Layout>Auto Constrain.

13 Content

Sets the current box to be a picture box, a text box, or a box with no content. This means that if you create a box with the wrong tool, you can switch it. Content>none is useful because the box won't have an X across it, as with an empty picture box, nor will it keep insisting on you putting text in when you double-click it by accident.

14 Shape

Converts different kinds of shapes. You can convert a regular shape into an editable curve (go to the shape that looks a bit like an artist's palette), convert a box into a line, or a line into a box, make a curved or angled line into an orthogonal line, and also quickly apply a couple of different kinds of corners. When converting a line, opt/alt-clicking joins the ends of the line to make the box. Regular clicking makes a shape with a very narrow content area.

Note that this is not the same as the Shape tools.

☐ Rectangle
☐ Rounded
☐ Bevelled
☐ Inset
○ Circular
╱ Line
+ Orthogonal
∿ Bézier
↺ Freeform

▲ The nine types of shape in QuarkXPress. Shapes created with Shapemaker are Freeform.

Menus

15 Merge or Split Paths

Merge or Split Paths provides a powerful toolbox for combining objects and paths. This is calculated from the item at the back forwards to those at the front.

Intersection—the area where the back shape intersects with one or more of the others.

Union—the total outline of all the shapes together.

Difference—the back minus the front shapes.

Reverse Difference—the front shapes minus the back.

Exclusive Or—only areas with an odd number of overlaps, ie, one item only, shape; two items, shape removed; three items, shape.

Combine—the same as Exclusive Or, except the points are constructed in a different way.

Join Endpoints—joins two lines if the points are close together.

Split Outside Paths—makes the outside path a separate shape you can work on with the Bézier tools.

Split All Paths—makes every shape a separate shape. Nb, this will mean that hollow shapes become filled shapes.

With a little creativity, these tools can create a vast array of shapes which can be text boxes, picture boxes, lines, or curves for text on a curve.

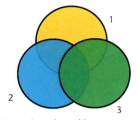

▲ *From these three objects, selected in order, here are the results using Merge/Split*

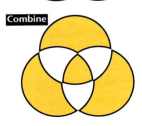

16 Point/Segment type

With the ☞ Point Tool selected, you can convert corner, smooth or symmetrical points and turn a straight segment into a curve or vice versa.

17 Convert text to boxes

Converts text to boxes. This is sometimes the only option if a font will not export or print. You can also use it to turn dingbats into editable shapes, to create text with a photographic background, or to insert a rotated character. This can anchor the new box where it was in the text, make it unanchored, or convert an entire box.

18 Edit Runaround/Clipping Path

Edits the runaround or clipping path of an appropriate object.

See Measurements>Runaround and Clipping, page 85.

19 Flip Shape

This flips the shape horizontally or vertically (rather than the content). From QX2018 this works on groups in addition to single objects.

20 Share, Unsynchronise size/item/content, Copy to Other Layout

These commands relate to sharing content. See the Content Palette for details, page 99.

21 Callout Anchor

Inserts a callout anchor, along with other options.

See the Callout Styles palette, page 93.

22 Composition Zones

Composition zones create a new layout from an area of the page. This layout can then be edited independently. You can add the layout to the Content palette by using the corner menu on that palette and then choosing Add.

There are two main uses for this.

First, if it is inconvenient to work on a part of the layout in the main document, creating a composition zone will let you work on it separately. This could be because it is highly complex and everything is going too slowly, or because it is layered underneath something else and you don't want to keep having to switch layers on and off, or because it is rotated, for example by 180˚ as part of a document that is going to be folded, but does not merit separate imposition. Once created, you can rotate the composition zone in the main layout so that it is the right way up for print, but work on it in a separate layout the right way up for editing. All changes you make on the composition zone layout immediately update in the main layout. If you want that composition zone layout to appear in the layout tabs, you can select this in the edit box from the Content palette.

The second use is if you designate an area of a document to be worked on by someone else. This could be a cover, an advertisement, a highly technical table, or because you are splitting up the spreads of a magazine across a department.

To do this, create a composition zone using the Composition Zone tool, or by clicking on an item and choosing Item>Composition Zones>Create. If you then choose Item>Composition Zones>Edit, you can see the layout you just created, and create anything in it that you want to be seen by your co-worker. Returning to the main layout, with the Composition Zone selected, go to the Content palette and Ctrl-click/right-click or click on the corner menu and choose Add. You can now double-click or choose the pencil to edit, brining up the shared item properties dialogue for layouts and composition zones. You can now make the zone available to all projects, and make it external, so that someone else can work on it. To tidy things up, you can make it internal again once it is ready.

You can also share entire layouts by the same method, making them shareable from Layout>Advanced Layout Properties or by Ctrl-clicking/right-clicking on the Layout tab at the top of the screen to give access to the same menu item.

▼ *To create a self-imposed fold-in-four card, create and rotate composition zones for the inverted pages*

23 Digital Publishing: Add to Reflow/Add Pages to Reflow/Auto tag

These replicate some of the features of the Articles palette, allowing you to add items into the Reflow for an ePub or Kindle, and to automatically tag an entire layout. See the Articles palette for more details, page 92.

24 New Box from Clipping

Creates a new box from a clipping path. See Measurements>Runaround and Clipping for details and examples, page 85.

▲ *Notes retain their screen size, no matter what page zoom you have. You set their font and size in Preferences>Notes. Knowing as you do that Comic Sans was created for this kind of communication, you can ironically use that font, though for no other purpose, ever.*

25 Note

Adds a sticky type note, deletes one, allows you to navigate between notes, to open notes and to close notes.

▲ *Notes retain their screen size, no matter what page zoom you have. You set their font and size in Preferences>Notes. Knowing as you do that Comic Sans was created for this kind of communication, you can ironically use that font, though for no other purpose, ever.*

26 Scale

This has the same function as the Scale palette. See page 129.

6 Page

▲ The Insert Pages dialogue is invoked by Page>Insert.

▼ The Move Pages dialogue enables you to move ranges of pages. You can also do this visually with the Page Layout palette, but doing it this way is often quicker.

1 Insert

This opens the Insert Pages dialogue, which allows you to insert any number of pages before a page, after a page, or at the end of the layout, optionally link them to the current text chain, and set which Master Page will apply to them. You can do the same thing visually in the Page Layout palette, but for a lot of pages, this is quicker, simpler, and more powerful.

2 Delete

Delete allows you to delete a specific range of page numbers. You cannot delete all the pages. If you want to delete them all, first create a blank page at the beginning of the document and then delete from 2 to the end.

3 Move

Move allows you to move a range of pages to before a particular page, after a page, or to the end of the document. Save first, and check that you have got everything where you want it before doing any more work.

Check especially carefully that things are not linking round each other. This is easy to miss, because going down with the cursor will take you to the correct page even if there are a hundred pages in between.

4 Master Guides & Grid

This is only available when working in Master Pages.

See the Page Layout palette, page 126.

5 Section

This enables you to create a new section. A section is essentially a new numbering sequence. You can prefix it, you can specify the start number, and you can specify Arabic or Roman numerals, or alphabeticals. You would often have the front-matter of a book done in this way. This reflects print house practice of the last two hundred years.

From QX2017, you can give a section a name. This only becomes relevant when creating a custom Table of Contents in the File>Export As options for a digital layout.

6 Previous, Next, First, Last, Go to...

Controls to navigate to other pages.

7 Display

Displays the Master Pages. See Page Layout palette page 126.

7 Layout

The Layout tabs are at the top of the layout window, just below the window controls. Ctrl-clicking/right-clicking gives access to New, Duplicate, Delete, New Layout Specification, Layout Properties and Advanced Layout Properties in the same way that this menu does.

1 New

This creates a new layout, opening the same dialogue as a new file. See File>New Project.

2 Duplicate

This duplicates the current layout and all its contents. Duplicate is the method by which you convert a print layout into a digital layout, or one size of digital layout into a different size. It is identical to the features from File>New Document, with one addition: Apply Adaptive Scaling. This allows you to have the document automatically adjust its elements based on parameters you specify in the Options. See the Window>Scale, page 129, for information.

3 Delete

This deletes the current layout and all its contents. It cannot be undone, though you can invoke File>Revert to Saved. You cannot delete the only layout.

4 New Layout Specification

This creates a new JDF Job Jacket layout specification. See Utilities>Job Jackets, page 173.

5 Layout Properties

This opens the Layout Properties dialogue. See File>New for a discussion of this, page 138.

6 Advanced Layout Properties

This is where you make a layout shareable. See Content, page 99.

7 Metadata

This opens the Metadata dialogue which is used both for PDF files and for eBooks/Kindles. QuarkXPress will add default data if you don't put anything in, so always fill this in. You can also set Title, Subject, Publisher, Copyright, ISBN, Language, Description and Keywords, separated by commas.

8 Autotag Layout

This opens up the Autotag Layout dialogue. See the Articles palette, page 92, for more details.

9 Previous, Next, First, Last, Go to

These navigate you to other Layout panes.

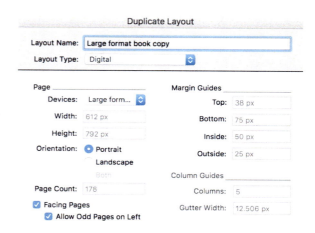

▲ For information on Adaptive Scaling, see the Scaling palette. In Duplicate Layout, Adaptive Scaling also offers content sharing.

Digital Layout

QuarkXPress originally only offered one kind of layout: print. Since QX2016, you have been able to publish HTML5 and fixed layout ePub or Kindle from the Digital Layout. Since QX2017 this also covers apps, and the layout is responsive, which is to say the browser will automatically choose the correct size, provided that you have created it.

To do this, you need to create a separate digital layout for each size of device that you want to use, and for each orientation. If you turn Adaptive Scaling on, QX will make a good job of rearranging the items and their scaling to work on a differently shaped page. It will not be perfect, but it will take you a long way. You can also turn on, in the options, shared content. This means that if you later update the text in one layout, it will update the text in all layouts. See the Content palette for more information. Not all features are supported in HTML5. In the Measurements panel of a Digital Layout, at the far right, you can click a check-box which turns text or other elements into graphics on export. Normally leave this unchecked, unless you see that your items render incorrectly.

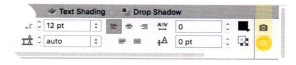

8 Table

Tables are created with the Table tool and mainly managed from the Measurements Panel, or, for Inline Tables, from the Tables Styles palette. The controls here are replicated in the Contextual Menu, which is usually a more convenient place to locate them. For most of these options to work, you have to have a table open and be at a cell or selection with the Text Content Tool. Generally, these commands do not apply to Inline Tables, which are managed from the Table Styles palette and are not directly editable for content in QuarkXPress.

Insert—opens a dialogue to insert a row or a column, offering above, below, number of rows, and the option to retain attributes.

Select—offers a wide range of choices for selecting rows, columns, headers, odds, evens, horizontal grids, vertical grids and the borders.

With ordinary tables, it is not possible to set the frames for individual cells, only for an entire vertical or horizontal grid, though combining cells will interrupt these, which may produce the desired effect. If you need to manage frames of individual cells, then either format until you are satisfied and then choose Table>Convert Table>to Group, which will enable you to work with every cell individually as they will now be frames, or else create your chart in Excel and import as an Inline Table.

Generally speaking, information placed in complex tables is ignored by readers of a narrative document, but is often the first information people examine when looking for specific data. Tables need to be constructed to make it easy to access information, rather than to make a particular point. For this reason, simplicity and clarity should always be at the top of the table maker's list.

Tables are often used by web designers and word processor users as the easiest way to lay out information in columns. Tables provided like this should usually be laid out in a more appropriate way.

Delete—Deletes an entire row or entire column.

Combine Cells—combine two or more cells, retaining only the content of the leftmost, topmost cell in the selection. It is worth setting a hot-key for combine/uncombine cells, because this is by far the most useful tool for creating distinctive tables which do not fit easily into one of the categories.

Table Break—this sets a number of key properties for managing tables, especially anchored tables, that run over more than one page or are likely to. You can set header and footer rows, and determine which are continued, and also control the maximum width (which should be just less than the column width, to prevent irresolvable reflow) and height.

Make separate tables—when you have tables that have broken across more than one page, you can use this to make them separate tables, which may be more manageable.

Header—only for a row selection including the top row, sets it to repeat as the header on each new page.

Repeat as Footer—same as for header, but at the bottom of the page.

Convert text to table—turns a properly tabbed set of text into a table. Copy and Paste from Word or import from Word will often bring across these kinds of tables, as well as importing tab delimited files. However, think carefully before you do this: many tables would be much happier simply set up as tabulated data. Generally speaking, if you can get all the information on one line, tabs will look better and be far easier to manage. On the other hand, if gridlines or shading are crucial, or if text is going to wrap frequently, a table is more likely to do the job.

Convert Table—to text, or group of boxes. If you copy and paste a table from Excel into QuarkXPress, it will come across as a table. It may be better to convert it to text, as discussed above, or to convert it to boxes. A table is also a convenient way of making a grid, which can then be converted to boxes. A table converted to text can be converted back. You cannot convert boxes back to a table, though Utilities>Linkster can make it much easier to manage a group of boxes.

Link text cells—if you did not choose that option when you created the table, you can change it here.

Maintain geometry—if your table is set to autofit rows or columns, Maintain Geometry switches that off and keeps the table the same shape. It isn't a bad workflow to start with Autofit, and, once you are happy, switch on Maintain Geometry to fine-tune.

▼*Making this Gantt chart using Chartwell Bars takes about five minutes, and data can be typed in directly or loaded from Excel. This chart is running text: it doesn't need to be anchored as a separate box.*

9 View

1 Fit in Window, 50%, 75%, Actual Size, 200%, Thumbnails

This sets the magnification. You can also type this in at the very bottom left hand corner of the layout screen. Typing T or selecting Thumbnails here goes to thumbnail mode. When two documents are in thumbnail mode, pages can be dragged from one to another. This is often a good way of rescuing a document which is showing signs of corruption.

2 Enter Full Screen

Enters full screen mode (Mac only)

3 Dynamic Guides

Dynamic guides are largely new in QuarkXPress 2016. By default all are on, which means that red guide measurements with double arrows or transitory guides appear whenever one of the following happens:
• Centres are aligned
• Edges are aligned
• Item is aligned to centre of page
• Equal dimensions in at least one direction with another box on the spread
• Equal spacing between other items.

Additionally, a measurement tooltip appears as you drag. You can turn any or all of them off here.

▲*Dynamic Guides appear vertically or horizontally whenever an element you are dragging matches that dimension of any other element on the layout. While you drag, a tooltip appears at the bottom right hand corner to tell you exact width and height in your preferred measurements.*

4 Guides

F7 turns the guides on or off, including page margins, box outlines and guides you have assigned. It's usually best to keep this assigned to a hot-key, as this is one of the most frequently used functions. On the one hand, the guides are necessary to ensure everything is in the right place, on the other they can create a false sense of bustle and, conversely, of structure.

5 Hide Selection

When Guides are off, the boundaries of the current box are still displayed. You can turn this off (but not for the rest of the text chain) with this function. However, it also hides drag- and shift-selected text highlighting, which makes it useful only for previewing, rather than for actual editing.

6 Page Grids, Text Box Grids

Shows Page and Text Box Grids.

7 Snap to Guides, Snap to Page Grids

Snaps to Guides or Page Grids. You can set the degree of snap in Preferences>Print Layout>Guides and Grid.

8 Rulers, Ruler Direction

▼ Soft proofing:
Off
Greyscale
RGB
CMYK

Turns the rulers on and off, and swaps the direction of measurement.

9 Invisibles, Visual Indicators

Shows the Invisibles: spaces, tabs, returns, and so on, and the Visual Indicators, which are non-typographic invisibles, such as the icons that go with HTML5 attributes.

10 Highlight Content Variables

Turns highlighting on and off for Content Variables.

11 Highlight Cross References

This turns highlighting on and off for Cross References.

12 Trim View

Turns on the Trim View, which hides everything which is off the printed page. This is essential for visualising full-bleed documents, where the bleed can give a false sense of page proportions.

13 Hide Suppressed

Hides items which are suppressed and will therefore not print or export. This is useful if you are using a non-printing template, such as for packaging or a book cover. It also hides other non-printing items, such as Index markers and notes.

14 Proof Output

This offers options for all of the Colour Output Setups you have created in Edit>Color Setups. Assuming that your workflow is properly colour managed, you can see a good rendering of output in greyscale, 100K black, CMYK, Spot, and so on. 100K black is 'true' printed black, as opposed to a black made from enriching black with other colours from the CMYK palette. When proofing on a laser printer, rich black, aka greyscale, will be blurrier, though the black itself will be very flattering. When printing to a true mono printing press, there will be no additional colours 'improving' the look of black, so greyscale 100K will give a truer proof.

When set to As is, soft proofing is off.

New in QX2018, Blend Transparencies work in the colour space of the output setup. If you are outputting to RGB composite, choose the RGB colour space for soft proofing. If you are outputting to CMYK composite, choose CMYK soft proofing. This is independent of the final output technology: you can output to RGB composite and still do final print to CMYK, as this conversion is handled in-RIP. In the examples, the blending has quite a different result in greyscale, RGB and CMYK.

15 Story Editor

This opens the Story Editor, which is a simple text editor built into QuarkXPress for working on the underlying text. This is useful if you have all kinds of transformations going on which make it hard to see where the cursor is going, or what you are editing. The story editor retains numbering, and also shows you where anchored graphics fall.

16 Hide Notes

Hides all notes. You can close rather than hide notes in Item>Notes>Close all notes.

17 View Sets

View sets are collections of decisions from the View menu, including Guides, Grids, Rulers, Ruler direction, Visual Indicators, Invisibles, Trim View and Hide Suppressed. Three presets are supplied: default, authoring view, which maximises the visual indicators, and output preview, which hides everything but the printed result. You can create your own from whatever settings you have when you create a new set. Use in conjunction with Window>Palette Sets.

▲ Story Editor is especially useful when working with complex layouts and with Open Type transformation fonts such as FF Chartwell.

▼ View Sets makes it easy to quickly switch views.

10 Utilities

1 Insert Character

This allows you to insert a variety of breaking and non-breaking characters that are typographically important, especially different kinds of spaces. It is also where you can find Conditional Style Markers. Some shortcut keys are assigned, but you can also assign others for characters you use frequently.

2 Content Variable

This is an alternative method of working with Content Variables.

See the Content Variables palette, page 100.

3 Check Spelling

This runs the spell checker. It works as most spell checkers do. However, if you want to build a glossary of proper nouns and other non-standard words, first create a new auxiliary spell check file before you run the spell checker. When you run it, add rather than skip words that are specific to the publication. When you have completed the spell check, you can open the Auxiliary Dictionary in a text processor. It will be in XML format, but very little tidying up is needed to produce a pristine list of words, which will become the basis for your glossary.

▲ Insert Character allows you to insert precise typographic spaces, different types of dash, and utility markers. It is worth memorising keyboard shortcuts for Indent Here and Right Indent Tab.

4 Word and Character Count

Counts the words and characters for the layout or the story. The dialogue gives word count, unique word count, character count and symbol count, as well as many East Asian counts. The count includes footnotes and endnotes.

Menus 171

▲ Line Check search criteria. These provide a high level of typographic sophistication. Text Box Overflow indicates a problem.

▲ Suggested Hyphenation for the word 'hyphenation'. Note that this gives all the possible legitimate hyphenations, and is not subject to hyphenation strictness in the H&Js.

▼ Example of picture information provided in Usage:

Full Path: /Documents/Writing/Martin M Turner Communications/Quark Book/Images/Vert-just-cond-style.png
File Size: 28K
Colour Depth: RGB
Type: PNG
Modification Date: 28/04/2016 12:16
Dimensions: 77.964 mm x 164.747 mm at 72 dpi

▲ Long path names can cause the information to wrap. Stretch the box to overcome this.

5 Line Check

Line check allows you to search for loose justification, auto-hyphenation, manual hyphenation, widows, orphans, and text box overflow. Computer typesetting should always be seen as the beginning rather than the end. In many cases it is better to turn off automatic controls for widows and orphans (in Paragraph styles), let the text flow as it will, and then manually add in the controls afterwards. Hyphenation can also be technically correct, but visually wrong.

6 Suggested Hyphenation

Suggests options for the 'correct' hyphenation from QuarkXPress's own algorithms. Some languages have very strict rules of hyphenation. Others, such as English, have conflicting rules and numerous exceptions. It is often better to turn off automatic hyphenation and then hyphenate manually, which this tool assists. Consider using hyphenation strictness in H&Js to limit automatic hyphenation and then supplement with this method.

7 Hyphenation Exceptions

Computers hyphenate 'doesn't' as 'does-n't' and 'didn't' as 'did-n't', which are clearly wrong. There are many other exceptions to computer algorithms, and even hyphenations considered correct a hundred years ago (and so still in dictionaries) but which are now wrong, because of shifts in pronunciation. You can enter hyphenation exceptions in this menu item which will apply only to the specified language in the current document. QuarkXPress will query this every time the document is loaded. A better way is either to set the hyphenation in the job jacket, or close all documents and set the hyphenation exceptions for the application. This will then apply to all new documents.

8 Convert Project Language

This converts every instance of a particular language in the project, including in style sheets, to a different language, or to a variant of the same language, for example from US English to International English, or from Portuguese (Portugal) to Portuguese (Brazil).

9 Usage

Usage brings up a dialogue box with six panes which cover the usage and updating or replacement options for Fonts, Pictures, Profiles, Composition Zones, Digital Publishing and Tables. Note that this relates only to the current layout.

Fonts
This lists all the fonts in the current layout, and gives you an information panel with details including internal font name, file name and location, type and version. It allows you to find the first usage of the font, and to replace it. This is particularly useful when you have inadvertently mixed two versions of the same typeface—for example, Microsoft Office-supplied Baskerville with ITC Baskerville.

Pictures
This shows all of the pictures in the document, with their names, page numbers, type and status (ok, modified or missing). 'PB' with a page number refers to a picture on the pasteboard—ie, which is off the page and will therefore not be printed.

Pictures pasted from the clipboard show less information because no disk file exists. Where the disk file does exist, further information is shown below. You can choose to show an image in the document, and to update it if it is modified or missing.

Profiles
This shows the Source colour profiles, as defined in Edit>Colour Setups>Source or loaded in with picture files. If you open a

profile that is used by a picture, the list of pictures using that profile is then shown. Technical profile information is given in the information panel. This is mainly useful if you discover that an image has come across with the wrong profile, or if you have an image that is printing differently from what you expect. The full path of the image is shown, and you can replace the profile with another if you wish to. Unless the image has a wrongly assigned profile, usually a result of user-error in another application, you should not need to do this.

Composition Zones
This shows any composition zones that have been made External, for example by adding them to the Content palette and then editing to make them external. It does not show composition zones that are only in the current project. The status is given (ok, modified, or missing) and you can update a modified composition zone file.

Digital Publishing
This does the same as the Pictures pane, but imported digital assets such as video files that are not pictures.

Tables
Works as the Pictures pane, but for linked Excel tables.

10 Item Styles Usage

The Item Styles Usage opens a dialogue box showing every usage of each item style, which page it appears on, and whether it has been modified. You can choose to show it, or to update it, though, in this case, 'update' means reverting a modified box back to the current version of the item style, even if that is older than the modification.

▼ *The Item Styles Usage shows every usage of each item style, giving its page number and whether it has been modified or not. Items can be updated (or rather, reconformed) to the original style.*

11 Job Jackets Manager

When you create a document in QuarkXPress, a Job Jacket is automatically created for it. Normally this is closed when you close the document, but you can create a separate Job Ticket which will make your Job Jacket persistent. Why? A Job Jacket contains a wide variety of specifications about how to make a file, and you can use it either to create a series of compatible documents, or (if you are careful) to automatically update a suite of documents as you work on them.

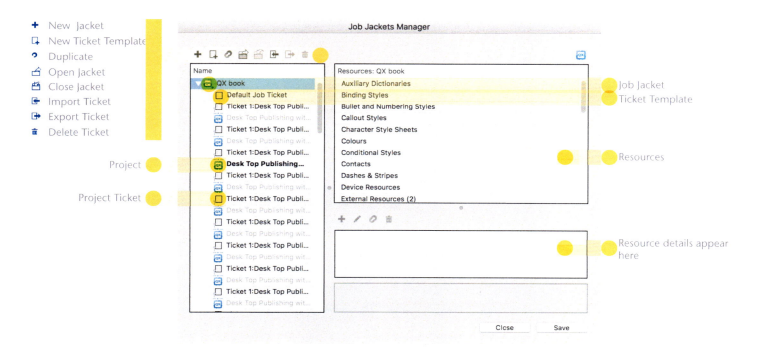

Job Jackets are a 'big' print industry specification, of which QuarkXPress desktop uses only a portion. There are changes you can make in the Job Jackets which won't have any effect on your files, though they may confuse a print house further down the production chain if you change them experimentally.

Essentially, the world of Job Jackets is in three parts.

The Jacket is like the old manilla folder you used to keep a client's work in. It contains everything you ever did for them, their phone numbers, their branding specifications, and some random notes you made about talking to Alfie at the print house because nobody else could make sense of the requirement.

The Ticket is the thing you fill in when you take on a particular job. This has a particular size, or set of sizes, may contain a subset of the colours, and so on.

The Project is the document in progress itself, like artwork in the folder.

You create specifications in the Job Jacket and then add them to Job Ticket, and you create art in the Project.

The Ticket is the intermediate. You don't create anything there except for **Layouts**, which are assembled from other components. For the rest, you just move specifications and resources into it from the Project or from the Jacket. Anything you put into the Ticket from the Project becomes part of the Jacket. Anything you put into the Ticket from the Jacket becomes available to the Project.

So far so good, but why are you doing this at all?

It makes sense when you go to File>New>Project from Ticket. Opening a previously created ticket will bring all of its colours, stylesheets, page descriptions, margins and master pagers (among others) into your new document. If you choose Share Jacket on import, then modifying the shared resources will modify them for all files sharing that jacket. This is ideal for managing a suite of co-branded documents. Changing the main body text size from 11 point to 10 point will reformat the other documents as they are opened.

▲ The job jacket contains all the resources which have been moved into the ticket. You can create some resources there—all those which are not greyed out.
▲ The job ticket contains only resources which have been brought in from the Ticket or the Project, except for Layout, which combines various resources from the Jacket.
▲ The project contains all the resources in the ticket, if it was created with File>New>From Ticket.

Procedure

Create a project. Set some paragraph styles.

Open Utilities>Job Jackets Manager.

Go to the job ticket, move in resources from the project by changing them from 'in project' to 'in ticket'. They are now in the Job Jacket.

Create some resources in the Job Jacket.

Create a new ticket template in the job jacket.

Move resources into the new template.

Use File>New>Project from Ticket, choosing your template ticket.

You now have a new file containing all the resources you moved into the ticket.

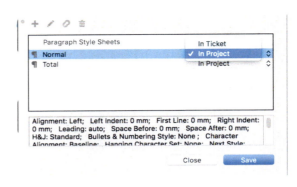

▲ With a project selected, you can move resources from 'In Project' to 'In Ticket'. Once you have put them into the Project's own ticket, they come into the Job Jacket. You can now move them from there into a new Ticket Template. Some resources, such as Paragraph Style Sheets and Colours, are created in the Project. Others are created in the Job Jacket.

▼ Creating a Layout Specification in the Job Jacket. This is one of the resources you create in the Job Jacket and then pull into the Ticket Template, in this case through the Layout Specification. The specification can include Master page margins, columns and grids, the number of pages to be created (and which are evaluated against), and the page size. You can have any number of Layout Specifications in a Job Jacket, and then you decide which to include in a particular ticket template.

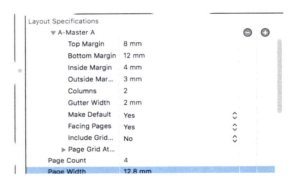

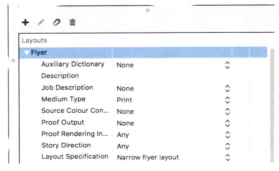

▲ In the Job Ticket, the only resource you can create is a Layout. This uses resources created in the Job Jacket. Before you can pull in a Job Jacket created layout specification (as above), you must first select Medium Type (Print or Digital). You can then click on Layout Specification for a drop-down menu of all the available specifications—only those you have in the Job Jacket.
▲ All other resources appear automatically in the list, and are marked as 'in Jacket' or 'in Project'. As above, you must move them to 'in ticket' if you want them to be included in the template.

12 Insert Placeholder Text

This inserts a string of faux-Latin text, sufficient to fill the selected text box. It will not, however, cause the text to overflow to the next page. If you prefer to use your own text, you can achieve this by creating a shared content text frame and filling it with your preference, for example in another alphabet, or with a different frequency of word-length, if you want to get an idea of how text will work in narrow columns. With box and text attributes turned off, you can then apply it wherever you like.

13 Cloner

The Cloner lets you clone a selection, range of pages, or an entire layout or project, putting it in the same layout, a new layout, a new project file, an existing Quark file, into many Quark projects at one page each, or into separate projects, one per layout. You can specify where the clone is inserted, and how many times, and you can choose to put the pages in sections, either contiguously even if you have selected discontinuous pages (eg, 1-3,7,15), or preserving the source section structure.

If cloning to a new project, all the style sheets in use will be automatically carried over. Click 'Copy Style Sheets' if you want to copy unused styles as well.

There are numerous uses for this. If you were making a set of personalised invitations, you could create as many identical pages as you need, and then, with a Master Page, run a single linked text box on each page right the way through. If you then paste a text file of names, the file will automatically populate, fully personalised.

▲ The cloner is a good way of moving layouts into documents, and pages from layout to layout or document to document. It is only useful for well-behaved documents. If you are having trouble with a document that keeps crashing, go to Thumbnail scale view and create a second document also at Thumbnail scale. Drag the pages from one to the other. This will solve most problems.

14 ImageGrid

The Image Grid creates a matrix of images across one or more pages to display a folder of picture files. The obvious use for this is to create a contact sheet of images, or else to create a display book. However, with a little thought, all kinds of results are possible, including laying out a long document that has previously been created as a PDF, and just needs headers, footers and page numbers reworking.

There are three ways it can work:

Autosize—fits the right number of pictures on the page for a specified number of rows and columns, with gap settings you specify.

Fixed size—every picture has the box size you specify, separated by the gap size.

Autofill—you set a size limit, and Image Grid attempts to fill each page using that limit.

There are a number of options:

Add picture info—puts the file name only or file name and type, size and colour information underneath the text.

Apply drop shadow—applies a default drop shadow with the offset you specify.

Box shape—allows you set the box shape to rectangular, rounded or round, optionally using your tool preferences.

Picture sizing—imports at a set percentage, fits proportionally to the box, or stretches to fit the box.

Fit box to picture—resizes the box to fit the picture.

Process subfolders—processes everything in the subfolders of the folder you specify.

Process Folder then activates it, once you have selected the folder to process.

OK does no more than save the settings. Cancel reverts to the previous settings.

As many pages as are necessary are created, but they do not use Master Pages. You can apply these afterwards, along with item styles.

It's worth playing around with ImageGrid, just to see what it can do, as it may be the solution to a problem you have not yet encountered.

▲ Image Grid can be used for a simple grid type layout like this, but you can also use it to import PDF files for do-it-yourself imposition, or to import every page of an entire book with a view to making blanket changes or selective conversion to native objects.

Linking text boxes

Linkster is a powerful tool for linking or unlinking many pages or boxes at once. The linking tool in the toolbar is more convenient in many cases, and, since QX2017, offers several of the functions of Linkster. See under Tools, above.

15 Linkster

Linkster links and unlinks boxes. You can link selected boxes, or you can specify pages, in which case the main auto-linking box is selected.

Unlinking offers four options. The icons are a bit difficult to decode, but once you have identified them they are intuitive.

The first ▦▦▦ (top left) breaks the selected box from both the box before and after it, and breaks the chain. In other words, you will have three separate stories.

The second ▦▦▦ (bottom left) unlinks the current box from the chain, but keeps the chain intact. Your selected box and its text are now a stand-alone box, but the rest of the story flows as before.

The third ▦▦▦ (top right) breaks the chain between this box and the previous one.

The fourth ▦▦▦ (bottom right), breaks the chain between this box and the next one.

You can also link, and choose to keep text in the same boxes, or allow it to flow freely. Always save first.

16 ShapeMaker

▲ Spirogram with arrow-heads Shapemaker largely reproduces the shape tools, but it has a couple of tricks they don't, including polygrams, spirograms, golden rectangles and double squares. Aside from these options, it works in the same way as the Shape tools.

ShapeMaker is a tool which creates mathematically defined shapes by changing their options and parameters. You don't need to understand the mathematics to make it work, though. With the exception of Spirograms, all of the ShapeMaker functions are now available directly from the Shape Tools with ☆⬠▢◇△▱◡✿.

There are four tabs: Waves, Polygons, Spirals, Rectangles. The previous Presets tab was replaced in QX2017 with a visual presets function which is also available for the Tools versions.

In each case you can create any kind of box, or just lines, and you can specify its width and height. If creating a text box, you can specify its columns and gutters. You can also alter the existing box.

The easiest way to get to grips with this is to open it up and play.

Waves—undulating lines on one or more sides of the box. These can also be square or triangular lines, depending on the wave type.

Polygons—all kinds of multi-sided shapes, not just the regular polygons they taught you in school. You can specify curves, twirls and other fancy options. Try the Spirogram type. This is also where you can make a golden rectangle or a double square.

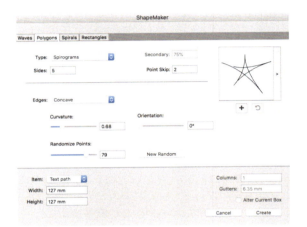

Spirals—golden, Archimedean and custom spirals. These are very good as templates for the overall layout of the page, if you are one of those people who believe that the golden section is a key aesthetic principle.

Rectangles—if you want complete control over the shape of rectangles, such as turning them into speech bubbles, this is where to look.

Presets—when you have a shape you like, type in a name here and add it. All the parameters will go into your new preset, which will appear with a silhouette of its shape.

Because the shapes are mathematically derived, they respond very fast in a layout. You can Super-Step-and-Repeat them, merge or combine them with other shapes, and edit them with the Bézier tools.

17 Font Mapping

This menu normally comes up if you open a document for fonts not installed on your system, and allows you to map a font you don't have to a font you do have. You can set this behaviour in Preferences>Application>Fonts.

Normally, when a project opens up and fonts are missing, the font mapping dialogue will come up. It will tell you which fonts are missing, and allow you to specify what to replace them with. You can edit, delete, import and export these rules, though you can't actually create them in this menu.

The rules then apply to your copy of QuarkXPress—they don't affect the document itself, which will open with the original fonts on other computers. So, for example, if you were working with a design agency that was setting a document in fonts you don't have, you could receive the project, edit it, and send it back, and it would be in the correct fonts when you did.

If you want to actually change the fonts—for example, because you have upgraded from True Type fonts to OpenType, use the Usage>Fonts dialogue to identify where they occur, then update the style sheets (easy if you have used structured style sheets), and then, from Usage>Fonts, replace any ad hoc uses.

18 Convert Old Underlines

This is a one-time utility which finds any legacy underlines from QuarkXPress 3.x and turns them into contemporary underlines.

19 PPD Manager

The PPD Manager lists all of the printer PPD files—which QuarkXPress needs to correctly control your printer—installed on your system. You can specify an auxiliary folder if you have downloaded a PPD but the system is not seeing it.

20 App Build Status

This gives access to the most recent iOS or Android app Build Status. You can also access this from the ❶ icon at the bottom of the screen when in a digital layout. This was new in QX2017 for iOS, and in QX2018 for Android.

21 Proxy Settings

If your network access requires a proxy, you can set it here for iOS or Android application building.

22 XTensions Manager

The XTensions Manager allows you to turn off XTensions, and also to see XTensions which have been turned off because of a problem. Clicking About will give you full details about an XTension, including contact details for support. You have to restart QuarkXPress for changes to take effect.

Normally, you shouldn't have to use this menu, but if there is a problem with an Xtension, for example one you have from a third party, you can use this to track it down. On a Mac, Xtensions are now installed differently from previously. Normally they should install themselves in the correct place, but you can open up the Help menu to find where they are to be located on your system.

23 Profile Manager

This is a simple list of installed colour profiles which allows you to switch them off, and also to use an auxiliary folder. Profiles are actually managed in Edit>Color Setups. You should not normally need this item, as there is generally no harm in having all of your profiles turned on, and ICC profiles that are embedded with imported documents should come across with them, and be visible in Utilities>Usage Profiles.

24 Make QR Code

This allows you to make an image (left icon) or vector (right icon) Quick Response Code, either with text or with a VCard. Once the 'next big thing' in youth and business advertising, they fell out of favour because an extra app was needed in iOS or Android to access them. With iOS 11, they are now directly accessible from the iPhone camera. On Android, if the user holds down the home button, the code will come up as a clickable Google link.

25 Redline

See the Redline palette for more information, page 129.

11 Window

1 New Window

You can open a new window of the current project. When you close the last open window of a project, QuarkXPress will prompt you to save it. If you try to open a project already open, QuarkXPress will tell you this, and offer you the option of opening a new window.

2 Split Window

Splits the window so that you can scroll to different parts of the document and compare them.

3 Bring All to Front

Brings all QuarkXPress windows to the front of the windows open on your computer.

4 Tile

Tiles the open windows on the screen. If you want to tile pages for print, this is in the File>Print>Pages pane.

Tile controls are also at the bottom of the screen.

At the bottom left of the layout window, the magnification box (100%), the page number (1), navigate by preview arrow ▲, page left ◄ and right ►, view master page 🗐, split horizontally 🗐, split vertically 🗐 export ↗ and HTML5 app preview ⊙ (digital layout only) may easily be hidden by the Measurements panel. When creating iOS or Android apps, you also have access to ⓘ for information on progress and errors.

5 Palette Sets

You can save the positions of all your open palettes and retrieve them with this item. This is convenient for different kinds of working, and also if you use a laptop that you connect to an external display, and want to preserve as much screen as possible on the laptop. You can also have all the palettes on an additional display if you want. Use this in conjunction with View>View Sets to quickly change the way QuarkXPress displays.

Pro-tip: to maximise the document window on a Mac without going to fullscreen, Option-Click the green button.

6 Turn Hiding On (Mac only)

With this you can hide palettes at the bottom, top, left or right, or all docked palettes. Docked palettes are ones which have become magnetically attached to one of the docking areas—you will see a grey background appear when you move a palette there. If palettes are hidden, they spring back into view when you hover the mouse over that area of the screen.

7 The palettes

See the Palettes section, above.

12 Script (Mac Only)

This gives access to a number of useful Apple Scripts. You can also create your own scripts and place them there. Almost all of the supplied scripts are also now given as JavaScripts, in the JavaScript menu, and are accessible on both platforms.

13 Help

This gives access to Help. Search allows you to find a feature in the menus. To open the Help file, choose Help Topics.

Convert Legacy Files enables you to open QuarkXPress 6.0 and earlier files. Later files open directly in QuarkXPress.

On Windows, the following items are available, which are in the QuarkXPress menu on a Mac:

Quark Cache Cleaner

About QuarkXPress

Edit Licence Code

Transfer Licence Code

Check for Updates

Quark Update Settings.

▼ On Windows, most of the items from the QuarkXPress menu (Mac) are in the Help menu. The exception is the Preferences, which are found under Edit>Preferences.

Menus

Index

A
A system 60
Adaptive scaling 3, 4, 5, 109, 129, 138, 146, 167
Add noise 115
Alpha Channel 85, 86, 111
Android 3, 4, 5, 35, 43, 53, 69, 91, 109, 141, 144, 145, 177, 178
Articles ii, 5, 52, 53, 63, 66, 67, 92, 126, 129, 130, 146, 163, 165, 167
Artifact 52, 67, 92, 163
Audiences 2
Auto constrain 137
Auto page insertion 127
auto-tag 67, 92

B
Bezier 3, 10, 74, 86
Binding 55
Bleed 10, 13, 53, 56, 60, 64, 106, 108, 121, 127, 138, 142, 143, 149, 151, 170
blending modes 49
Blends 4, 5, 97, 104, 108, 143, 144
Books 93
borders 4, 5, 49, 76, 82, 84, 85, 88, 90, 104, 113, 134, 137, 141, 158, 168
brand 35
brightness and contrast 117

C
Callouts 93
character style 12, 14, 15, 77, 97, 102, 130, 131, 134, 154, 160
Circle 10, 41, 73, 74, 83, 100, 104, 118
CMY 33
CMYK 33
Coating 43, 54, 60, 61, 68
Colour balance 118
Colour Field 41
Colour fonts 3, 4, 5, 77, 78
Colour picker 4, 94
Colours ii, 2, 14, 31, 32, 33, 34, 35, 43, 47, 49, 56, 60, 61, 75, 77, 79, 81, 82, 83, 84, 85, 88, 90, 92, 93, 94, 95, 96, 97, 104, 106, 108, 113, 118, 120, 135, 141, 142, 148, 149, 150, 152, 153, 159, 170, 174
COLR 5
Column rules 4, 80, 81, 82
Column splitting 4, 81

Composite workflow 142
Composition ii, 3, 18, 19, 29, 56, 63, 73, 75, 99, 111, 129, 143, 144, 165, 172, 173
Compression 53, 142
Conditional Styles ii, 12, 15, 44, 51, 88, 97, 99, 123, 134, 152, 153
Content variables ii, 2, 3, 4, 5, 12, 50, 51, 62, 63, 99, 100, 101, 127, 139, 170, 171
Creation Date 100
Cross-reference 100, 101, 122, 161
Curves are like Levels, except that instead of just specifying the 117

D
Dashes and Stripes 158
Delivery 2
Desaturate 120
Despeckle 111
Digital Press 56
DOCX 4, 51, 63, 140
drop shadow 89

E
Edge detection 115
Emboss 114
emotion 31
Endnotes 4, 102, 103, 160, 161, 171
EPS 3, 4, 5, 53, 86, 137, 140, 141, 143, 151, 159
ePub 2, 3, 4, 5, 43, 53, 63, 66, 67, 69, 92, 108, 109, 125, 129, 141, 145, 146, 159, 165, 167
Excel 3, 12, 44, 50, 51, 63, 74, 75, 90, 133, 140, 151, 152, 168, 169, 173
export 2, 3, 4, 10, 33, 39, 42, 44, 49, 52, 53, 60, 63, 64, 66, 67, 68, 69, 82, 83, 89, 91, 92, 94, 96, 101, 107, 109, 110, 112, 121, 125, 128, 130, 133, 134, 137, 138, 140, 141, 142, 143, 145, 146, 148, 149, 151, 153, 159, 163, 164, 166, 167, 170, 173, 177, 178
Extended Gamut Colour 33

F
File Name 100
Find Edges 113
Find/Change 4, 12, 99, 123, 124, 136, 142, 152, 153, 161
First Aid 13
Fixed-layout eBook 4
Flexo 57
Flip groups 4, 163
Folding 54
font 23
Footnote 102
Footnotes 4, 14, 39, 102, 103, 123, 140, 146, 153, 160, 161, 171
Format painter 4, 73, 75
Frame gradients 4
Frames 3, 4, 5, 76, 84, 88, 104, 108, 132, 137, 168
Freehand 10, 74, 75

G
Gamma Correction 119
Gaussian Blur 111
Gene Davis 41
Glyphs 103
Gradients 104
GREP 4, 12, 50, 51, 99, 124, 153
Grid ii, 10, 12, †18, 19, 21, 51, 62, 63, 64, 65, 79, 93, 96, 103, 104, 105, 106, 107, 123, 127, 128, 129, 131, 132, 133, 137, 138, 151, 156, 157, 166, 168, 170, 175
guides 105

H
Hanging Characters 155
Heading Style 14, 52, 67, 130, 131
House Style 38
HTML5 ii, 2, 3, 4, 5, 35, 43, 53, 68, 69, 77, 91, 92, 108, 109, 117, 141, 144, 145, 159, 167, 170, 178
hyperlinks 141
Hyperlinks 110
Hyphenation 3, 4, 5, 14, 21, 77, 78, 93, 131, 137, 156, 157, 172
Hyphenation quality 3, 4, 5, 156

I
ICC 4, 57, 178
IDML 3, 4, 39, 62, 138
Import 3, 4, 34, 39, 44, 51, 62, 63, 73, 74, 96, 99, 133, 136, 138, 140, 141, 146, 153, 159, 168, 173, 174, 175, 177
InDesign 3
Index ii, 65, 66, 93, 101, 121, 122, 123, 146, 170

Inline tables 4, 5, 12, 51, 75, 90, 133, 137, 168
Invert 120
iOS 3, 4, 5, 35, 43, 69, 91, 109, 141, 144, 145, 177, 178
Item eye-dropper 10
Item Styles ii, 12, 14, 74, 94, 99, 123, 151, 153, 158, 160, 173, 175
Item tool 10, 72, 73, 75

J
JavaScript ii, 3, 4, 5, 12, 34, 38, 39, 42, 50, 51, 62, 103, 110, 124, 141, 144, 153, 179
Job Jackets 12, 34, 93, 136, 138, 143, 148, 153, 167, 173, 174
Justification 4, 21, 78, 82, 156, 157, 158, 172

K
Kerning 158
Kindle 2, 7, 26, 43, 53, 66, 67, 92, 108, 125, 126, 129, 141, 145, 146, 159, 165, 167

L
Laser Printer 56
Layout Tab 10, 165
Leading 3, 4, †18, 20, 21, †22, 23, 25, 46, 63, 65, 78, 102, 105, 131, 132, 137, 155, 156
Letraset 7, 41, 44
Levels 116
Line between 81
Line draw tool 10
line length 20, 21, 76
Link text boxes tool 10
Linking tool 4, 72, 75, 176
Lists ii, 63, 64, 65, 80, 93, 101, 110, 121, 125, 126, 141, 153, 154, 156, 172, 177

M
Magnification 10, 75, 107, 126, 169, 178
master page 10, 19, 51, 60, 64, 65, 93, 105, 107, 122, 126, 127, 128, 166, 174, 175, 178
Master Pages 126
Masters and Guides 12
Measurements ii, 4, 10, 11, 12, 13, 14, 21, 22, 23, 45, 49, 72, 73, 74, 75, 76, 79, 80, 81, 83, 84, 85, 87, 88,

90, 91, 107, 123, 129, 130, 131, 132, 134, 135, 137, 155, 158, 160, 161, 162, 163, 164, 165, 167, 168, 169, 178
Median 116
Merge or Split Paths 164
Merge text boxes 4, 39, 152, 162
Messages 2
Metadata 52, 66, 67, 141, 146, 167
Modification Date 101
Multi-gradients 4

O
Offset 57
Open Type 3, 4, 5, 15, 44, 77, 99, 103, 136, 137, 144, 152, 153, 155, 160, 171
OpenType 3, 4, 5, 44, 50, 130, 137, 177
Optical Margin Alignment 155
Outcomes 2
Output Preview 13, 171

P
Page number 10, 51, 62, 63, 64, 65, 100, 101, 122, 126, 127, 141, 161, 172, 173, 178
Page Reference 101
Pan 10, 72, 73, 75, 109
Pantone Extended Gamut 142
paragraph style 14, 21, 51, 64, 78, 80, 99, 102, 105, 122, 125, 126, 128, 130, 131, 134, 155, 160, 174
PDF ii, 2, 3, 4, 5, 14, 33, 34, 39, 44, 45, 52, 53, 57, 60, 61, 62, 63, 64, 67, 86, 92, 93, 96, 101, 110, 111, 121, 129, 130, 131, 133, 136, 138, 140, 141, 142, 143, 145, 146, 147, 148, 149, 151, 152, 159, 160, 162, 163, 167, 175
photography 29
Picture content tool 10, 73, 75, 84
Posterize 120
Preferences 13, 21, 23, 39, 66, 74, 77, 102, 105, 106, 122, 127, 128, 135, 136, 138, 139, 140, 148, 149, 151, 153, 157, 159, 160, 161, 163, 165, 170, 175, 177, 179
Proportional leading 4
PSD 91
publishing process 38

Q
Quark Cache Cleaner 13, 135, 139, 179
Quark Rescue 13, 139
QX2015 4, 5, 23, 52, 129
QX2016 4, 5, 34, 62, 77, 103, 108, 144, 167
QX2017 4, 5, 23, 34, 49, 72, 76, 77, 78, 80, 81, 82, 84, 85, 94, 104, 110, 128, 129, 131, 134, 135, 136, 139, 140, 141, 145, 152, 155, 160, 161, 162, 166, 167, 176, 177
QX2018 4, 5, 13, 14, 15, 34, 38, 42, 45, 49, 51, 52, 62, 67, 76, 77, 78, 84, 91, 92, 95, 99, 100, 103, 108, 124, 129, 130, 131, 138, 141, 144, 145, 152, 153, 155, 156, 160, 163, 164, 170, 177

R
Rectangle 10, †18, 40, 74, 75, 136, 163, 176
RGB 33
Risograph 57
Running Header 101
Running headers 4, 51, 64, 101, 127

S
Safety 108
SBIX 5
Scale images to 5000% 4
sections 128
Selective Colour 119
Shapemaker tools 4, 72
Shared Item Properties 99
Smart single quotes 4
Space/Align 87
Span Columns 80
Spanning 4, 11, 80
spell checker 171
Split Columns 80
Spot Colour 33
Standard Paper Sizes 60
Stock weights 54
Stroke live text 4
Style Sheets ii, 2, 4, 11, 12, 13, 14, 15, 52, 63, 67, 72, 92, 93, 125, 130, 134, 147, 153, 160, 172, 174, 175, 177
Super Step and Repeat 162
SVG 5, 77

T
Table of Contents 144, 146
Table styles ii, 3, 4, 5, 75, 90, 123, 133, 163, 168
Table tool 10, 74, 75, 90, 133, 137, 168
Tagged PDF ii, 4, 5, 14, 52, 67, 92, 129, 130, 131, 141, 146, 163
Text content tool 10, 72, 75, 168
Text framing 4, 5
text on a line 82
Text shading ii, 3, 4, 5, 14, 88, 123, 130, 131, 134, 154, 155, 160
Thermal 57
Threshold 120
thumbnail 18, 19, 63, 75, 141, 169, 175
Tools ii, 4, 12, 13, †21, 24, 29, 32, 41, 46, 63, 69, 72, 73, 74, 75, 76, 86, 106, 119, 133, 136, 137, 143, 153, 159, 163, 164, 176
Trace Contour 115
Transparency 3, 4, 5, 14, 41, 48, 49, 52, 53, 76, 78, 82, 83, 84, 85, 86, 88, 91, 94, 110, 113, 115, 123, 143, 144, 149, 151
transparency blend 3, 5, 48, 49, 53, 84, 94, 110, 143, 144
typeface 21, 23, 25, 34, 65, 121, 122, 152, 159, 172
Typographer's ragged text 156

U
Unlink text boxes tool 10
Unsharp Masking 112
URLs 38
UV 43, 60, 61, 91, 159

V
View Sets 13, 171, 179
visual identity 34

W
Wave 10, 40, 41, 42, 74, 75, 176
weight 43

X
XPress Tags 12, 39, 51, 63, 140, 147

Z
Zoom tool 10, 75

Made in the USA
San Bernardino, CA
22 July 2018